Abortion from the Religious and Moral Perspective

Abortion from the Religious and Moral Perspective

An Annotated Bibliography

George F. Johnston

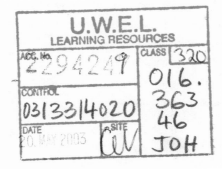
Bibliographies and Indexes in Religious Studies,
Number 53

PRAEGER

Westport, Connecticut
London

Library of Congress Cataloging-in-Publication Data

Johnston, George F., 1946–
    Abortion from the religious and moral perspective : an annotated bibliography / George F. Johnston.
      p. cm. —(Bibliographies and indexes in religious studies, ISSN 0742–6836; no. 53)
    Includes indexes.
      ISBN 0–313–31402–0 (alk. paper)
      1. Abortion—Bibliography. 2. Abortion—Religious aspects—Bibliography. I. Title. II. Series.
Z6671.2.A2 J64   2003 HQ767.2
016.36346—dc21   2002042584

British Library Cataloguing in Publication Data is available.

Library of Congress Catalog Card Number: 2002042584
ISBN: 0–313–31402–0
ISSN: 0742–6836

First published in 2003

Praeger Publishers, 88 Post Road West, Westport, CT 06881
An imprint of Greenwood Publishing Group, Inc.
www.praeger.com

Printed in the United States of America

The paper used in this book complies with the
Permanent Paper Standard issued by the National
Information Standards Organization (Z39.48–1984).

10 9 8 7 6 5 4 3 2 1

To my late wife, Penny, who loved
all children, born and unborn, this
book is affectionately dedicated.

CONTENTS

INTRODUCTION

      For about the last three decades, the issue of abortion has polarized this nation. Some have argued strenuously that abortion should be legal through all nine months of pregnancy, and for almost any reason, whereas others have argued just as strenuously that abortion is the killing of a human being, and so should not be legal, except perhaps when a pregnancy endangers the life of the mother. In the middle are those who argue for a more moderate position, either by limiting the number of valid reasons for obtaining an abortion, or by limiting when during a pregnancy one can be obtained, or through a combination of the two. Many of the people who have been involved in the abortion debate, especially on the pro-life side, though they certainly are not absent from the pro-choice side, are religious people, who hold their particular view on abortion because of their religious convictions. Many Christian groups, including the Catholic Church and a number of Protestant denominations, have taken official stands on abortion one way or the other. Other people, while not particularly religious, have developed rational, philosophical arguments either for permitting, or not permitting, abortion. These arguments are often based on general moral principles that are thought to be universally true, and independent of one's particular religious convictions. This brings us to the reason for this book.

      It is the purpose of this bibliography to bring together as many citations as possible on how abortion intersects with religion and morality. Any way in which religion and morality impinge on abortion is considered in scope in this bibliography. A quick look at the table of contents will reveal the particular topics considered in scope for this bibliography. For example, items that discuss the following topics are all covered in this bibliography: the status of the fetus (is it a person or not), as well as the morality or immorality of abortion, whether the items are written from a religious or a philosophical vantage point. Also included are citations to literature that discuss how religious groups have gotten involved in the abortion controversy, as well as discussions of to what extent they should get involved. This naturally gets into church-state issues. Items that discuss the question of imposing one's morality on others as well as whether a Christian politician can legitimately take the position of "personally opposed, but publically in favor" are both included. Items that show how one's religion, church attendance, and so on, affect one's attitudes toward abortion are also included. Finally, this bibliography includes citations to official documents from many different Christian groups, both Catholic and Protestant.

Citations from all points of view are included. They range from the extreme conservative position that all abortions, even when the mother's life is in danger, are seriously immoral, to the extreme liberal position that both abortion, through all nine months of pregnancy, and even infanticide, are morally unobjectionable. There are, of course, a lot of views in between these extremes that are also included, as well as review articles, which generally review what others have written on abortion. With the sole exception of the chapter of official Protestant documents, all items within one topical section are listed alphabetically by author, regardless of the particular position taken by the author on that subject. The annotations provided should be sufficient to show the vantage point taken by each particular author.

As mentioned before, there are also included two chapters of the official documents of various religious groups. Because of the importance of the Catholic Church in the abortion controversy, one whole chapter is devoted to Catholic documents. Anything from the Pope, the Vatican, various groups of bishops, as well as speeches, letters, and so on, written by individual bishops in the conduct of their office are included. Another chapter includes the official statements on abortion taken by a number of different Protestant denominations. Neither of these chapters pretends to be complete. In particular, there are several Protestant denominations not represented here. It is hoped, however, that all the major denominations have been included, as well as some minor ones.

All of the citations, except for those in the two chapters of official documents, are annotated. These annotations are intended to be brief, objective statements of what the author of the piece actually says, basically summarizing the contents. The compiler has studiously avoided making subjective comments. A word about terminology is in order here. Some terms such as "show" or "demonstrate" may sometimes connote an evaluative judgment. The reader should be careful not to read such an evaluative judgment into these terms. Thus, when the annotation reads "The author shows that ....," this should not be taken to mean that the compiler feels the author has conclusively demonstrated his point. Likewise, the use of "attempts to show" should not be read to mean that the compiler feels the author tried, but somehow failed, to demonstrate a particular point. The word "claims" has sometimes been used to avoid this problem, but in order not to overuse it, the words "show" or "attempts to show" have also been used. The compiler, like most other people, does have his own very considered opinion on the morality of abortion, one arrived at as a result of his own religious convictions. He has attempted, however, to leave those opinions aside in the writing of the annotations. It is for the reader to decide if he has succeeded in this effort.

The two chapters of official documents are not annotated. Many official statements from religious groups, especially those from Protestant denominations, are very short resolutions, many times taking only half a page or so. As a result, it was felt that an annotation would almost be counter-productive, and would probably say nothing more than whether it was a pro-choice or a pro-life statement. The chapter of Protestant material is divided into three sections, however, that show the basic position taken by each denomination: Pro-Choice, Moderate, and Pro-Life. These sections are meant to take the place of an annotation describing the position of the denomination. All materials in the chapter of Catholic material are, of course, pro-life, because of the unabashedly pro-life position taken by the Catholic hierarchy, so this chapter does not need to be sub-divided. Some materials have been written by Catholics who are pro-choice. These are not included in this chapter, but rather are found in chapter two. Since the Catholic Church is officially pro-life, anything by individual Catholics who are pro-choice cannot be said to be an "official" document. Also, though the chapter of Catholic official material is not annotated, in the proper sense of that term, the compiler has, when he felt it necessary, given the venue in which a particular statement was made.

Why yet another bibliography on abortion, one may ask? That is a legitimate question, and one the compiler had to face before beginning this project. Most other bibliographies on abortion have approached the subject broadly. That is to say, they have included citations that discuss abortion from a multitude of perspectives. They have included the religious and moral perspective, to be sure, but they have also included citations discussing it from the legal, sociological, political, and medical perspectives. As a result, they have necessarily had to be rather selective in what they included. Many have actually included the word "selected" in their title. This book attempts to narrow the focus to just the religious and the moral perspective, but to be as comprehensive as possible within that more narrow scope. No bibliography, of course, can hope to be exhaustive. This bibliography is no exception. But it is the compiler's hope that he has included all of the most important publications within scope, as well as many of the less important items.

In order to aid researchers in finding relevant items, this bibliography is presented in a topical arrangement. A quick look at the table of contents will show this topical breakdown. As a result of this type of arrangement, the compiler has felt free to duplicate citations when they seemed to fit into more than one topic. Thus, one particular citation may appear in more than one place in the bibliography. This will allow researchers to jump to any section that is of interest to them, and be able to find publications of at least some relevance to his interest. There is also the subject index, which will provide access to very particular subjects, or to things not brought out in the particular topical arrangement provided. Because items by particular authors are necessarily scattered throughout the bibliography due to this topical arrangement, an author index is also included. One will note that the citatō ns in this bibliography are all numbered, in one sequential arrangement, regardless of section or chapter breaks. The numerical references in the indexes refer to the citation number, not the page number.

This bibliography includes citations for books, journal articles, essays appearing in books prepared under editorial direction, academic dissertations, and some material found on the world wide web. In cases where a book is prepared under editorial direction, with a number of contributors, I have included any articles in the book considered to be within the scope of this bibliography. In addition, if the book as a whole was considered to be in scope, I have included a citation for the book as well. In other cases, however, the in-scope essays are found in books of too general a nature to be considered in-scope for this bibliography, such as a book on today's ethical problems. In those cases, only the in-scope articles are cited, but not the book as a whole. In cases where an article has been published several times, such as a piece that first appears as a journal article and is later republished as part of a collection of essays, the compiler has made every effort to find the first publication of the article and cite that. On occasion, however, where the original was difficult to obtain, or where the reprint was deemed to be more available than the original, he has cited the reprint and made a note about the original publication. Due to the difficulty in finding them, he has not, however, included citations to videos and sound recordings. This weakness is to be lamented, but was felt to be unavoidable.

One will note that throughout this bibliography, the compiler has shown a preference for substantive articles rather than news articles. For example, in chapter three, the compiler could have included many news-related articles, such as "Religious groups protest outside of Supreme Court Building." Due to their sheer number, however, including them would have brought this bibliography to unmanageable proportions, and in the end, not provided access to anything really important. Rather, the compiler decided early on to provide access to more substantive articles, such as ones that discuss to what extent Christian groups should be involved in protesting abortion. If one desires access to the news items, he may quickly find them in various periodical indexes, such as the *Readers' Guide to Periodical Literature,* as well as the indexes to most major metropolitan newspapers. It is this preference for the more substantive material, by the way, that at least partially explains the omission of videos and sound recordings from this bibliography.

1 PERSONHOOD AND THE STATUS OF THE FETUS

RELIGIOUS DISCUSSIONS

1.   Allen, Sydney. "Immortality of the Soul and the Abortion of the Body." In *Abortion: Ethical Issues and Options,* edited by David R. Larson, 89-98. Loma Linda, Calif.: Loma Linda University, Center for Christian Bioethics, 1992.

     Argues that the fetus has, what she calls, "latent" or "innate" immortality. As a result, we must treat it with great reverence and respect, but it does not have the same rights and privileges as those already born.

2.   Atkinson, David. "Some Theological Perspectives on the Human Embryo." *Ethics and Medicine* 2 (1986): 8-10; 2 (1986): 23-24, 32.

     The author lays out some biblical themes which contribute to a theological account of the status of the human embryo.

3.   Bajema, Clifford E. *Abortion and the Maning of Personhood.* Grand Rapids, Mich.: Baker Book House, 1974.

     Argues from both biology and theology that personhood begins at conception. Answers the question whether abortion is murder, and closes with the view that abortion, except to save the life of the mother, is wrong.

4.   Baughman, Charles W. "The Breath of Life: What Does the Bible Say in a Crucial Question in the Abortion Debate: When Does Human Life Begin?" *Christian Social Action* 9, no. 3 (1996): 30-34.

     Through a study of several biblical passages, the author attempts to show that the Bible does not view the fetus as a person, or even alive in the sense of human life. He claims that according to the Bible, life enters the child at birth.

5.   Bazak, Jacob. "The Legal Status of the Fetus in Jewish Halacha and in Israeli Law." In *Jewish Law Association Studies, VIII*, 1-5. Atlanta: Scholars Press, 1996.

The legal status of the fetus is discussed in both its criminal and in its civil aspects.

6.   Boyd, Kenneth. "The Moral Significance of the Embryo and the Fetus." In *Abortion in Debate*, 49-61. Edinburgh: Quorum Press, 1987.

Begins with a discussion of the theological and moral context from which he bases his opinions, and then proceeds to present an argument for saying that the fetus becomes more and more a person as it grows and develops.

7.   Cahill, Lisa Sowle. "Abortion, Autonomy, and Community." In *Abortion and Catholicism: The American Debate*, edited by Patricia Beattie Jung and Thomas A. Shannon, 85-97. New York: Crossroad, 1988.

The author concedes that the precise value and rights of human fetal life remains an open question, but argues that the fetus deserves considerable respect from conception on. Serious considerations must be present to justify abortion even relatively early in pregnancy.

8.   Channer, J. H., ed. *Abortion and the Sanctity of Human Life.* Exeter, Eng.: Paternoster Press, 1985.

A collection of articles that together argue, on medical, philosophical, and moral-theological grounds, that abortion is immoral because it is the deliberate killing of an innocent and helpless human being.

9.   Connery, John R., S.J. "Abortion: Unspeakable Crime." *National Catholic Reporter*, 18 Feb. 1977, 33.

A review of the church's teaching on abortion from the earliest times. He points out that there is no historical precedent for the current view that the fetus is not yet a human being, and so may be aborted. In the past, he says, the fetus was seen as a potential human being, and it was sacred for that reason.

10.   Crosby, Tim. "Abortion: Some Questionable Arguments." In *Abortion: Ethical Issues and Options*, edited by David R. Larson, 55-69. Loma Linda, Calif.: Loma Linda University, Center for Christian Bioethics, 1992.

The author takes many of the biblical passages pro-lifers use to say that human life begins at conception, and shows that, generally speaking, they push these passages too far. He finds nothing in Scripture to prove that the embryo is a person. Nonetheless, he opposes all abortions of convenience.

11. Culliton, Joseph T. "Rahner on the Origin of the Soul: Some implications regarding Abortion." *Thought* 52 (1978): 203-214.

Outlines the thought of the theologian Karl Rahner on the origin of the soul, and then presents the implications of that thought on the issue of abortion.

12. Diamond, James J. "Abortion, Animation, and Biological Hominization." *Theological Studies* 36 (1975): 305-324.

After a study of empirical biology, the author concludes that this data tilt toward the conclusion that fertilization does not represent the beginning of definitive life of an individualized homo. He submits that the moral theologian should more accurately divide acts into anti-fertilizational, anti-conceptive, and abortional (the induction of organismal death in a living human organism, thus a homicide).

13. Donceel, Joseph F. "Immediate Animation and Delayed Hominization." *Theological Studies* 31 (1970): 76-105.

The author claims that Thomas Aquinas' view that the soul does not enter the body at conception, but rather sometime between conception and birth, should be revived. He examines several reasons that induce him to expect such a revival.

14. ———. "A Liberal Catholic's View." In *The Problem of Abortion.* 2nd ed., edited by Joel Feinberg, 15-20. Belmont, Calif.: Wadsworth Pub. Co., 1984.

A defense of Thomas Aquinas' view that the soul is not infused into the body until the fetus begins to show human shape and possesses the basic human organs.

15. Drutchas, Geoffrey G. *Is Life Sacred?* Cleveland: Pilgrim Press, 1998.

The author argues that a belief in the *sanctity* of human life does not cohere well with either biblical teaching or with church tradition. Rather he argues for a more modest *respect* for human life.

16.   Enquist, Roy J. "Abortion and the Image of God." *Dialog* 22 (1984):
        198-201.

        Using the doctrine of the image of God, the author attempts to reconsider
        the theological basis for our interpretation of the moral basis for abortion.

17.   Fairweather, Eugene. "The Child as Neighbour: Abortion as a Theologi-
        cal Issue." In *The Right to Birth: Some Christian Views on Abortion*,
        edited by Eugene Fairweather and Ian Gentles, 41-55. Toronto: The
        Anglican Book Centre, 1976.

        The author examines the view of the early church on children, and
        concludes that they held children, from the time of conception, to be very
        precious, and a gift from God. He then proceeds to give a theological
        justification for viewing abortion as immoral, except perhaps when the
        mother's life is endangered by continuing a pregnancy.

18.   Fisher, Rev. Anthony, O.P. "'When Did I Begin?' Revisited." *Linacre
        Quarterly* 58, no. 3 (1991): 59-68.

        A review of *When Did I Begin*, by Norman M. Ford (see citation # 99).
        This article in particular criticizes Ford's contention that there is no human
        individual soul present in the embryo until two or three weeks after
        fertilization.

19.   Frame, John M. "Abortion from a Biblical Perspective." In *Thou Shalt
        not Kill: The Christian Case against Abortion*, edited by Richard L. Ganz,
        43-75. New Rochelle, N.Y.: Arlington House, 1978.

        The author deals with a great many biblical passages which can be used
        to determine the Bible's attitude toward abortion and the personhood of
        the fetus. He shows that, while we cannot *prove* from Scripture that the
        fetus is a person from the moment of conception, and thus entitled to a
        right to life, the Christian is under Scriptural obligation to act on the
        assumption that the fetus is a person in the sight of God from the moment
        of conception. He then considers if there are any cases in which abortion
        is permitted, concluding that the oly possible justification for abortion
        would be to save the life of the mother.

20.   Gentry, Kenneth L, Jr. *The Christian Case against Abortion.* Revised and
        updated. Memphis: Footstool Publications, 1989.

        Presents a Christian case against abortion by first examining the scientific
        evidence, and then the biblical evidence on the beginning of human life,
        followed by the biblical view of the value of prenatal life.

21.   Green, Ronald M. "Jewish Teaching on the Sanctity and Quality of Life." In *Jewish and Catholic Bioethics: An Ecumenical Dialogue,* edited by Edmund D. Pellegrino and Alan I. Faden, 25-42. Washington, D.C.: Georgetown Univ. Press, 1999.

The author outlines the "sanctity of life" view and the "quality of life" view, as they relate to abortion and euthanasia. He then examines Orthodox Jewish teaching, and shows that, contrary to popular opinion, it tends to favor the "quality of life" view.

22.   Hauerwas, Stanley. "Why Abortion is a Religious Issue." In *The Ethics of Abortion: Pro-Life vs. Pro-Choice.* Rev. ed., edited by Robert M. Baird and Stuart E. Rosenbaum, 149-169. Buffalo: Prometheus Books, 1993. First published in *A Community of Character: Toward a Constructive Christian Social Ethic.* Univ. of Notre Dame Press, 1981.

Presents the argument that the first question should not be "is the fetus a human being," but rather, "How should the Christian regard and care for the fetus as a child?"

23.   Heaney, Stephen J. "Aquinas and the Presence of the Human Rational Soul in the Early Embryo." In *Abortion: A New Generation of Catholic Responses,* edited by Stephen J. Heaney, 43-71. Braintree, Mass.: Pope John Center, 1992.

A critique of Thomas Aquinas, and those who follow his thinking, that the soul does not enter the body at conception, but rather some time later. He says that such a view suggests that we must have a human ontological individual before the soul comes. He claims, however, that it is the soul which makes this matter to be a human ontological individual.

24.   Higginson, Richard. "The Fetus as a person." In *Abortion in Debate,* 37-48. Edinburgh: Quorum Press, 1987.

The author presents an argument that the fetus is a person from the moment of conception, and then asks in what cases, if ever, it is morally permissible to abort this person/fetus.

25.   Hinthorn, Daniel R. "When Does Human Life Begin?" *Christianity Today,* 24 March 1978, 35-37.

A Christian physician looks at the Bible and medicine, and determines that human life begins at fertilization. When the soul is infused into the body, however, is a different question. The author disputes the view that the soul is infused at fertilization, as twinning doesn't occur until later. He concludes that we have no evidence that God recognizes the living mass of cells in the mother as a person until implantation occurs.

26.   Irving, Dianne Nutwell. "Philosophical and Scientific Analysis of the Nature of the Early Human Embryo." Ph.D. diss., Georgetown University, 1991.

Claims that arguments for delayed hominization are flawed because the various biological "marker events" they use cannot be sustained logically, philosophically, or scientifically. She presents a case for immediate hominization, that is, that the original human zygote is a living, individual, rational human being.

27.   Kreeft, Peter. "Human Personhood Begins at Conception." *Journal of Biblical Ethics in Medicine* 4 (1990): 8-13.

An argument for personhood beginning at conception.

28.   Maguire, Marjorie Reiley. "Personhood, Covenant, and Abortion." *Annual of the Society of Christian Ethics* (1983): 117-145

An argument from a Christian ethical perspective that the fetus is not a person at the point of conception, but that it does become one at some point before birth. She claims that the Scripture nowhere asserts that life is sacred, only that the people of God are sacred. She thus concludes that a woman is only obligated to carry to term those fetuses for whom she is physically, emotionally, psychologically, and economically prepared to carry out the demands of covenant after birth.

29.   McCartney, James J. "Some Roman Catholic Concepts of Person and their Implications for the Ontological Status of the Unborn." In *Abortion and the Status of the Fetus,* edited by William B. Bondeson, H. Tristram Engelhardt, Jr., Stuart F. Spicker, and Daniel H. Winship, 313-323. Dordrecht: D. Reidel Pub. Co., 1983.

Examines the views of several Roman Catholic writers on the concept of personhood, and shows the implications these concepts have for the ontological status of the unborn.

30.   ———. *Unborn Persons: Pope John Paul II and the Abortion Debate.* American University Studies, Series VII, Theology and Religion, vol. 21. New York: Peter Lang, 1987.

Discusses the philosophic and moral thought of Pope John Paul II, especially on personhood and abortion. He traces the theological and philosophical influences that shaped his thought, and then examines his thought on personhood.

31.   McCormick, Richard A., S.J. "Who or What is the Preembryo?" *Kennedy Institute of Ethics Journal* 1 (1991): 1-15.

Using both science and Catholic theology, the author presents his conclusions that, while the pre-embryo is not yet a person, we should consider it to be one.

32.   Minturn, Leigh. "The Birth Ceremony as a Rite of Passage into Infant Personhood." In *Abortion Rights and Fetal 'Personhood,'* 2nd ed., edited by Edd Doerr and James W. Prescott, 81-88. Long Beach, Calif.: Centerline Press, in cooperation with Americans for Religious Liberty, 1990.

An anthropological study which concludes that in most societies, including Christian societies, personhood is conferred on infants via birth ceremonies, and that human infants do not become legal entities until adults in the social group have purified and/or blessed the child in a particular rite.

33.   Montgomery, John Warwick. "The Fetus and Personhood." *Human Life Review* 1, no. 2 (1975): 41-49.

Saying that we may regard "soul" as a theological term for "person," the author goes on to present a theological discussion of the soul, and when it begins to exist, and the application this has to the issue of abortion.

34.   Morecraft, Joe, III. "What Are You Doing about the American Holocaust? (What the Bible Says about Abortion)." *Counsel of Chalcedon,* December 1988, 4-8, 39.

Presents an outline of the Bible's teaching on abortion, showing that it begins with the basic principle that we are to preserve and protect human life because it is made in the image of God, and that human life begins at conception.

35.   O'Donovan, Oliver. "Again: Who is a Person?" In *Abortion and the Sanctity of Human Life,* edited by J. H. Channer, 125-137. Exeter, Eng.: Paternoster Press, 1985.

Using the parable of the Good Samaritan as a backdrop, and in particular the way in which Jesus answered the question "Who is my neighbor?," the author presents an argument that we should see personhood in the same way that Jesus defined one's neighbor. Thus we discover the personhood of another by his dealings with us.

36.   O'Mathúna, Dónal P. "The Bible and Abortion: What of the Image of God?" In *Bioethics and the Future of Medicine: A Christian Appraisal,* edited by John F. Kilner, Nigel M. de S. Cameron, and David L. Scheidermayer, 199-211. Grand Rapids: Eerdmans Pub. Co., 1995.

Discusses the question of what the Bible means when it speaks of man being in the image of God, and then discusses the implications of that on the abortion issue.

37.   Outler, Albert C. "The Beginnings of Personhood: Theological Considerations." *Perkins Journal* 27, no. 1 (1973): 28-34.

Examines the theological issues in the beginning of personhood. Concludes that no one can prove conclusively when personhood begins.

38.   Poundstone, Tom. "The Catholic Debate on the Moral Status of the Embryo." In *The Silent Subject: Reflections on the Unborn in American Culture,* edited by Brad Stetson, 169-175. Westport, Conn.: Praeger, 1996.

Presents an historical and theological account of the Catholic view on when ensoulment occurs, and of the moral status of the fetus.

39.   Preston, Willard F. "The Unborn Child." *Linacre Quarterly* 46 (1979): 50-54.

An address by a Catholic pro-life physician before the Delaware Legislature, in which he gives an argument for the sanctity of all human life, born and unborn.

40.   Provonsha, Jack W. "Reverence for Life and the Abortion Issue." In *Abortion: Ethical Issues and Options,* edited by David R. Larson, 113-123. Loma Linda, Calif.: Loma Linda University, Center for Christian Bioethics, 1992.

The author describes the "reverence for life" ethic of Albert Schweitzer, and urges it as an approach to the abortion issue.

41.   Ramsey, Paul. "The Morality of Abortion." In *Abortion: The Moral Issues,* edited by Edward Batchelor, 73-91. New York: Pilgrim Press, 1982. Originally published in Daniel H. Labby, ed. *Life or Death: Ethics and Options* (Seattle: Univ. of Washington Press, 1968).

The author presents the range of views that have been held regarding when human life begins. He says, however that from an authentic Christian perspective, none of them matter very much, because ultimately, the sanctity of human life is grounded not in something inherent in man, but rather in the value that God places on it.

42. Rankin, John C. "The Corporeal Reality of *Nepeš* and the Status of the Unborn. *Journal of the Evangelical Theological Society* 31 (1988): 153-160.

Using Genesis 2:7 and a word study of the Hebrew word *nephesh* (soul) as a basis, the author presents an argument that, biblically speaking, the one celled zygote, from the point of conception, is, in the fullest theological sense, a person made in the image of God, deserving of the same protection we give to all human beings.

43. Rogerson, J. W. "Using the Bible in the Debate about Abortion." In *Abortion and the Sanctity of Human Life,* edited by J. H. Channer, 77-92. Exeter, Eng.: Paternoster Press, 1985.

The author shows that, while many of the biblical texts that Christians use to argue against abortion are questionable in terms of their proper application to abortion, nonetheless the Bible does challenge us to include unborn children along with the defenseless, which the Bible everywhere tells us to defend.

44. Scott, Graham A. D. "Abortion and the Incarnation." *Journal of the Evangelical Theological Society* 17 (1974): 29-44.

Through a survey of biblical passages, the author comes to the conclusion that human life begins at conception, but he also calls for Christians not to condemn those who have had an abortion, but are repentant.

45. Shannon, Thomas A., and Allan B. Wolter, O.F.M. "Reflections on the Moral Status of the Pre-Embryo." *Theological Studies* 51 (1990): 603-626.

Reviews the contemporary biological data about the early human embryo, and compares that with the philosophical and Catholic theological claims made about it. They conclude that personhood does not begin until about the third week after fertilization.

46. Simmons, Paul D. "The Fetus as Person: A Biblical Perspective." In *Abortion Rights and Fetal 'Personhood,'* 2nd ed., edited by Edd Doerr and James W. Prescott, 15-28. Long Beach, Calif.: Centerline Press, in cooperation with Americans for Religious Liberty, 1990.

An examination of biblical teaching which concludes that the Bible is silent on the issue of abortion.

47.   Smyth, Harley. "The Bible and the Unborn Child: Reflections on Life Before Birth." In *The Right to Birth: Some Christian Views on Abortion,* edited by Eugene Fairweather and Ian Gentles, 25-39. Toronto: The Anglican Book Centre, 1976.

An examination of biblical statements, trying to discern what they say about life before birth.

48.   Stott, John R. W. "Reverence for Human Life." *Christianity Today,* 9 June 1972, 8-12.

Seeks to find a guiding principle in Christian faith that can guide us through the labyrinth of medical-moral problems of life. He finds such a principle in what he terms a "reverence for human life," and defends this principle on theological grounds. He then applies the principle to medical practice and to some burning medical issues.

49.   Talone, Patricia. "Sanctity of Life in Catholic and Jewish Thought: Convergence and Divergence." In *Religions of the Book,* edited by Gerard S. Sloyan, 209-224. Lanham, Md.: University Press of America, 1996.

Explores the concept of sanctity of life as found in Jewish and Christian (particularly Catholic) thought. She then examines how the two traditions apply these principles in the issues of euthanasia and abortion.

50.   Thomasma, David C. "The Sanctity-of-Human-Life Doctrine." In *Jewish and Catholic Bioethics: An Ecumenical Dialogue,* edited by Edmund D. Pellegrino, and Alan I. Faden, 54-73. Washington, D.C.: Georgetown Univ. Press, 1999.

The author examines the sanctity of life doctrine as taught in Judaism and in Christianity. He finds that it has a plethora of meanings, as well as several attacks on it. He then presents a reconstruction of the sanctity of life doctrine.

51.   Verhey, Allen. "The Body and the Bible: Life in the Flesh according to the Spirit." In *Embodiment, Morality, and Medicine,* edited by Lisa Sowle Cahill and Margaret A. Farley, 3-22. Dordrecht: Kluwer Academic Publishers, 1995.

Examines the views of two Protestant theologians – Joseph Fletcher and Paul Ramsey – on the issue of personhood, and the relation of the person to the body. He then tests both these views from a biblical perspective, and finds the views of Paul Ramsey as being closer and more faithful to biblical teaching.

52. Waltke, Bruce K. "Reflections from the Old Testament on Abortion." *Journal of the Evangelical Theological Society* 17 (1976): 3-13.

The author presents an analysis and exegesis of several Old Testament passages, coming to the conclusion that the fetus is a human being and deserving of a right to life, and that abortion should only be allowed in cases where the mother's life is in danger.

53. Wernow, Jerome R. "Saying the Unsaid: Quality of Life Criteria in a Sanctity of Life Position." In *Bioethics and the Future of Medicine: A Christian Appraisal,* edited by John F. Kilner, Nigel M. de S. Cameron, and David L. Schiedermayer, 93-111. Grand Rapids: Eerdmans Pub. Co., 1995.

Discusses the general Evangelical position on quality of life criteria in bioethical decisions such as abortion, infanticide and euthanasia. Explores the validity of the claim that qualified sanctity of life positions are unarticulated and obtuse.

54. White, Andrew A. "The Corporeal Aspect and Procreative Function of the Imago Dei and Abortion." *Journal of Biblical Ethics in Medicine* 6 (1992): 19-24.

Based on the Christian doctrine of the image of God, in particular on its corporeal aspects, the author makes an argument against abortion.

PHILOSOPHICAL DISCUSSIONS

55. Barry, Rev. Robert P., O.P. "Personhood: The Conditions of Identification and Description." *Linacre Quarterly* 45 (1978): 64-81.

Demonstrates the logical necessity of ascribing personhood to the developing stages of life. Delineates the conditions, events, and states that make the ascription of personhood to the developmental stages of human life a necessity.

56. ———. "Self-Consciousness and Personhood." *Linacre Quarterly* 46 (1979): 141-148.

A critique of Michael Tooley's article, "Abortion and Infanticide." (see citation # 146).

57.   Bassen, Paul. "Present Stakes and Future Prospects: The Status of Early
         Abortion." *Philosophy and Public Affairs* 11 (1982): 314-337.

         If abortion is murder, then obviously there must be a victim. The author
         argues that the real question is not whether the fetus is a person, but
         whether it can be a victim. He concludes that in the early stages, before
         two months, the fetus cannot be a victim, and so may be aborted without
         consequence. Once we reach the third trimester though, the fetus can be
         a victim. In between, he says, is a grey area, where it is difficult to make
         a hard and fast rule.

58.   Bauer, Joe. "The Right of Choice." *American Atheist* 32 (April 1990):
         48-49.

         A critique of the pro-life argument that, since the fetus has the entire
         genetic make-up of an adult human being, it is therefore a human being,
         with a right to life.

59.   Becker, Lawrence C. "Human Being: The Boundaries of the Concept."
         Philosophy and Public Affairs 4 (1975): 334-359.

         Argues that we can define when human life begins and ends, and that we
         can do so biologically. He argues that human life begins when the
         organism has achieved its basic morphology and its inventory of
         histologically differentiated organs is complete. The end of human life
         occurs when the system of those reciprocally dependent processes are
         arrested in such a way that the organism itself cannot reverse.

60.   Bedate, Carlos A., and Robert C. Cefalo. "The Zygote: To Be or Not to
         Be a Person." *Journal of Medicine and Philosophy* 14 (1989): 641-645.

         On biological grounds, the authors argue against the moral and theological
         statement that the zygote is a person because it contains all the informa-
         tion necessary to produce the specific biological character of the future
         adult. They claim that while the zygote makes possible the existence of
         a human being, it does not possess sufficient information to form it. It has
         sufficient information to produce exclusively human tissue, but not to
         become an individual human being.

61.   Berquist, Richard. "Abortion and the Right to Life before Personhood."
         In *Abortion: A New Generation of Catholic Responses,* edited by Stephen
         J. Heaney, 121-132. Braintree, Mass.: Pope John Center, 1992.

         Presents the argument that abortion is always a violation of the right to
         life, whether the aborted embryo is an actual person yet or not.

62.   Bigelow, John, and Robert Pargetter. "Morality, Potential Persons, and Abortion." *American Philosophical Quarterly* 25 (1988): 173-181.

        The authors start with the premise that an action is morally permissible if it harms no one, including future persons, unless there is some over-riding consideration against it. They apply this principle to the cases of contraception and abortion. They conclude that contraception, and early abortion are morally permissible because there is not an actual future person being harmed.

63.   Biggers, John D. "Generation of the Human Life Cycle." In *Abortion and the Status of the Fetus*, edited by William B. Bondeson, H. Tristram Engelhardt, Jr., Stuart F. Spicker, and Daniel H. Winship, 31-53. Dordrecht: D. Reidel Pub. Co., 1983.

        Using science and biology, the author comments that there is a complete cycle from fertilization to birth to maturity to death, and that some people in the maturity stage may participate in the process of reproduction that renews the life cycle. As a result, he claims that we cannot point to fertilization as the point at which life begins.

64.   Bok, Sissela. "Who Shall Count as a Human Being? A Treacherous Question in the Abortion Discussion." In *Abortion: Pro and Con*, edited by Robert L. Perkins, 91-105. Cambridge, Mass.: Schenkman Pub. Co., 1974.

        The author claims that efforts to decide when human life begins are deceptive at best, and do not help us solve the abortion debate. She says that we should rather decide what are the common principles we have for the protection of life; why do we consider life to be sacred? She lists several reasons for protecting life, and claims that these reasons do not apply to a fetus in the early stages of pregnancy.

65.   Bole, Thomas J., III. "Metaphysical Accounts of the Zygote as a Person and the Veto Power of Facts." *Journal of Medicine and Philosophy* 14 (1989): 647-653.

        The author argues that the metaphysical claim that the soul of a human person is infused at conception is negated by biological fact, because the zygote itself is not yet determined to be an individual human.

66.   Bondeson, William B., H. Tristram Engelhardt, Jr., Stuart F. Spicker, and Daniel H. Winship, eds. *Abortion and the Status of the Fetus*. Philosophy and Medicine, vol. 13. Dordrecht: D. Reidel Pub. Co., 1983.

A collection of articles, from various perspectives, on the moral and legal status of the fetus, and the implications that may have for issues such as abortion, infanticide, euthanasia, and *in vitro* fertilization.

67.   Bracken, W. Jerome. "Is the Early Embryo a Person?" In *Life and Learning VIII: Proceedings of the Eighth University Faculty for Life Conference, June 1998 at the University of Toronto,* edited by Joseph W. Koterski, S.J., 443-467. Washington, D.C.: University Faculty for Life, 1999.

       Presents a critique of the arguments for the non-personhood of the early embryo, and proposes counter-arguments for saying that the early embryo is a person.

68.   Brandt, R. B. "Hare on Abortion." *Social Theory and Practice* 15 (1989): 15-24.

       A critique of Hare's article, "A Kantian Approach to Abortion." (see citation # 109).

69.   Brody, Baruch. A. "Fetal Humanity and the Theory of Essentialism." In *Philosophy and Sex,* edited by Robert Baker and Frederick Elliston, 338-355. Buffalo: Prometheus Books, 1975.

       What properties are essential to being human, and when does the fetus acquire them? That is the question the author attempts to answer. He concludes that the fetus acquires them sometime between the end of the second week and the end of the twelfth week after conception, and that abortion after this is morally wrong.

70.   ———. "On the Humanity of the Foetus." In *Abortion: Pro and Con,* edited by Robert L. Perkins, 69-90. Cambridge, Mass.: Schenkman Pub. Co., 1974.

       The author asks the question whether there is an objective point at which it can be said that the fetus at that point becomes a living human being. He concludes that there is, and that point is at about the sixth week, when fetal brain activity commences. He also criticizes those who take the view that we *cannot* know when human life begins, and we must merely *decide* when it begins.

71.   Brungs, Robert. "Human Life vs. Human Personhood." In *What is a Person?,* edited by Michael F. Goodman, 281-291. Clifton, N.J.: Humana Press, 1988.

The author notes that as a result of *Roe v. Wade,* two ideas have crept into our thinking – that there is a difference between human biological life and human personal life, as well as the idea of quality of life as opposed to the sanctity of life. He then shows how these twin ideas have already begun to, and will continue to lead to some very unwelcome things, eugenics being one of them.

72.   Cahalan, John C. "A Prolegomenon to any Future Ethics of Abortion." In *Life and Learning VIII: Proceedings of the Eighth University Faculty for Life Conference, June 1998 at the University of Toronto,* edited by Joseph W. Koterski, S.J., 327-362. Washington, D.C.: University Faculty for Life, 1999.

The author defends the view that human life, or personhood, begins at conception by saying that the point when killing a fetus is as wrong as killing an adult is that point when, according to objective evidence an entity that is oriented to the kinds of things that give value to our choices first exists.

73.   Cahill, Lisa Sowle. "The Embryo and the Fetus: New Moral Contexts." *Theological Studies* 54 (1993): 124-142.

Addresses the interplay of scientific information about embryonic development with philosophical interpretations of personhood to see if full moral status can be tied to a particular physiological indicator.

74.   Callahan, Daniel. "The 'Beginning' of Human Life: Philosophical Considerations." In *What is a Person?,* edited by Michael F. Goodman, 29-55. Clifton, N.J.: Humana Press, 1988.

Examines the various views on when human life begins in order to point out the various factors that must be taken into consideration in any philosophical investigation of the question.

75.   ———. "Rights of the Fetus Uncertain." *National Catholic Reporter,* 18 Feb. 1977, 32.

Shows that the question of the fetus has not been answered. Since the status of the fetus is uncertain, he concludes that we should leave abortion legal. Yet, at the same time, he is concerned that by doing so, we are merely choosing one good (freedom of the woman) at the expense of another good (life).

76.   Callahan, Sidney. "Moral Duty to the Unborn and Its Significance." In *The Silent Subject: Reflections on the Unborn in American Culture,* edited by Brad Stetson, 43-49. Westport, Conn.: Praeger, 1996.

Argues that the unborn human being has value because it is a member of the human family and shares in the heritage of the human species.

77.   Carter, W. R. "Once and Future Persons." In *What is a Person?*, edited by Michael F. Goodman, 185-197. Clifton, N.J.: Humana Press, 1988.

Presents the thesis that there are degrees of personhood; that is that a given entity, whether it be a fetus, an infant, or an older person, may "fit" the definition of person more or less loosely.

78.   Childress. James F. "A Response to Ronald Green 'Conferred Rights and the Fetus.'" *Journal of Religious Ethics* 2, no. [1] (1974): 77-83.

A critique of Ronald Green's article, "Conferred Rights and the Fetus." (see citation # 106).

79.   Cooney, William. "The Fallacy of All Person-Denying Arguments for Abortion." *Journal of Applied Philosophy* 8 (1991): 161-165.

The author claims that arguments in favor of abortion which deny the personhood of the fetus do not work.

80.   Crosby, John F. "The Personhood of the Human Embryo." In *Life and Learning: Proceedings of the Third University Faculty for Life Conference,* edited by Joseph W. Koterski, S.J., 177-199. Washington, D.C.: University Faculty for Life, 1993.

Presents a critique of the argument that, while the human embryo may indeed be fully human, it is not yet a person, as personhood requires consciousness.

81.   ———. "Why Persons Have Dignity." In *Life and Learning IX: Proceedings of the Ninth University Faculty for Life Conference, June 1999, at Trinity International University, Deerfield, Ill.,* edited by Joseph W. Koterski, S.J., 79-92. Washington, D.C.: University Faculty for Life, 2000.

Attempts to answer the question, what gives a human being dignity? Why do we recognize dignity in a person? He does this, as much as possible, without resorting to theological reasons, so as to provide a much broader base for appeal.

82.   Daniels, Charles B. "Abortion and Potential." *Dialogue* 18 (1979): 220-223.

A critique of Pluhar's article, "Abortion and Simple Consciousness" (see citation # 133) on the basis that he has not established that potentially conscious beings have actual rights, nor that the rights they do have devolve from a degree of consciousness they have the potential to achieve.

83.   Devine, Philip E. "Abortion." In *Contemporary Issues in Bioethics,* 2nd. ed., edited by Tom L. Beauchamp and LeRoy Walters. Belmont, Calif.: Wadsworth Pub. Co., 1982.

Argues that the grounds for asserting the humanity of an infant are also present in the fetus. Thus, the fetus, from conception on, is also a human person.

84.   ———. "Fetuses and 'Human Vegetables.'" In *Ethics for Modern Life.* 4th ed., edited by Raziel Abelson, and Marie-Louise Friquegnon, 174-185. New York: St. Martin's Press, 1991.

The author begins with the claim that if infanticide is murder, then abortion must be murder as well, for the only grounds for asserting the humanity of the infant also apply to the fetus. The author then goes on to discuss the question of the personhood of the fetus, and when it begins. He concludes that we should ascribe a right to life to the fetus from the sixth week of gestation at the latest.

85.   ———. "The Scope of the Prohibition against Killing." In *The Abortion Controversy: 25 Years after Roe v. Wade: A Reader.* 2nd ed., edited by Louis P. Pojman and Francis J. Beckwith, 234-256. Belmont, Calif.: Wadsworth Pub. Co., 1998. First published in *The Ethics of Homicide.* Ithaca, N.Y.: Cornell Univ. Press, 1978.

The author asks what kinds of beings are protected by the rule against homicide. He presents several principles, and comes to the conclusion that, in most cases, abortion is immoral, as it is the killing of a member of the human species.

86.   Di Ianni, Albert R. "Is the Fetus a Person?" *American Ecclesiastical Review* 168 (1974): 309-326.

Examines the question, What is a person? While he prefers the conservative position that the fetus is a person with a right to life, he admits that it might be plausible to place the beginning of personhood not at conception, but rather several weeks later.

87.   Dore, Clement. "Abortion, Some Slippery Slope Arguments, and Identity over Time." *Philosophical Studies* 55 (1989): 279-291.

The author presents his own version of the slippery slope argument against abortion. This argument states that since there is no identifiable point in gestation when it can be indubitably stated that personhood begins at that point, therefore we are forced to say that personhood begins at conception.

88.   Duden, Barbara. *Disembodying Women: Perspectives on Pregnancy and the Unborn.* Translated from the German by Lee Hoinacki. Cambridge, Mass.: Harvard Univ. Press, 1993.

The goal of this treatise is to show historically that the human fetus, as conceptualized today, is not a creature of God or a natural fact, but an engineered construct of modern society.

89.   Dupré, Louis. "A New Approach to the Abortion Problem." *Theological Studies* 34 (1973): 481-488.

The author presents an approach to solving the abortion dilemma on the basis of personhood.

90.   Duska, Ronald. "On Confusing Human Beings and Persons." In *Realism,* edited by Daniel O. Dahlstrom, 158-165. Washington, D.C.: American Catholic Philosophical Association, 1984.

A review of the thought of three philosophers with different conceptions of human beings vs. persons. He concludes that we cannot base human rights on personhood. Rather, he speculates that we may have to base it on sanctity.

91.   Edwards, Rem B. "Abortion Rights: Why Conservatives are Wrong." *National Forum* 69, no. 4 (1989): 19, 21, 23-24.

Gives legal and philosophical reasons for rejecting the conservative position that the fetus is a human person from the moment of conception.

92.   Engelhardt, H. Tristram, Jr. "The Beginnings of Personhood: Philosophical Considerations." *Perkins Journal* 27, no. 1 (1973): 20-27.

An exploration of the concepts involved in determining what personhood is, and when it begins.

93.   ———. "The Ontology of Abortion." *Ethics* 84 (1974): 217-234.

This article focuses on the question of whether, and to what extent, the fetus is a person. He concludes that it is impossible to establish a basis for holding that the fetus is a human person. The fetus, he claims, is an example of human life but not of personal life. There are, he claims, two categories of human life: biological and personal. The fetus, he says, is nonpersonal, and merely biological.

94. English, Jane. "Abortion and the Concept of a Person." *Canadian Journal of Philosophy* 5 (1975): 233-243.

Examines the concept of a person and concludes that no single criterion can capture the entire concept, and no sharp line can be drawn as to when personhood begins. It also argues that even if the fetus is a person, the principle of self-defense allows a woman to have an abortion in some cases, especially in the early months of a pregnancy. On the other hand, even if the fetus is not a person, it is too much like a baby in the later stages of a pregnancy to permit an abortion.

95. Feinberg, Joel. "Abortion." In *Matters of Life and Death,* edited by Tom Regan, 183-217. Philadelphia: Temple Univ. Press, 1980.

Examines what personhood is, and applies this to the moral status of the fetus. He then examines the rights of others involved in the abortion decision, primarily those of the mother. He weighs the rights of the fetus with the rights of the mother.

96. ———. "Potentiality, Development, and Rights." In *The Problem of Abortion.* 2nd ed., edited by Joel Feinberg. 145-150. Belmont, Calif.: Wadsworth Pub. Co., 1984.

Presents a modified view of potentiality, such that the rights of the fetus grow steadily and gradually throughout gestation, until they are mature at birth. Thus, abortions at a very early stage (before three months), are unproblematic, but after three months, the rights of the fetus do begin to play a role in the decision. As the fetus grows more and more, its rights will more and more outweigh the rights of the mother.

97. Fletcher, Joseph F. "Four Indicators of Humanhood: The Enquiry Matures." *Hastings Center Report* 4, no. 6 (1974): 4-7.

A sequel to his earlier article (see citation # 98), in which he defines four indicators, or traits, which he says are the *sine qua non* of personhood.

98. ———. "Indicators of Humanhood: A Tentative Profile of Man." *Hastings Center Report* 2, no. 5 (1972): 1-4.

The author outlines the criteria he believes are necessary for true humanhood, or personhood. He also shows the implications of these criteria on abortion and euthanasia.

99.   Ford, Norman M. *When Did I Begin? Conception of the Human Individual in History, Philosophy and Science.* Cambridge: Cambridge Univ. Press, 1988.

Using the disciplines of philosophy and scientific embryology, along with the history of each, the author presents a case for saying that a human individual does not exist until there is no longer any possibility of twinning, which occurs at about the fourteenth day of gestation.

100.   Foster, J. "Personhood and the Ethics of Abortion." In *Abortion and the Sanctity of Human Life,* edited by J. H. Channer, 31-53. Exeter, Eng.: Paternoster Press, 1985.

The author presents an argument that abortion is morally tantamount to murder, on the basis of the status of the fetus and on the question of whether there are circumstances in which abortion is morally permissible, and thus not tantamount to murder.

101.   Gallagher, John. *Is the Human Embryo a Person? A Philosophical Investigation.* Human Life Institute Research Reports, no. 4. Toronto: Human Life Research Institute, 1985.

A philosophical investigation into the question of when the human person begins to exist. Comes to the conclusion that the human person begins at the point of fertilization.

102.   Galvin, Richard Francis. "Noonan's Argument against Abortion: Probability, Possibility and Potentiality." *Journal of Social Philosophy* 19, no. 2 (1988): 80-89.

A critique of Noonan's article, "An Almost Absolute Value in History." (see citation # 129). This article takes Noonan to task for his argument that human life begins at conception.

103.   Gardell, Mary Ann. "Moral Pluralism in Abortion." In *Abortion and the Status of the Fetus,* edited by William B. Bondeson, H. Tristram Engelhardt, Jr., Stuart F. Spicker, and Daniel H. Winship, 325-331. Dordrecht: D. Reidel Pub. Co., 1983.

The author displays the wide variety of views on the status of the fetus, and the implications these have for abortion. She shows that it is not likely that agreement can be reached by general rational argument, as the differences are generally the result of differing presuppositions and world-views. This, she says, is reason enough, in pluralistic societies, not to proscribe abortion by law.

104. Goldman, Alan H. "Abortion and the Right to Life." *The Personalist* 60 (1979): 402-406.

A critique of Michael Tooley's article "Abortion and Infanticide" (see citation # 146) on the basis that the self-conscious desire to continue living is not a necessary condition to have a right to life.

105. Goodman, Michael F., ed. *What is a Person?* Contemporary Issues in Biomedicine, Ethics, and Society. Clifton, N.J.: Humana Press, 1988.

A collection of articles on the concept of personhood – what it is, when it begins, etc. This question has application to the issues of abortion, infanticide, and euthanasia.

106. Green, Ronald M. "Conferred Rights and the Fetus." *Journal of Religious Ethics* 2, no. [1] (1974): 55-75.

The author seeks to determine the moral status of the fetus by means of a rational theory of rights. He argues that all agents with a rational and moral capacity have full rights; those who do not, have their rights conferred on them by other rational, moral agents. He concludes that most rational, moral agents would choose not to sacrifice their liberty by conferring substantial rights on the fetus.

107. Grisez, Germain. "When Do People Begin?" In *The Ethics of Having Children*, edited by Lawrence P. Schrenk, 27-47. Washington, D.C.: National Office of the American Catholic Philosophical Society, 1990.

The author lays out his own definition of personhood, which leads him to the conclusion that most human persons begin at conception, although some begin during the next two or three weeks by the dividing of embryos.

108. Hare, R. M. "Abortion: Reply to Brandt." *Social Theory and Practice* 15 (1989): 25-32

A reply to Brandt's critique (see citation # 68) of his thesis.

109. ———. "A Kantian Approach to Abortion." *Social Theory and Practice* 15 (1989): 1-14.

Some have argued that since the fetus is a potential person, that is, since, left to itself, the fetus will develop into a person like us, that this provides a good argument against abortion. The author presents a critique of this potentiality principle.

110.   Hartshorne, Charles. "Concerning Abortion: An Attempt at a Rational View." *Christian Century* 98 (1981): 42-45.

Presents an argument that the fetus is not human in the normal sense, but is only potentially a person.

111.   Holland, Alan. "A Fortnight of My Life is Missing: A Discussion of the Status of the Human 'Pre-Embryo.'" *Journal of Applied Philosophy* 7 (1990): 25-37.

The author demonstrates that the moral arguments used to deny that human beings begin to exist at conception are weak. He concludes by saying that there is no good reason to deny that human beings begin to exist at conception.

112.   Honnefelder, Ludger. "The Concept of a Person in Moral Philosophy." In *Sanctity of Life and Human Dignity*, edited by Kurt Bayertz, 139-160. Dordrecht: Kluwer Academic Publishers, 1996.

The author presents his own definition of personhood. He also examines the current state of the debate, and looks at the metaphysical implications.

113.   Iglesias, Teresa. "What Kind of Being Is the Human Embryo?" *Ethics and Medicine* 2 (1986): 2-7.

The author disputes the notion that it is not important to determine if the embryo is a person, but rather ask the question how are we to act towards it. She also disputes the view that the embryo is only a potential human person, and thus there is no ham in destroying it. She presents her conviction, grounded on biological knowledge, philosophical reflection, and Christian faith, that the human embryo is a human person with an eternal destiny.

114.   Joyce, Robert E. "Personhood and the Conception Event." In *What is a Person?*, edited by Michael F. Goodman, 199-211. Clifton, N.J.: Humana Press, 1988.

Presents an argument that the *conceptus,* or the human zygote, is specifically and truly a person, though less developed. He claims that a one-celled individual at conception is not a potential person, but an actual person with great potential for development and self-expression.

115.   Kohl, Marvin. "Is the Fetus a Human Being?" *The Humanist* 32, no. 3 (1972): 8

Claims that it is not "a fact beyond dispute" that each unborn human infant is a human being. A fetus in the early stages of development, he says, has rights, but they are not human beings' rights. The rights of humans between birth and death take moral precedence over the rights of other beings.

116.   Lee, Patrick. "Personhood, the Moral Standing of the Unborn, and Abortion." *Linacre Quarterly* 57, no. 2 (1990): 80-89.

A critique of the view that sentience is the criterion for moral standing, and of the view that there are degrees of moral standing, such that early abortions are permissible, but late abortions usually are not.

117.   ———. "Self-Consciousness and the Right to Life." In *Abortion: A New Generation of Catholic Responses*, edited by Stephen J. Heaney, 73-84. Braintree, Mass.: Pope John Center, 1992.

The author presents a critique of two common arguments for saying that the fetus is a human being, but not a person. He claims that such arguments must show, not just that the fetus lacks those qualities necessary to have moral rights, but also why having these qualities is a necessary precondition for having basic moral rights. He claims that most such arguments do not take this latter step.

118.   Lenzen, Wolfgang. "Value of Life vs. Sanctity of Life – Outlines of a Bioethics that Does without the Concept of *Menschenwürde.* In *Sanctity of Life and Human Dignity*, edited by Kurt Bayertz, 39-55. Dordrecht: Kluwer Academic Publishers, 1996.

This paper aims to reinforce the claim of the moral redundancy of the concept of *Menshcenwürde* by outlining a system of bioethics that does without it. The main point of this system is to replace the idea of "sanctity of life" with the idea of "value of life. The author then applies this to the issues of assisted suicide, euthanasia, abortion and contraception, and *in vitro* fertilization.

119.   Li, Chenyang. "The Fallacy of the Slippery Slope Argument on Abortion." *Journal of Applied Philosophy* 9 (1992): 233-237.

Demonstrates that arguments that we do not have to draw a clear cut-off line in the development of the fetus into a person in order to contend that the fetus is not a person are valid arguments. In particular, he criticizes the article by William Cooney (see citation # 79).

120.   Li, Hon Lam. "Abortion and Degrees of Personhood: Understanding Why
        the Abortion Problem (and the Animal Rights Problem) Are Irresolvable."
        Public Affairs Quarterly 11 (1997): 1-19.

        A claim that there are degrees of personhood, and that as the fetus grows,
        it develops a higher degree of personhood, and hence a higher value.

121.   Lomasky, Loren E. "Being a Person—Does it Matter?" In *The Problem
        of Abortion,* 2nd ed., edited by Joel Feinberg, 161-172. Belmont, Calif.:
        Wadsworth Pub. Co., 1984.

        In the debate over abortion, many people assume that it is of critical
        importance to determine if the fetus is a person or not. The author,
        however, argues that being a person is not a morally significant property.

122.   Maguire, Marjorie Reiley. "Symbiosis, Biology, and Personalization."
        In *Abortion Rights and Fetal 'Personhood,'* 2nd ed., edited by Edd Doerr
        and James W. Prescott, 5-14. Long Beach, Calif.: Centerline Press, in
        cooperation with Americans for Religious Liberty, 1990.

        Presents a definition of personhood which basically puts the beginning of
        personhood with birth. The author also states that there is only one case
        when personhood will begin before birth, and that is when the mother
        wants the child. It is the consent of the woman to continuing a pregnancy
        that marks the beginning of personhood.

123.   May, William E. "What Makes a Human Being to be a Being of Moral
        Worth?" *The Thomist* 41 (1976): 416-443.

        The author presents a case for the view that all members of the human
        species are also persons, or, to use his words, beings of moral worth.

124.   Miller, Monica Migliorino. "The Preborn and Prejudice." In *When Life
        and Choice Collide: Essays on Rhetoric and Abortion,* edited by David
        Mall. Vol. 1. Libertyville, Ill.: Kairos Books, 1994.

        An examination of abortion from the civil rights perspective in terms of
        prejudice. The author claims that attitudes that the unborn are either less
        than human, or non-persons, are a form of prejudice against the unborn,
        one born out of ignorance and fear. She claims that respect for human
        rights will never be complete unless this prejudice toward the unborn is
        abolished.

125.   Mitchell, John A., and Scott B. Rae. "The Moral Status of Fetuses and
        Embryos." In *The Silent Subject: Reflections on the Unborn in American
        Culture,* edited by Brad Stetson, 19-32. Westport, Conn.: Praeger, 1996.

Lays out a metaphysical foundation for ethical decision making concerning human rights at both ends of life. Comes to the conclusion that zygotes, embryos and fetuses are fully and equally human beings.

126. Moraczewski, Albert S. "Human Personhood: A Study in Person-alized Biology." In *Abortion and the Status of the Fetus*, edited by William B. Bondeson, H. Tristram Engelhardt, Jr., Stuart F. Spicker, and Daniel H. Winship, 301-311. Dordrecht: D. Reidel Pub. Co., 1983.

The author outlines what he believes to be the essential elements of personhood, and shows the human fetus, from the point of fertilization, meets those criteria. He then answers common objections to this position.

127. Moussa, Mario, and Thomas A. Shannon. "The Search for the New Pineal Gland: Brain Life and Personhood." *Hastings Center Report* 22, no3 (1992): 30-37.

Some have tried to link personhood with "brain life." Once the brain is alive, a person exists. The authors of this article dispute that link, saying that brain life is neither a defensible, nor a useful notion.

128. Newton, Lisa H. "Humans and Persons: A Reply to Tristram Engelhardt." *Ethics* 85 (1975): 332-336.

A critique of Engelhardt's article, "The Ontology of Abortion" (see citation # 93), on the basis that he fails to distinguish between two very different questions: Is this a living human being, and, is this a person. The first question, the author says, is a question of fact; the second is a question of value.

129. Noonan, John T. "An Almost Absolute Value in History." In *The Morality of Abortion: Legal and Historical Perspectives*, edited by John T. Noonan, 1-59. Cambridge, Mass.: Harvard Univ. Press, 1970.

The author takes the position that it is impossible to draw a line as to when personhood begins, as it is present from conception. A being with a complete set of human genes is by definition a full human being who possesses all human rights.

130. Pahel, Kenneth R. "Michael Tooley on Abortion and Potentiality." *The Southern Journal of Philosophy* 25 (1987): 89-107.

A critique of Michael Tooley's book, *Abortion and Infanticide* (see citation # 147)

131.   Pastrana, Gabriel, O.P. "Personhood and the Beginning of Human Life."
        The Thomist 41 (1977): 247-294.

        Presents a philosophical analysis of two questions: (1) When does human
        life begin?, and (2) What is a person? He argues that these concepts are
        essentially philosophical and that one must establish the philosophical
        meaning of human life and personhood before discussing the legal,
        sociological, and moral considerations.

132.   Perkoff, Gerald T. "Toward a Normative Definition of Personhood." In
        Abortion and the Status of the Fetus, edited by William B. Bondeson, H.
        Tristram Engelhardt, Jr., Stuart F. Spicker, and Daniel H. Winship, 159-
        166. Dordrecht: D. Reidel Pub. Co., 1983.

        Speaking as a physician, the author presents an overview of various
        philosophical and religious views of what personhood is, and the effects
        this has on the abortion decision, in order to aid physicians who need to
        make decisions about fetal life, abortion, and fetal experimentation.

133.   Pluhar, Werner S. "Abortion and Simple Consciousness." *Journal of
        Philosophy* 74 (1977): 159-172.

        Presents an argument for establishing sentience, or simple consciousness,
        as the point at which a fetus gains personhood.

134.   Pojman, Louis P. "Abortion: A Defense of the Personhood Argument."
        In *The Abortion Controversy: 25 Years after Roe v. Wade: A Reader*. 2nd
        ed., edited by Louis P. Pojman and Francis J. Beckwith, 275-290.
        Belmont, Calif.: Wadsworth Pub. Co., 1998.

        The author presents several pro-abortion arguments, and shows that only
        one of them, the argument that the fetus does not have the properties that
        characterize personhood, is valid. He then argues for a moderate position
        on abortion.

135.   Puccetti, Roland. "The Life of a Person." In *Abortion and the Status of
        the Fetus*, edited by William B. Bondeson, H. Tristram Engelhardt, Jr.,
        Stuart F. Spicker, and Daniel H. Winship, 169-182. Dordrecht: D. Reidel
        Pub. Co., 1983.

        The author claims that personhood can only be attributed to a subject of
        conscious experiences. Thus abortion, and certain forms of infanticide are
        allowed, as well as the euthanasia of those who no longer have sufficient
        conscious functions.

136.　Sass, Hans-Martin. "The Moral Significance of Brain-Life Criteria." In *The Beginning of Human Life,* edited by Fritz K. Beller and Robert F. Weir, 57-70. Dordrecht: Kluwer, 1994.

Argues that just as the cessation of brain activity has been almost universally accepted as the definition of when death occurs, we should establish that human life begins with the beginning of brain function, or at about the tenth week of gestation.

137.　Schwartz, Lewis M. "An Essay on the Moral Status of Abortion." In *New Essays on Abortion and Bioethics,* edited by Rem B. Edwards, 267-301. Greenwich Conn.: JAI Press, 1997.

Critically examines the arguments of those who claim that the status of the fetus does not change from the time of conception to the time of birth, and finds them defective. He then examines the arguments of those who claim that the status of the fetus does not remain constant, but rather changes as it develops. He finds these arguments more defensible.

138.　Schwarz, Stephen D. "Personhood Begins at Conception." In *The Abortion Controversy: 25 Years after Roe v. Wade: A Reader.* 2nd ed., edited by Louis P. Pojman and Francis J. Beckwith, 257-274. Belmont, Calif.: Wadsworth Pub. Co., 1998. First published in *The Moral Question of Abortion.* Chicago: Loyola Univ. Press, 1990.

Argues that the fetus is an actual person from the time of conception, not just a potential person. He thus condemns abortion and infanticide as abuses of power.

139.　Shannon, Thomas A. "Fetal Status: Sources and Implications." *Journal of Medicine and Philosophy* 22 (1997): 415-422.

Examines four social contexts, and shows how they offer differing, and often contradictory, views on the status of the fetus: abortion, prenatal diagnosis, fetal research, and fetal transplantation.

140.　Sherwin, Susan. "The Concept of a Person in the Context of Abortion." *Bioethics Quarterly* 2 (1981): 21-34.

Investigates the significance of the fetus's status as a person in resolving the moral issue of abortion.

141.　Solomon, Robert C. "Reflections on the Meaning of (Fetal) Life." In *Abortion and the Status of the Fetus,* edited by William B. Bondeson, H. Tristram Engelhardt, Jr., Stuart F. Spicker, and Daniel H. Winship, 209-226. Dordrecht: D. Reidel Pub. Co., 1983.

Presents an argument that self-consciousness is not the sole criterion for establishing personhood, but becomes so only within a social network. Self-consciousness is neither a necessary, nor a sufficient condition for personhood and rights. These conditions emerge only in a more general sense of social worth.

142.   Steinbock, Bonnie. *Life Before Birth: The Moral and Legal Status of Embryos and Fetuses.* New York: Oxford Univ. Press, 1992.

Presents a view of the moral standing of persons based on the interest view, i.e., a being must be capable of caring about what is done to himself in order to have moral status. He must be capable of being made, if only rudimentarily, happy or miserable, comfortable or distressed. The author then applies this principle to the question of abortion.

143.   Stone, Jim. "Why Potentiality Matters." *Canadian Journal of Philosophy* 17 (1987): 815-829

Some have criticized the potentiality argument – that a fetus has a right to life because it is a potential human being – on the basis that potential properties have nothing to do with current rights, and on the basis that it may lead to moral absurdities. This author answers these arguments and presents a positive case for the importance of potentiality in the abortion argument.

144.   Strong, Carson. "The Moral Status of Preembryos, Embryos, Fetuses, and Infants." *Journal of Medicine and Philosophy* 22 (1997): 457-478.

Presents moral arguments for saying that the moral status of the fetus increases during pregnancy.

145.   Thomas, Larry L. "Human Potentiality: Its Moral Relevance." *The Personalist* 59 (1978): 266-272.

A critique of Michael Tooley's article, "Abortion and Infanticide" (see citation # 146). This author claims that, contrary to what Tooley says, potentiality is a morally relevant factor with respect to having a right to life.

146.   Tooley, Michael. "Abortion and Infanticide." *Philosophy and Public Affairs* 2 (1972): 37-65.

The author presents the properties he believes an entity must possess in order to have a right to life. He then shows that both fetuses and infants do not have these properties, and thus do not have a right to life.

147.   ———. *Abortion and Infanticide.* Oxford: Clarendon Press, 1983.

The author begins with an account of philosophy in general, and ethics in particular, along with important techniques used in thinking about ethical issues. He then uses these principles as a springboard for discussing the ethics of abortion and infanticide. He defines the properties needed to have a right to life in such a way that fetuses and infants do not qualify. He concludes that both abortion and infanticide are therefore permissible.

148.   Tushnet, Mark, and Michael Seidman. "A Comment on Tooley's 'Abortion and Infanticide.'" *Ethics* 96 (1986): 350-355.

A critique of Michael Tooley's book, *Abortion and Infanticide* (see citation # 147). The authors claim that even if his premise is true, the conclusions he draws do not necessarily follow.

149.   Veatch, Robert M. "The Beginning of Full Moral Standing." In *The Beginning of Human Life,* edited by Fritz K. Beller and Robert F. Weir, 19-33. Dordrecht: Kluwer, 1994.

Surveys the status of the question as to when an individual gains full moral standing, and then proposes that our current debate over the definition of death can be useful in coming to a conclusion on this question.

150.   Wade, Francis C. "Potentiality in the Abortion Discussion." *The Review of Metaphysics* 29 (1975): 239-255.

A critique of H. Tristram Engelhardt's thesis (see citation # 93) that, since potentiality is no more than a promise, and is not an actuality, then we should make a clear distinction between human life and personal life.

151.   Walker, Vern R. "Presumptive Personhood." *Linacre Quarterly* 45 (1978): 179-186.

The author argues that the fetus has a right to life because there is a reason to presume that the fetus is a person until good reason is brought forward for classifying it otherwise. He claims that the burden of proof should rest with those who claim that the fetus is not a person, rather than with those who claim that it is.

152.   Warren, Mary Anne. "The Moral Significance of Birth." *Hypatia* 4, no. 3 (1989): 46-65.

Presents an argument that birth remains the most appropriate place to mark the existence of a new legal person.

153.   ————. *Moral Status: Obligations to Persons and Other Living Things.*
             Oxford: Clarendon Press, 1997.

             Discusses the concept of "moral status," and argues that it is multi-
             criterial, that is, there is more than one valid criterion of moral status, and
             there is more than one type of moral status, with different types implying
             different obligations. The author then applies this concept of moral status
             to the issues of euthanasia, abortion, and the moral status of non-human
             animals.

154.   ————. "On the Moral and Legal Status of Abortion." *The Monist* 57
             (1973): 43-61.

             Argues that the fetus is not a person deserving of the same rights as one
             already born, and that therefore, abortion is permissible.

155.   Weiss, Roslyn. "The Perils of Personhood." In *What is a Person?*, edited
             by Michael F. Goodman, 115-126. Clifton, N.J.: Humana Press, 1988.

             Shows that the concept of personhood is the natural and logical conse-
             quence of a rights-centered approach to abortion. She claims, however,
             that rights alone do not form a solid basis for the moral issue of abortion,
             and proposes instead that the concept of duties be used as a basis.

156.   Wendler, Dave. "Understanding the 'Conservative' View on Abortion."
             Bioethics 13 (1999): 32-56.

             An examination of philosophical literature would make one believe that
             the conservative view on abortion is based on the claim that the fetus is a
             person from the point of conception. The author argues, however, that the
             conservative view on abortion is based, not on the personhood of the fetus,
             but rather on the natural process of fetal development.

157.   Werner, Richard. "Abortion: The Moral Status of the Unborn." *Social
             Theory and Practice* 3 (1974): 201-222.

             Presents arguments in favor of three positions: (1) that embryos and
             fetuses are indeed human beings; (2) that the moral obligation against the
             taking of human life is strong enough to rule out most abortions; and (3)
             that being human, rather than being a persons is, for abortion, the morally
             relevant criterion.

158.   ————. "Abortion: The Ontological and Moral Status of the Unborn."
             In *Today's Moral Problems*, 2nd. ed., edited by Richard A. Wasserstrom,
             51-74. New York: Macmillan, 1979.

A revision of the previous article, the author presents arguments (1) that the fetus is a human being from conception onward; (2) that personhood as the criterion for full membership in the moral community is a defective criterion, and (3) that being a sentient human being is the relevant criterion for being a full member of the moral community. He concludes that abortion of the non-sentient unborn is permissible.

159. White, Patricia D. "The Concept of Person, the Law, and the Use of the Fetus in Biomedicine." In *Abortion and the Status of the Fetus,* edited by William B. Bondeson, H. Tristram Engelhardt, Jr., Stuart F. Spicker, and Daniel H. Winship, 119-157. Dordrecht: D. Reidel Pub. Co., 1983.

Examines the question of whether there is a connection between the concept of person (as defined in the law), and the proper use of the fetus in bio-medicine. She finds that the law has not developed a coherent concept of person, but even if one could find a coherent concept of person in the law, it is not clear how that would help one come to any moral conclusions on abortion.

160. Wreen, Michael J. "The Possibility of Potentiality." In *Values and Moral Standing,* edited by Wayne Sumner, Donald Callen, and Thomas Attig, 137-154. Bowling Green, Ohio: The Applied Philosophy Program, Bowling Green State University, 1986.

The author defends the potentiality principle by showing the weaknesses in the arguments against it. The potentiality principal states that the fetus is a potential human being, and so has a right to life.

161. ———. "The Power of Potentiality." *Theoria* 52 (1986): 16-40.

The author presents positive arguments in favor of the potentiality principle that the fetus has a right to life because it is a potential human being.

162. Zaitchik, Alan. "Viability and the Morality of Abortion." *Philosophy and Public Affairs* 10 (1981): 18-26.

The author argues against the view that viability, because it is a shifting standard, is a morally arbitrary cut off point for determining the personhood of the fetus.

2 ABORTION IN RELIGIOUS THOUGHT

GENERAL RELIGIOUS VIEWS

163.   *Abortion, Religion, and the State Legislator after Webster: A Guide for the 1990's*. Chicago: The Park Ridge Center for the Study of Health, Faith, and Ethics, 1990.

A guide for legislators, designed to give them a better understanding of the religious dimensions of the abortion controversy, without taking sides on the issue.

164.   Kenyon, Edwin. "Values, Morals and Religion." Chap. 2 in *The Dilemma of Abortion*. London: Faber and Faber, 1986.

Discusses the different moral concepts employed by those who have evaluated the morality of abortion. Also discusses the views on abortion taken by different religious groups, Christian and non-Christian alike.

165.   LaFleur, William R. "Contestation and Consensus: The Morality of Abortion in Japan." *Philosophy East and West* 40 (1990): 529-542.

Outlines the Buddhist, Confucian, and Shinto views of abortion as found in Japan.

166.   Melton, J. Gordon, and Gary L. Ward, eds. *The Churches Speak on – Abortion: Official Statements from Religious Bodies and Ecumenical Organizations*. The Churches Speak series. Detroit: Gale Research, 1989.

A compilation of statements on abortion from various religious groups.

167.   Muldoon, Maureen. "The Positions of Religious Denominations."
        Chap. 3 in *The Abortion Debate in the United States and Canada: A
        Source Book.* New York: Garland Publishing, Inc., 1991.

        A detailed presentation of the positions on abortion taken by many
        different religious denominations and traditions.

168.   Simmons, Paul D. "Religious Approaches to Abortion." In *Abortion,
        Medicine, and the Law,* 4th ed., completely revised, edited by J. Douglas
        Butler and David F. Walbert, 712-728. New York: Facts on File, 1992.

        Gives a brief description of the position taken by many different religious
        groups, both Christian and non-Christian alike.

169.   Wenz, Peter S. *Abortion Rights as Religious Freedom.* Philadelphia:
        Temple University Press, 1992.

        While agreeing with the conclusion reached by the Supreme Court in its
        Roe v. Wade decision, the author criticizes its reasoning. He claims that
        the High Court should not have used the right to privacy as its main reason
        for allowing abortion, but rather, should have considered abortion as a
        form of religious freedom.

170.   Weston, Mark. "Faith and Abortion: Where the World's Major Religions
        Disagree." *Washington Post.* 23 Jan. 1990, Health Section.

        Presents a synopsis of the positions taken on abortion by 29 major
        religious groups, 20 of whom are Christian.

CHRISTIAN VIEWS

171.   *Abortion in Debate.* Edinburgh: Quorum Press, 1987.

        A book sponsored by the Board of Social Responsibility of the Church of
        Scotland. It presents several articles on Christianity and abortion, from
        varying perspectives.

172.   "The America We Seek: A Statement of Pro-Life Principles and Con-
        cern." *First Things,* May 1996, 40-44.

        A public statement of their pro-life position, signed by forty-five leaders
        of the movement.

173.   Anderson, David Earle. "Abortion and the Churches: 'Clarification' or
        Rollback?" *Christianity and Crisis* 51 (1991): 60-65

Discusses mainline churches' current and historic attitudes toward abortion, arguing that although these attitudes have shifted somewhat, they have not turned away from their basic stance in favor of abortion rights.

174.   Anderson, John O. *Cry of the Innocents: Abortion and the Race towards Judgement.* With Doug Brendel. South Plainfield, N.J.: Bridge Publishing, 1984.

Using the biblical book of Hosea as a backdrop, the author compares the ancient practice of child sacrifice with the modern practice of abortion. He predicts that just as God punished Israel for its sin, he will punish the United States for its sin of abortion.

175.   Andreasen, Niels-Erik. "A Biblical Perspective on Abortion." In *Abortion: Ethical Issues and Options,* edited by David R. Larson, 43-53. Loma Linda, Calif.: Loma Linda University, Center for Christian Bioethics, 1992.

A Seventh-Day Adventist author, while admitting that the Bible says nothing about abortion explicitly, shows how it does have a unique understanding of early life processes from conception to birth, and on the potential disruptions to that process.

176.   Andrusko, Dave. "Echoes of Nuremberg." *Fundamentalist Journal* 8 (April 1989): 30-33.

A Christian refutation of the practice of using fetal tissue for transplantation.

177.   Atkinson, Gary M. "The Church's Condemnation of Procured Abortion: A Philosophical Defense." In *Abortion: A New Generation of Catholic Responses,* edited by Stephen J. Heaney, 101-119. Braintree, Mass.: Pope John Center, 1992.

The author presents a philosophical defense of the Catholic Church's position against abortion. His main thesis is that the right to life is possessed by all members of the human species.

178.   Banner, Michael. "Christian Anthropology at the Beginning and End of Life." *Scottish Journal of Theology* 51 (1998): 22-60.

Christian medical ethics, the author says, is obliged to start from its own presupposition, the Gospel of Jesus Christ, the "I Am," who is without beginning and without end, the first and the last. The author then goes on to argue that both abortion and euthanasia deny this reality, and so must be opposed by Christian medical ethics.

179.   Barnes, Peter. *Open Your Mouth for the Dumb: Abortion and the Christian.* Edinburgh: The Banner of Truth Trust, 1984.

Shows that the Bible is the standard by which controversies are to be judged, and then goes on to show that the Bible is opposed to abortion.

180.   Barry, Rev. Robert P., O.P. "The Roman Catholic Position on Abortion." In *New Essays on Abortion and Bioethics,* edited by Rem B. Edwards, 151-182. Greenwich, Conn.: JAI Press, 1997.

Traces the historical development of the Catholic position on abortion, and explains the Catholic teaching on the concept of the person, and closes with a defense of the Roman Catholic position on abortion.

181.   Batchelor, Edward, ed. *Abortion: The Moral Issues.* New York: Pilgrim Press, 1982.

A collection of articles by leading religious ethicists which survey the present debate over abortion.

182.   Baum, Gregory. "Abortion: An Ecumenical Dilemma." *Commonweal* 99 (1973): 231-235.

The author, a Pro-life Catholic, calls people to look with respect on the views of those with whom he disagrees. He shows how liberal Protestants have developed their pro-abortion view because of their own view of life.

183.   Beckwith, Francis J. "Abortion and Argument: A Response to Mollenkott." *Journal of Biblical Ethics in Medicine* 2 (1989): 48-56.

A critique of Mollenkott's thesis (see citation # 327) that the pro-choice position is more consistent with Christian ethics than is the pro-life position.

184.   ———. "Brave New Bible: A Reply to the Moderate Evangelical Position on Abortion." *Journal of the Evangelical Theological Society* 32 (1990): 489-508.

A critique, from a Pro-Life perspective, using biblical and logical arguments, of an article by Dolores Dunnett (see citation # 237).

185.   ———. "A Critical Appraisal of Theological Arguments for Abortion Rights." *Bibliotheca Sacra* 148 (1991): 337-355.

Presents a pro-life response to the arguments of those scholars who claim that the Bible does not specifically condemn abortion, or that the Bible actually supports the pro-choice position.

186.   Beem, Teresa. "The 'Hard Cases' of Abortion." In *Abortion: Ethical Issues and Options,* edited by David R. Larson, 155-169. Loma Linda, Calif.: Loma Linda University, Center for Christian Bioethics, 1992.

Using Christian principles as well as case studies, the author presents reasons for not allowing abortion even in the hard cases of rape, AIDS, and the life of the mother.

187.   Bernardin, Cardinal Joseph. "The Consistent Ethic of Life after Webster." *Origins* 19 (1990): 741, 743-748.

Examines the status of the consistent ethic of life, especially in light of the Supreme Court's *Webster v. Reproductive Health Services* decision.

188.   ———. "The Consistent Ethic: What Sort of Framework?" *Origins* 16 (1986): 345, 347-350.

A Catholic cardinal presents an overview of his "consistent ethic of life" and examines its implications for public policy, citizens, and public officials.

189.   ———. "Linkage and the Logic of the Abortion Debate." In *Consistent Ethic of Life,* edited by Thomas G. Fuechtmann, 20-26. Kansas City, Mo.: Sheed & Ward, 1988.

The author, a noted Roman Catholic cardinal, demonstrates a linkage between abortion and other life related issues such as care of the handicapped and the terminally ill. He argues for what he calls a "consistent ethic of life," that is, a pro-life stance on all these issues.

190.   ———. "The Precious but Fragile Gift of Human Life." *Origins* 15 (1986): 563-564.

An address at a March for Life vigil in Washington, D.C., Jan. 21, 1986, calling for a respect for human life.

191.   Bettenhausen, Elizabeth. "Abortion Catechisms: Creator and Cause." *Christianity and Crisis* 50 (1990): 30-31.

Argues that the fact that God is creator does not necessarily imply that God causes every fertilization of ovum and sperm that takes place.

192.   Bevere, Allan R. "Abortion: Philosophical and Theological Consider-
        ations." *Ashland Theological Journal* 28 (1996): 45-59.

        Presents several theological and philosophical arguments against the pro-
        abortion position.

193.   Blanshard, Paul, and Edd Doerr. "Is Abortion Murder?" *The Humanist*
        32, no. 3 (1972): 8-9.

        A critique of the Catholic and Evangelical Protestant view that abortion
        is tantamount to murder.

194.   Bonner, Gerald. "Abortion and Early Christian Thought." In *Life and
        Learning IV: Proceedings of the Fourth University Faculty for Life
        Conference held at Fordham University June 1994,* edited by Joseph W.
        Koterski, S.J., 230-252. Washington, D.C.: University Faculty for Life,
        1995.

        A review of the early Church's teaching on abortion and infanticide.

195.   Bosgra, Tj. *Abortion, The Bible and the Church.* Honolulu: Hawaii Right
        to Life Educational Foundation, 1980.

        Presents an argument that the Judeo-Christian tradition, as found in the
        Bible, is unabashedly anti-abortion. He also presents quotations from the
        official positions on abortion of many different Christian denominations,
        and presents ideas on what Christians can do to change the situation
        regarding abortion in the United States today.

196.   Bottum, J. "Facing up to Infanticide." *First Things,* Feb. 1996, 41-44.

        The author shows how, in response to persuasive logic from the pro-life
        community, pro-choice advocates have changed their arguments for
        abortion. He shows that they now admit what Pro-Lifers have been saying
        all along, that abortion is the killing of a human being, and that it is tragic.
        He argues, however, that Pro-Life people should not assume that they
        have won the battle. Rather, he says, the more that people tolerate
        abortion, the closer they come to tolerating infanticide.

197.   Broach, Claude U., ed. *Seminar on Abortion: The Proceedings of a
        Dialogue Between Catholics and Baptists.* Charlotte, N.C.: The Ecumeni-
        cal Institute, 1975.

        Papers delivered at a conference on abortion sponsored by the Bishops'
        Committee for Ecumenical and Inter-Religious Affairs and the Ecumeni-

cal Institute of Wake Forest University and Belmont Abbey College, November 10-12, 1975.

198.   Brown, Harold O. J. *Death before Birth.* Nashville: T. Nelson, 1977.

Presents the case against abortion from a Christian perspective.

199.   ———. "Legal Aspects of the Right to Life." In *Thou Shalt not Kill: The Christian Case against Abortion,* edited by Richard L. Ganz, 111-126. New Rochelle, N.Y.: Arlington House, 1978.

Presents a critique of the Supreme Court's *Roe v. Wade* decision from a Christian perspective.

200.   ———. "Protestants and the Abortion Issue: A Socio-Religious Prognostication." *Human Life Review* 2, no. 4 (1976): 131-139.

Comments on the fact that, while many Protestants are pro-life, there are also quite a few, especially in the United States, who are pro-choice. The author sees the reason for this in differences on the issue of the relationship of church and state.

201.   Brown, John B. "The Larger Context of Abortion." In *Affirming Life: Biblical Perspectives on Abortion for the United Church of Christ,* edited by John B. Brown and Robin Fox, 33-50. [S.l.]: United Church of Christ Friends for Life, 1991.

Abortion does not occur in a vacuum. It was preceded by a change in society's world-views, resulting in a new ethic. The author outlines the prevailing assumptions of this new ethic, as well as the assumptions of evangelical Christians who oppose abortion.

202.   Brown, John B., and Robin Fox, eds. *Affirming Life: Biblical Perspectives on Abortion for the United Church of Christ.* [S.l.]: United Church of Christ Friends for Life, 1991.

A collection of articles on abortion from the pro-life perspective, written by members of the United Church of Christ who believe that their denomination has erred in taking an official position favoring abortion.

203.   Brun, John C. "Adventists, Abortion, and the Bible." In *Abortion: Ethical Issues and Options,* edited by David R. Larson, 27-42. Loma Linda, Calif.: Loma Linda University, Center for Christian Bioethics, 1992.

Shows how Seventh-Day Adventist authors have used the Bible in their discussion of abortion, and closes with some suggestions of his own.

204.   Bryan, G. McLeod. "Abortion: An Historical Survey of Catholic and Baptist Positions." In *Seminar on Abortion: The Proceedings of a Dialogue Between Catholics and Baptists*, edited by Claude U. Broach, 10-36. Charlotte, N.C.: The Ecumenical Institute, 1975.

An overview of both Catholic and Baptist teachings on abortion.

205.   Bullock, C. Hassell. "Abortion and Old Testament Prophetic and Poetic Literature." In *Abortion: A Christian Understanding and Response*, edited by James K. Hoffmeier, 65-71. Grand Rapids, Mich.: Baker Book House, 1987.

Presents an evaluation of what the prophetic and the poetic portions of the Old Testament have to say about abortion, along with guidelines on how to interpret them.

206.   Burtachell, James T. "A Call and a Reply." *Christianity and Crisis* 36 (1977): 270-271.

A response to the "Call to Concern." (see citation # 211).

207.   ———. *Rachel Weeping and other Essays on Abortion.* Kansas City, Kans.: Andrews & McMeel, 1982. Reprint, *Rachel Weeping: The Case against Abortion.* San Francisco: Harper & Row, 1984.

Essays by a Catholic theologian opposed to abortion.

208.   Cahill, Lisa Sowle. "Abortion." In *The Westminster Dictionary of Christian Ethics*, edited by James F. Childress and John Macquarrie, 1-5. Philadelphia: The Westminster Press, 1986.

A review of the teaching on abortion from the vantage point of Christian ethics and Christian theology.

209.   ———. "Abortion: Roman Catholic Perspectives." In *Encyclopedia of Bioethics.* Rev. ed., edited by Warren Thomas Reich. Vol. 1. New York: Macmillan, 1995.

A discussion of Roman Catholic teaching on abortion.

210.   Calhoun, Byron, M.D. "Am I a Murderer?" *Journal of Biblical Ethics in Medicine* 2 (1989): 46-47.

The author lays out the biblical arguments against abortion, and then discusses his personal odyssey – from favoring abortion before becoming a Christian, to being totally against abortion, to being persuaded to perform a few abortions in cases of severely deformed fetuses, to now not doing any abortions for any reason.

211.   "A Call to Concern." *Christianity and Crisis* 36 (1977): 222-223.

An ad, signed by a number of theologians, that expresses their support for maintaining the legality of abortion in the face of what they call the absolutist position that abortion is always wrong.

212.   Callahan, Daniel. "The Roman Catholic Position." In *Abortion: The Moral Issues*, edited by Edward Batchelor, 62-72. New York: Pilgrim Press, 1982. Reprinted from his *Abortion: Law, Choice and Morality* (New York: Macmillan, 1977).

The author presents, and at the same time, criticizes, the typical Roman Catholic argument against abortion.

213.   Callahan, Sidney. "Is Abortion ever a Legitimate Moral Choice? A Response." In *The Befuddled Stork: Helping Persons of Faith Debate Beginning-of-Life Issues*, edited by Sally B. Geis and Donald E. Messer, 112-118. Nashville: Abingdon Press, 2000.

Presents moral arguments against abortion on demand. At the same time, however, the author admits that there are some circumstances when it is allowable.

214.   Cameron, Nigel M. de S. "Kindness that Kills." In *Abortion in Debate*, 9-19. Edinburgh: Quorum Press, 1987.

Presents biblical and theological arguments against abortion, and answers some arguments given in favor of it.

215.   Cameron, Nigel M. de S., and Pamela F. Sims. *Abortion: The Crisis in Morals and Medicine.* Leicester, Eng.: Inter-Varsity Press, 1986.

Examines what the Bible says about abortion, as well as what the church historically has said. They then examine the current situation. They argue that abortion is wrong, except to save the life of the mother.

216.   Casanova, Judith Boice, Jean Lambert, and Marjorie Suchocki. "What about Abortion?" In *What's a Christian to Do?*, edited by David P. Polk, 113-136. St. Louis: Chalice Press, 1991.

A presentation of both sides of the abortion controversy, concluding that the best theological response is that we should have a fundamental trust in God, recognizing that while we make decisions with integrity, likewise others will, with their own integrity, make decisions opposite to ours. The authors also call for an openness and respect for one another in the public debate.

217.   Catholic Committee on Pluralism and Abortion. "Statement on Pluralism and Abortion." *Origins* 14 (1984): 414.

A statement in which this committee states that the position of the Catholic hierarchy against abortion is not the only legitimate Catholic position.

218.   Churchill, Craig. "Churches of Christ and Abortion: A Survey of Selected Periodicals." *Restoration Quarterly* 38 (1996): 129-143.

The author surveys selected periodical literature by Christian writers to see how faithfully they reflect these elements: (1) a clear, coherent opposition to abortion, (2) a solid theological and philosophical framework, (3) an awareness of the broad range of issues involved, and (4) an appreciation of the need for supportive contexts from which life-affirming decisions can be promoted.

219.   Colson, Charles, and Nancy Pearcey. "Why Max Deserves a Life." *Christianity Today*, 16 June, 1997, 80.

Reflecting onhis own autistic grandson, the author, a well-known evangelical Christian, presents a vigorous defense for not aborting handicapped children.

220.   Congdon, Robert N. "Exodus 21:22-25 and the Abortion Debate." *Bibliotheca Sacra* 146 (1989): 132-147.

An exegesis of Exodus 21:22-25, showing that this passage cannot, as is often done, be used to justify abortion.

221.   Conley, John J., S.J. "Coherence and Priority: Evaluating the Consistent Ethic." In *Life and Learning VII: Proceedings of the Seventh University Faculty for Life Conference, June 1997 at Loyola College*, edited by Joseph W. Koterski, S.J., 39-53. Washington, D.C.: University Faculty for Life, 1998.

A critique of Cardinal Joseph Bernardin's consistent ethic of life.

222.   Connery, John R., S.J. *Abortion: The Development of the Roman Catholic Perspective.* Chicago: Loyola Univ. Press, 1977.

Traces the history of Catholic thought on abortion from the earliest times to the middle of the twentieth century.

223.   ————. "A Seamless Garment in a Sinful World." In *Abortion and Catholicism: The American Debate,* edited by Patricia Beattie Jung and Thomas A. Shannon, 272-278. New York: Crossroad, 1988.

Examines how to apply a consistent ethic of life – one that respects life in all stages and situations, unborn, infant, handicapped, adult, and aged – in a sinful and far from perfect world. He argues that holding a consistent ethic of life does not automatically mean that there must be an absolute prohibition on any action resulting in a loss of life.

224.   Corriden, James A. "Church Law and Abortion." *The Jurist* 33 (1973): 184-198.

Discusses abortion as found in Catholic Church law, using three questions as a framework: (1) What have been the prohibitions and penal sanctions against abortion? (2) What has been the sacramental discipline regarding the baptism of an expelled fetus, and (3) What is the relationship between these ordinances and the moral teaching or pastoral practices of the church? He also presents some recommendations for reform of canon law.

225.   Cottrell, Jack W. "Abortion and the Mosaic Law." *Christianity Today,* 16 March 1973, 6-9.

Many pro-choice advocates point to Exodus 21:22-25 as teaching that God puts less value on a fetus than he does on the mother. The author disputes that interpretation, saying that the phrase "her fruit depart" (American Standard Version), refers to a normal, premature birth, not a miscarriage.

226.   Craig, Judith. "Is Abortion ever a Legitimate Moral Choice? A Response." In *The Befuddled Stork: Helping Persons of Faith Debate Beginning-of-Life Issues,* edited by Sally B. Geis and Donald E. Messer, 104-111. Nashville: Abingdon Press, 2000.

While admitting that there is no ethical room for a casual decision regarding abortion, the author also says there are tragic circumstances when it is allowable. There are no circumstances, she says, in which we can say that an abortion should never be performed. She sees no absolutes in this area, only ambiguities, with the one constant that God is gracious.

227.   Crook, Roger H. "Abortion: An Ethical Perspective." In *Seminar on Abortion: The Proceedings of a Dialogue Between Catholics and Baptists*, edited by Claude U. Broach, 69-83. Charlotte, N.C.: The Ecumenical Press, 1975.

Presents the author's own Baptist view on the morality of abortion. Concludes that abortion is neither always morally wrong, regardless of circumstances, nor is it always morally permissible, without need for justification.

228.   Cunningham, James Justin. "Abortion Against a Biblical Background: The Reflections of a Roman Catholic." In *Seminar on Abortion: The Proceedings of a Dialogue Between Catholics and Baptists*, edited by Claude U. Broach, 49-58. Charlotte, N.C.: The Ecumenical Press, 1975.

A Catholic perspective on what the Old Testament and the New Testament teach about abortion.

229.   Curran, Charles E. "Abortion: Law and Morality in Contemporary Catholic Theology." *The Jurist* 33 (1973): 162-183.

Presents the state of the abortion question in Roman Catholic theology, along with suggestions on how Catholics can and should approach both the legal and the moral aspects of abortion.

230.   Davies, James A., and Jerry Jenkins. "Abortion – A Biblical and Educational Perspective." In *The Christian Educator's Handbook on Family Life Education*, edited by Kenneth O. Gangel and James C. Wilhoit, 269-285. Grand Rapids, Mich.: Baker Books, 1996.

Briefly presents the Evangelical position against abortion and answers objections of pro-choice advocates. The authors then discuss how the church can and should teach on the subject of abortion.

231.   Davis, John Jefferson. "Abortion." Chap. 6 in *Evangelical Ethics: Issues Facing the Church Today*. 2nd ed. Phillipsburg, N.J.: P & R Publishing, 1993.

A wide ranging discussion of abortion from a Christian perspective. The author gives historical background, and covers the medical and psychological aspects of abortion, and shows that the Bible and Christian theology condemn abortion, except to save the life of the mother.

232.   ———. *Abortion and the Christian: What Every Believer Should Know.* Phillipsburg, N.J.: Presbyterian and Reformed Pub. Co., 1984.

The author, a leading Evangelical Christian, surveys the leading ethical positions on abortion, the medical facts regarding fetal life, and what the Bible says about abortion. He uses this to help the Christian face the many practical questions that face him when he considers the question of abortion. The author himself takes the position that abortion, except when the mother's life would be threatened by a continued abortion, is immoral, and an affront to God.

233.   Diegel, Matthew H. "Two Canadian Responses to Abortion." *Consensus* 22, no. 1 (1996): 29-45.

Compares and contrasts the statements on abortion from two Lutheran denominations in Canada: The Eastern Canada Synod of the Lutheran Church in America, and the Evangelical Lutheran Church in Canada.

234.   Dobson, James, and Gary L. Bauer. *Children at Risk: The Battle for the Hearts and Minds of Our Kids.* Dallas: Word Publishing, 1990.

An examination by two leading Evangelical Christians of the current attitude of our society towards children and the family, together with a call to value all children, born and unborn, as well as the family as the very foundation of human society.

235.   Doerr, Edd, and James W. Prescott, eds. *Abortion Rights and Fetal 'Personhood.'* 2nd ed. Long Beach, Calif.: Centerline Press, in cooperation with Americans for Religious Liberty, 1990.

A collection of articles on various aspects of abortion, all written from a pro-choice perspective.

236.   Dombrowski, Daniel A., and Robert Deltete. *A Brief, Liberal, Catholic Defense of Abortion.* Urbana: Univ. of Illinois Press, 2000.

A defense of abortion on the basis of Catholic principles. The authors claim that the Catholic pro-choice position is just as compatible, if not more so, with Catholic tradition, as is the church's current anti-abortion stance.

237.   Dunnett, Dolores E. "Evangelicals and Abortion." *Journal of the Evangelical Theological Society* 32 (1990): 215-225.

Using the Bible, early church thought, and modern ethics, the author argues that abortion for mere convenience is wrong, but that abortion in the following circumstances is permissible: abortion before viability, abortion in order to save the life of the mother, and abortion in cases of rape, incest, and grave physical or mental defects.

238.   "The Durham Declaration: To United Methodists on Our Church and
        Abortion." In *The Church and Abortion: In Search of New Ground for
        Response*, edited by Paul T. Stallsworth, 11-16. Nashville: Abingdon
        Press, 1993.

        While the United Methodist Church has officially taken a pro-choice
        position, in this declaration a group of United Methodists call on the
        United Methodist Church to take a pro-life position, which they say is a
        scriptural, theological, and pastoral approach to abortion.

239.   Eggebroten, Anne, ed. *Abortion–My Choice, God's Grace: Christian
        Women Tell Their Stories*. Pasadena: New Paradigm Books, 1994.

        A collection of personal stories from Christian women who have decided
        to have an abortion, despite church strictures against it.

240.   Eidum, Charles D. "Life Before Birth." Editorial. *The Evangel*, no. 79
        (1998): 7.

        A call to Lutherans to support the pro-life position, along with answers to
        three common pro-choice arguments.

241.   Fairweather, Eugene and Ian Gentles, eds. *The Right to Birth: Some
        Christian Views on Abortion*. Toronto: The Anglican Book Centre, 1976.

        A series of articles from different members of the Anglican Church of
        Canada, this work is intended to carry further the philosophical and
        theological discussions begun in the document *Abortion, an Issue for
        Conscience*, (see citation # 795) which that denomination had passed in
        1973.

242.   Fairweather, Ian C. M. "Abortion: Christian Traditions not Unanimous."
        In *Abortion in Debate*, 73-86. Edinburgh: Quorum Press, 1987.

        Claims that historically, the church has treated abortion as a serious
        matter, only to be done in special and infrequent circumstances, but that
        it is wrong to conclude that the church has historically been totally
        opposed to abortion.

243.   Farraher, Rev. Joseph J., S.J. "Abortion and Probabilism." In *Abortion:
        A New Generation of Catholic Responses*, edited by Stephen J. Heaney,
        151-162. Braintree, Mass.: Pope John Center, 1992.

        Some Catholics have sought to defend abortion, at least in certain
        circumstances, on the basis of the principle of probabilism. This principle
        states that a truly doubtful law does not oblige; or that a doubtful

obligation is no obligation. The author of this article claims that this principle, while valid when used properly, has been misused in trying to defend abortion.

244.   *Fearfully and Wonderfully Made: A Collection of Sermons on Life by Presbyterians.* Burke, Va.: Presbyterians Pro-Life, 1995.

A collection of sermons on abortion by pro-life ministers of the Presbyterian Church (U.S.A.).

245.   Fehring, Richard J. "Contraception and Abortion: Fruits of the Same Tree." In *Life and Learning VI: Proceedings of the Sixth University Faculty for Life Conference, June 1996, at Georgetown University,* edited by Joseph W. Koterski, S.J., 149-162. Washington, D.C.: University Faculty for Life, 1997.

Pope John Paul II, in his encyclical *Evangelium Vitae,* links abortion and contraception as issues with similar characteristics, but different moral magnitudes. Conventional wisdom rejects such a link. This paper explains why this link of abortion and contraception is valid, by analyzing the pope's statements, and by analyzing how abortion and contraception both violate basic assumptions of health, nursing, and biological laws of nature.

246.   Ferraro, Barbara, and Patricia Hussey. "Statement by Two Abortion Ad Signers." *Origins* 16 (1986): 188-189.

Two Catholic nuns who favor abortion rights present a statement saying that the Church's reference to the New York Times ad they signed as being "pro-abortion" is mistaken, and that dissent on all controversial issues, including abortion, is necessary for the life of the church.

247.   Ficarra, Bernard J. "Religion and Abortion." Chap. 5 in *Abortion Analyzed.* Old Town, Maine: Health Educator Publications, 1989.

An examination of what various religious groups in the United States have taught about abortion, focusing particular attention on the Catholic Church.

248.   Fletcher, Joseph F. "Abortion and the True Believer." *Christian Century* 91 (1974): 1126-1127.

A refutation of the Catholic, conservative Christian, and Orthodox Jewish position that abortion is morally wrong.

249.   Fowler, Paul B. *Abortion: Toward an Evangelical Consensus.* Critical
        Concern Books. Portland, Ore: Multnomah Press, 1987.

        Examines biblical statements and Christian theology on life, and comes to
        the conclusion that abortion is wrong.   Also examines the various
        arguments usually given in favor of abortion, and shows how they are
        either weak or biblically unsound.

250.   Fowler, Richard A., and H. Wayne House. "Abortion and Euthanasia."
        Part 2 in *Civilization in Crisis: A Christian Response to Homosexuality,
        Feminism, Euthanasia, and Abortion.* 2nd. ed.   Grand Rapids, Mich.:
        Baker Book House, 1988.

        A refutation, from the Bible and Christian theology, of a permissive
        attitude toward abortion and euthanasia.

251.   Fox, Robin. "Historical Perspectives on Abortion."   In *Affirming Life:
        Biblical Perspectives on Abortion for the United Church of Christ,* edited
        by John B. Brown and Robin Fox, 13-31. [S.l.]: United Church of Christ
        Friends for Life, 1991.

        Traces the attitudes of the Judeo-Christian tradition toward abortion
        throughout history, examining the practice of abortion in light of the
        prevailing culture in which it was practiced.

252.   Fredericks, Richard. "A Compassionate and Christian 'Quality of Life'
        Ethic." In *Abortion: Ethical Issues and Options,* edited by David R.
        Larson, 125-142. Loma Linda, Calif.: Loma Linda University, Center for
        Christian Bioethics, 1992.

        The author criticizes the modern day "quality of life" ethic as being
        unbiblical, and says that Christians must oppose abortion, but that they
        should do so with compassion and empathy for the women caught in crisis
        pregnancies.

253.   Gaffney, Edward McGlynn. "Law and Theology: A Dialogue on the
        Abortion Decision." *The Jurist* 33 (1973): 134-152.

        A theological critique of the Supreme Court's two abortion decisions in
        early 1973: *Roe v. Wade,* and *Doe v. Bolton.*

254.   Ganz, Richard L. "Psychology and Abortion: The Deception Exposed."
        In *Thou Shalt not Kill: The Christian Case against Abortion,* edited by
        Richard L. Ganz, 26-42. New Rochelle, N.Y.: Arlington House, 1978.

The author demonstrates that the psychiatric and psychological profession's claim that its analysis of abortion is entirely neutral is far from true. He shows that it presupposes a materialistic atheistic humanism in its statements on abortion.

255.   ———— , ed. *Thou Shalt not Kill: The Christian Case against Abortion.* New Rochelle, N.Y.: Arlington House, 1978.

A collection of articles by Christians active in various disciplines. Each author presents an argument against abortion from the framework of his own discipline.

256.   Gardner, R. F. R. "The Ethical Question: Is Abortion ever Justified? The Search for a Christian Answer." Part II of *Abortion, the Personal Dilemma: A Christian Gynaecologist Examines the Medical, Social, and Spiritual Issues.* Grand Rapids, Mich.: Eerdmans, 1972.

The author claims that religion is essential in the issue of abortion, and then examines what the Old and New Testaments have to say about abortion, as well as what light Christian theology sheds on the subject.

257.   Garton, Jean Staker. *Who Broke the Baby?* Minneapolis: Bethany Fellowship, 1979.

The author takes many of the common arguments made in support of abortion, and answers them from a Christian perspective.

258.   Garvey, John, and Frank Morriss. *Abortion.* Catholic Perspectives. Chicago: Thomas More Press, 1979.

Two Catholic authors present their own views on why abortion is wrong.

259.   Geis, Sally B., and Donald E. Messer, eds. *The Befuddled Stork: Helping Persons of Faith Debate Beginning-of-Life Issues.* Nashville: Abingdon Press, 2000.

A collection of articles by Christians debating various beginning of life issues, including *in vitro* fertilization, abortion, and cloning. Each issue has two respondents, presenting contrasting opinions on the issue.

260.   Gerard, Joseph E. "Abortion and the Word of God." *The Baptist Bulletin,* September 1983, 8-10.

Shows that, according to the Bible, God is not only aware of, but actually involved in, the conception and development of the unborn.

261.   Gordon, Victor R. "Abortion and the New Testament." In *Abortion: A Christian Understanding and Response*, edited by James K. Hoffmeier, 73-85. Grand Rapids, Mich.: Baker Book House, 1987.

The author shows that, though the New Testament has nothing to say about abortion specifically, the broader theological and ethical perspective of the New Testament shows that it has a negative attitude toward abortion.

262.   Gorman, Michael J. "Abortion and the Biblical Metaphor of God as Mother." In *Life and Learning IV: Proceedings of the Fourth University Faculty for Life Conference held at Fordham University June 1994*, edited by Joseph W. Koterski, S.J., 253-270. Washington, D.C.: University Faculty for Life, 1995.

Examines the Bible's maternal metaphors for God, and shows how these images figure prominently in feminist theology and ethics. The author argues that, contrary to the claim of many feminist theologians, the Bible's metaphor of God as mother implies a comprehensive ethic of protecting all life, including fetal life.

263.   ———. *Abortion and the Early Church: Christian, Jewish and Pagan Attitudes in the Greco-Roman World.* New York: Paulist Press, 1982.

Presents a description of the attitudes toward abortion in the ancient pagan world, the ancient Jewish world, and in the early Christian Church. Closes with the relevance of this information to the church today.

264.   ———. "Ahead to Our Past: Abortion and Christian Texts." In *The Church and Abortion: In Search of New Ground for Response*, edited by Paul T. Stallsworth, 25-43. Nashville: Abingdon Press, 1993.

The author first identifies and explores the significance of the Durham Declaration's (see citation # 238) New Testament foundations, and then examines early Christian attitudes and practices regarding abortion. The author claims that the New Testament, both in principle, and as embodied in early Christian communities, leads us away from abortion, and toward protecting the unborn and giving compassionate care to those in need. He shows that the Durham Declaration is in agreement with this assertion.

265.   ———. "The Use and Abuse of the Bible in the Abortion Debate." In *Life and Learning V: Proceedings of the Fifth University Faculty for Life Conference, June 1995, at Marquette University*, edited by Joseph W. Koterski, S.J., 140-176. Washington, D.C.: University Faculty for Life, 1996.

Shows how both pro-life and pro-choice religious groups have misused the Bible to make it say what they want it to say on abortion. He then proposes an alternate method, where one lets the Bible speak for itself, and the Bible becomes the lens through which one views abortion.

266. Gudorf, Christine E. "To Make a Seamless Garment, Use a Single Piece of Cloth." In *Abortion and Catholicism: The American Debate,* edited by Patricia Beattie Jung and Thomas A. Shannon, 279-296. New York: Crossroad, 1988.

Argues that abortion should be kept separate from the consistent ethic of life. She argues that in the Catholic Church's teaching on abortion and war, there are two significantly different methods of moral decision making, despite claims for a consistent ethic of life.

267. Haldane, John J. "The Ethics of Life and Death." *Scottish Journal of Theology* 38 (1985): 603-611.

From the point of view of Christian ethics, the author argues that nuclear warfare and abortion are both the taking of innocent human life.

268. Hanks-Harwood, Ginger. "Abortion and Adventist Interpretation: Significant Theological Themes." In *Abortion: Ethical Issues and Options,* edited by David R. Larson, 99-112. Loma Linda, Calif.: Loma Linda University, Center for Christian Bioethics, 1992.

A Seventh-Day Adventist presents several biblical themes, and applies these to the issue of abortion. She says that in order to be truly "pro-life," people must also work to rectify the various social problems that make abortion desirable – poverty, a too casual view of sexuality, etc.

269. Harakas, Stanley S. "The Orthodox Christian View of Abortion." Chap. 22 in *Contemporary Moral Issues Facing the Orthodox Christian.* Minneapolis: Light and Life Pub. Co., 1982.

Presents the position of the Eastern Orthodox Church on abortion. This position is a pro-life position, which will allow abortion only in cases where the mother's life is at stake. In all other situations, abortion is not allowed.

270. ———. "The Supreme Court Abortion Decision." Chap. 36 in *Contemporary Moral Issues Facing the Orthodox Christian.* Minneapolis: Light and Life Pub. Co., 1982.

Presents a brief outline of the Supreme Court's *Roe v. Wade* decision, analyzes it from an Eastern Orthodox perspective, and declares that it is unscientific and not in accordance with Orthodox Christian truth.

271.   Hardon, John A. "Euthanasia and Abortion: A Catholic View." *Human Life Review* 1, no. 4 (1975): 88-100.

A presentation of the Catholic view on euthanasia and abortion.

272.   Häring, Bernard. "A Theological Evaluation." In *The Morality of Abortion: Legal and Historical Perspectives,* edited by John T. Noonan, 123-145. Cambridge, Mass.: Harvard Univ. Press, 1970.

The author presents his own position on abortion, but within the confines of general Catholic tradition.

273.   Harrison, Beverly Wildung. "Abortion: Protestant Perspectives." In *Encyclopedia of Bioethics.* Rev. ed., edited by Warren Thomas Reich. Vol. 1. New York: Macmillan, 1995.

Traces early and modern Protestant views on abortion.

274.   ———. "Free Choice: A Feminist Perspective." *Church and Society,* March/April 1981, 6-21.

A Christian ethicist challenges the traditional Christian teaching on abortion.

275.   ———. "Theology of Pro-Choice: A Feminist Perspective." In *Abortion: The Moral Issues,* edited by Edward Batchelor, 210-226. New York: Pilgrim Press, 1982.

A feminist defense of abortion, criticizing the Christian theology of abortion as misogynist.

276.   Harrison, Beverly Wildung, and Shirley Cloyes. "Theology and Morality of Procreative Choice." In *Abortion: A Reader,* edited by Lloyd Steffen, 319-339. Cleveland: The Pilgrim Press, 1996.

A feminist defense of abortion, criticizing the conservative view toward abortion as being misogynist. They say that the typical Christian theology must be converted to one which is more respectful of women.

277.   Hauerwas, Stanley. "Abortion: Once Again." In *New Perspectives on Human Abortion,* edited by Thomas W. Hilgers, Dennis J. Horan, and

David Mall, 420-439. Frederick, Md.: Aletheia Books, University Publications of America, 1981.

The author defends the thesis that Christians should regard abortion as an unfortunate practice, and should avoid it in their lives. Moreover, they should do all they can to help others likewise avoid it. However, there are circumstances where abortions are morally permissible, if still morally tragic. The Christian community should therefore use all of their linguistic skill to discriminate between morally permissible and impermissible abortions.

278. ———. "Abortion, Theologically Understood." In *The Church and Abortion: In Search of New Ground for Response,* edited by Paul T. Stallsworth, 44-66. Nashville: Abingdon Press, 1993.

In a lecture addressed to the United Methodist Church's Evangelical Fellowship during its 1990 Annual Conference, the author first presents a sermon on abortion by the Rev. Terry Hamilton-Poore, and then an ethical commentary on it. The point of the sermon, and the ensuing commentary, is to show that the church's duty is not so much to take a position on the legality of abortion, as to give support and aid to women caught in crisis pregnancies, as well as to any children that might result from those pregnancies.

279. Hauerwas, Stanley, and Joel Shuman. "Is Aborting a 'Problematic' Fetus Ethically Acceptable? A Response." In *The Befuddled Stork: Helping Persons of Faith Debate Beginning-of-Life Issues,* edited by Sally B. Geis and Donald E. Messer, 129-136. Nashville: Abingdon Press, 2000.

The authors point out that all children are in some sense "problematic," and they show the devastating effect of the notion that children with disabilities would be better off if they had never been born. They propose instead that in our baptism, we are reminded that our lives and the lives of our children are not our own, but are gifts from God. They suggest that the question should not be whether it is ethically acceptable to abort a problematic fetus, but rather, what has happened that Christians have come to believe that this is indeed the right question to ask.

280. Heaney, Stephen J., ed. *Abortion: A New Generation of Catholic Responses.* Braintree, Mass.: Pope John Center, 1992.

A collection of articles in which the individual authors present their own views of abortion, but all of them in line with general Catholic teaching on abortion.

281.   Heimburger, Douglas C. "The Scriptures on Abortion." *Journal of Biblical Ethics in Medicine* 2 (1989): 77-79.

The author brings together a number of biblical passages which, taken together, he says, comprise a powerful argument against abortion.

282.   Hill, Andrew E. "Abortion in the Ancient Near East." In *Abortion: A Christian Understanding and Response,* edited by James K. Hoffmeier, 31-48. Grand Rapids, Mich.: Baker Book House, 1987.

A review of abortion and birth control in the ancient Near East as found in the medical and legal documents of peoples such as the Sumerians, the Assyrians, the Egyptians, and the Persians.

283.   Hinlicky, Paul R. "War of Worlds: Re-Visioning the Abortion Dilemma." *Pro Ecclesia* 2 (1993): 187-207.

The author claims that abortion is a violation of the right to live which God has bestowed on nascent life. Thus, the question as to whether or not the fetus is a person is irrelevant. Abortion is wrong because it forecloses the future God opens.

284.   Hodges, Fredrica F. "The Assaults on Choice." In *Abortion Rights and Fetal 'Personhood,'* 2nd ed., edited by Edd Doerr and James W. Prescott, 1-4. Long Beach, Calif.: Centerline Press, in association with Americans for Religious Liberty, 1990.

Examines and criticizes two tactics of the pro-life movement: their teaching that the Bible condemns abortion, and their rhetoric.

285.   Hoffmeier, James K. "Abortion and the Old Testament Law." In *Abortion: A Christian Understanding and Response,* edited by James K. Hoffmeier, 49-63. Grand Rapids, Mich.: Baker Book House, 1987.

The author shows that, while the Old Testament has little to say specifically about abortion, one can tell from the whole tone and theology of the Old Testament that it puts the life of the unborn on the same par as the person outside the womb.

286.   ———., ed. *Abortion: A Christian Understanding and Response.* Grand Rapids, Mich.: Baker Book House, 1987.

A collection of essays, all by faculty members at Wheaton College, which discuss abortion from a Christian perspective.

287.   Holmes, Arthur F. "Some Ethical Questions." In *Abortion: A Christian Understanding and Response,* edited by James K. Hoffmeier, 103-113. Grand Rapids, Mich.: Baker Book House, 1987.

Admitting that the Bible is silent on such issues as abortion in cases of rape, incest, the life of the mother, and the possibility of therapeutic abortion, the author uses other resources such as inference, extra-biblical insights (including philosophical ethics), and the history of Christian ethics to reach conclusions about these issues.

288.   House, H. Wayne. "Miscarriage or Premature Birth: Additional Thoughts on Exodus 21:22-25." *Westminster Theological Journal* 41 (1978): 108-123.

Many have pointed to Exodus 21:22-25 as giving support for the view that the Bible views the fetus as something less than fully human, and thus able to be aborted. This author critiques that interpretation of the passage, saying that it speaks of a premature birth, not a miscarriage, and thus says nothing at all about abortion.

289.   Houston, Joseph. "The Church's Traditional Teaching about Abortion." In *Abortion in Debate,* 66-72. Edinburgh: Quorum Press, 1987.

Analyzes what the church has historically taught regarding abortion, and shows how this analysis can assist us in our current moral reflection.

290.   Howell, Nancy R. "Abortion and Religion." In *New Essays on Abortion and Bioethics,* edited by Rem. B. Edwards, 125-149. Greenwich, Conn.: JAI Press, 1997.

Argues that the typical Conservative Protestant view of abortion, with its emphasis on the personhood of the fetus, and on fetal rights, creates an impasse with the pro-choice position. The author encourages the Christian community to address new questions and enlarge the global and ecological scope of the abortion enquiry.

291.   Hoyt, Robert G. " A Call to Reflection." *Christianity and Crisis* 36 (1977): 253-255.

A critique of the "Call to Concern" (see citation # 211).

292.   Inch, Morris A. "What Does the Church Say?" In *Abortion: A Christian Understanding and Response,* edited by James K. Hoffmeier, 127-138. Grand Rapids, Mich.: Baker Book House, 1987.

A review of how the evangelical church expresses itself on social issues, including both historical as well as theoretical considerations, and then makes specific comments on the abortion issue as a case in point.

293.   Jones, D. Gareth. *Brave New People: Ethical Issues at the Commencement of Life.* Rev. ed. Grand Rapids, Mich.: Eerdmans, 1985.

Discusses issues such as contraception, abortion, and *In vitro* fertilization from a Christian perspective. He explores ways in which Christians can attempt to formulate adequate responses to these issues in the light of biblical, biological, and medical information.

294.   Jung, Patricia Beattie, and Thomas A. Shannon, eds. *Abortion and Catholicism: The American Debate.* New York: Crossroad, 1988.

A collection of articles on abortion written from the Catholic perspective.

295.   Klein, Leonard R. "Why the Church Opposes Abortion." *Lutheran Forum* 32, no. 4 (1998): 21-23.

The author lays out in simple terms why he believes the devout Christian should oppose abortion.

296.   Kline, Meredith G. "*Lex Talionis* and the Human Fetus." *Journal of the Evangelical Theological Society* 20 (1977): 193-201.

While favoring the pro-life interpretation of Exodus 21:22-25, the author suggests a different exegetical base for it.

297.   Klotz, John W. *A Christian View of Abortion.* Contemporary Theology Series. St. Louis: Concordia Pub. House, 1973.

Presents an overview of the abortion problem in the United States, and the issues it presents. He then provides a Christian and biblical answer to these issues, written from a conservative Christian vantage point.

298.   Koop, C. Everett, M.D. "Deception on Demand." *Moody Monthly,* May 1980, 24-29.

Claiming that the whole issue of abortion has been foisted upon us by deception, the author answers some pro-choice arguments, and calls on the evangelical churches to become more active in the Pro-Life movement.

299.   ———. "A Physician Looks at Abortion." In *Thou Shalt not Kill: The Christian Case against Abortion,* edited by Richard L. Ganz, 8-25. New Rochelle, N.Y.: Arlington House, 1978.

A well-known Christian physician, using both medical science and Christian theology, presents his reasons for rejecting abortion.

300.   ————. *The Right to Live, the Right to Die.* Wheaton, Ill.: Tyndale House, 1976.

A Christian physician presents arguments against abortion, euthanasia, and infanticide. He also gives his thoughts on the use of life support systems to prolong life.

301.   Kurz, William S., S.J. "Genesis and Abortion: An Exegetical Test of a Biblical Warrant in Ethics." *Theological Studies* 46 (1986): 668-680.

The author examines the argument that the human dominion over the creation found in Genesis 1:26-28 can be used as a justification for sometimes choosing abortion as necessary for responsible stewardship over creation. He presents an exegesis of Genesis 1:26-28 which shows that argument to be weak, and an unwarranted deduction from that passage.

302.   Lake, Donald M. "A Theological Perspective on Abortion." In *Abortion: A Christian Understanding and Response,* edited by James K. Hoffmeier, 87-100. Grand Rapids, Mich.: Baker Book House, 1987.

Shows that a proper understanding of Christian theology leads to the view that abortion is wrong.

303.   Lamb, James I. "Pro-Life is not an Option." *The Evangel,* Jan.-Feb. 2000, 1.

The Executive Director of Lutherans for Life calls on Christians to recognize that being pro-life is not an option--that is, it is not like a choice in some political debate; rather, he says, being pro-life is a biblical imperative.

304.   Larson, David R., ed. *Abortion: Ethical Issues and Options.* Loma Linda, Calif.: Loma Linda University, Center for Christian Bioethics, 1992.

A collection of essays originally presented at a conference of Seventh-Day Adventists held in 1988. All the essays are by Seventh-Day Adventists, but from differing perspectives on the abortion issue.

305.   Law, Cardinal Bernard. "The Consistent Pro-Life Ethic." *Origins* 14 (1984): 312-313.

An address before the Massachusetts Citizens for Life, in which the archbishop of Boston argues for a consistent ethic of life, that is a concern for all the life issues.

306.   ———. "What it Means to Be Pro-Life." *Origins* 30 (2001): 733, 735-738.

An address April 17, 2001 in Evansville, Indiana, at the annual banquet of the Vanderburgh County Right to Life Committee, in which he states that the pro-life movement must recognize the link between abortion, euthanasia, and all other assaults on the inviolability of human life.

307.   Leithart, Peter J. "Attacking the Tabernacle." *First Things,* November 1999, 15-16.

Presents an exegesis of Psalm 139:13 showing that abortion does not merely kill a child of God, it attacks the house of God. Thus, abortion is not just murder, it is sacrilege, an even worse offense against God.

308.   Lostra, Hans. *Abortion: The Catholic Debate in America.* New York: Irvington, 1985.

An analysis and evaluation of Catholic thought on abortion.

309.   Maguire, Daniel C. "Abortion: A Question of Catholic Honesty." *Christian Century* 100 (1983): 803-807.

The author maintains that the Catholic hierarchy insists that there can be only one Catholic position on abortion, the anti-abortion position. The author disputes that contention, saying that there is more than one normative Catholic position on abortion.

310.   ———. "Catholic Options in the Abortion Debate." In *Guide for Prochoice Catholics: The Church, the State, and Abortion Politics,* 15-19. Washington, D.C.: Catholics for a Free Choice, 1990.

Presents the view that, contrary to popular opinion, moral rigidity on moral matters is not the Catholic way. Thus, in the issue of abortion, he says, there is no one "Catholic" position.

311.   ———. "A Catholic Theologian at an Abortion Clinic." In *The Ethics of Abortion: Pro-Life vs. Pro-Choice.* Rev. ed., edited by Robert M. Baird and Stuart E. Rosenbaum. Buffalo: Prometheus Books, 1993.

A Catholic moral theologian describes several visits he made to an abortion clinic. He then concludes with his reasons why abortion should remain legal for women who feel they need it.

312. Maguire, Daniel C., and James T. Burtachell. "The Catholic Legacy and Abortion: A Debate." *Commonweal* 114 (1987): 657-663, 668-674.

The text of a debate between a pro-choice and a pro-life Catholic.

313. Mangan, Joseph T., S.J. "The Wonder of Myself: Ethical-Theological Aspects of Direct Abortion." *Theological Studies* 31 (1970): 125-148.

The author concludes that Catholic teaching on abortion is based on a sufficiently solid foundation for it to maintain that all direct abortion, whether as a means, or as an end in itself, is contrary to divine law, and admits no exceptions.

314. Martin, Walter R. *Abortion: Is it Always Murder?* Santa Ana, Calif.: Vision House, 1977.

Using the Bible as his foundation, the author argues that abortion for social reasons – for population control, as a means of birth control, or simply to control ones body – is wrong, and can be called murder. On the other hand, abortion in the cases of rape and the life of the mother are not wrong, and cannot biblically be called murder.

315. Martz, Judy C., and Harvey C. Martz. "Is Aborting a 'Problematic' Fetus Ethically Acceptable? A Response." In *The Befuddled Stork: Helping Persons of Faith Debate Beginning-of-Life Issues,* edited by Sally B. Geis and Donald E. Messer,121-128. Nashville: Abingdon Press, 2000.

Using Christian principles, the authors argue that aborting a fetus with significant genetic problems may be ethically appropriate, but they outline steps that they feel the parents must take before making that decision.

316. May, William E. "Abortion and Man's Moral Being." In *Abortion: Pro and Con,* edited by Robert L. Perkins, 13-35. Cambridge, Mass.: Schenkman Pub. Co., 1974.

State the official teaching of the Roman Catholic Church on abortion, along with a status of the debate among Catholic moralists. Closes with the author's own reasons why the direct, intentional killing of a human fetus is wrong.

317. ———. "Abortion, Moral Absolutes, and Dissent from Magisterial Teaching." In *Abortion: A New Generation of Catholic Responses,* edited

by Stephen J. Heaney, 277-296. Braintree, Mass.: Pope John Center, 1992.

Pope John Paul II advanced the teaching that there are certain acts which are intrinsically evil, independently of the circumstances. The moral norms against these acts are absolute norms in that they have no exceptions. Direct abortion is one of these acts. This article is a defense of this teaching, over against current revisionist theologians who claim that there are no moral absolutes.

318.   McCarthy, Donald G. "Ethics and Embryo Rights." *Origins* 14 (1984): 174-176.

A statement by a Catholic priest before the House Science and Technology Committee, Aug. 9, 1984, in which he argues against experimentation with embryos, including procedures such as the freezing, discarding, or destroying of embryos, and surrogate parenting.

319.   McCarthy, Donald G., and Albert S. Moraczewski, eds. *An Ethical Evaluation of Fetal Experimentation: An Interdisciplinary Study.* St. Louis: Pope John XXIII Medical-Moral Research and Education Center, 1976.

A report submitted by the Center's Task Force on Fetal Experimentation. It outlines, in light of general Catholic teaching, the moral, ethical and religious aspects of fetal experimentation. It also includes a discussion of the personhood of the fetus.

320.   McCormick, Richard A., S.J. "Notes on Moral Theology: The Abortion Dossier." *Theological Studies* 35 (1974): 312-359.

Reviews of a number of writings on abortion by various religious thinkers.

321.   ———. "Procreative Technologies." *Origins* 14 (1984): 173-174.

Testimony before the House Science and Technology Committee, Aug. 9, 1984, in which this Catholic theologian argues against experimentation on human embryos, including such things as *In Vitro* fertilization, artificial insemination by donor, surrogate motherhood, and embryo freezing.

322.   Meehan, Mary. "Theologians and Abortion: Not Their Finest Hour." *Human Life Review* 12, no. 4 (1986): 50-74.

Examines what she calls the "fuzzy thinking" of many theologians who support abortion, and shows it to be weak.

323.   Meilaender, Gilbert. "Against Abortion: A Protestant Proposal." *Linacre Quarterly* 45 (1978): 165-178.

The author provides a Protestant pro-life position which uses the best of Catholic theology on the subject, while avoiding, or modifying, those aspects of Catholic thought which cause Protestants problems.

324.   Miller, Kevin E. "The Politics of a Culture of Life." In *Life and Learning VI: Proceedings of the Sixth University Faculty for Life Conference, June 1996 at Georgetown University,* edited by Joseph W. Koterski, S.J., 245-266. Washington, D.C.: University Faculty for Life, 1997.

An examination of the political dimension of Pope John Paul II's encyclical, *Evangelium Vitae* ("The Gospel of Life"). He does this by examining the political implications of the "culture of life" of which John Paul speaks.

325.   Mirkes, Sister Renée, O.S.F. "Selective Termination: Doing Evil to Achieve Good?" In *Abortion: A New Generation of Catholic Responses,* edited by Stephen J. Heaney, 177-186. Braintree, Mass.: Pope John Center, 1992.

An ethical evaluation of the practice of selectively aborting several fetuses in a multi-fetal pregnancy in the hope that the remaining fetuses will have a greater chance to develop normally. The author sees this as doing evil to achieve a good. She claims that we should rather pursue the good and avoid the evil, and leave the unforeseeable consequences to God.

326.   Mohler, Albert R., Jr. "Is It Moral to Make 'Test-Tube Babies'? A Response." In *The Befuddled Stork: Helping Persons of Faith Debate Beginning-of-Life Issues,* edited by Sally B. Geis, and Donald E. Messer, 57-66. Nashville: Abingdon Press, 2000.

The author presents a Christian ethical argument against *in vitro* fertilization.

327.   Mollenkott, Virginia Ramey. "Reproductive Choice: Basic to Justice for Women." *Christian Scholar's Review* 16 (1988): 286-293.

Argues that if Christians really desire to give justice to women, they would advocate the woman's right to have an abortion. Justice for women, she argues, is impossible, without granting them reproductive choice.

328.   Montgomery, John Warwick. *Slaughter of the Innocents: Abortion, Birth Control and Divorce in the Light of Science, Law and Theology.* Westchester, Ill.: Cornerstone Books, 1981.

         Presents a critique of abortion, saying that it is a slaughter of the innocents, and that God would have us return to the respect for fetal life which he himself manifested in the giving of his own Son for salvation.

329.   Murphy, Jeremiah Timothy. "The 'Catholic Moment' and Abortion." Ph.D. diss., University of Southern California, 1996.

         Argues for the justification of a public policy of limited abortion, as opposed to abortion on demand and no abortion. The author claims that limited abortion is compatible with the Catholic Church's teaching on abortion. He also calls on the Catholic Church to take the lead in proposing such a public policy of limited abortion.

330.   National Council of the Churches of Christ in the U.S.A. *Abortion: A Paper for Study.* New York: Department of Publication Services, National Council of Churches, 1973.

         Reviews the various factors member churches have had to take into consideration in developing position statements on abortion – the societal situation, and their theological perspectives – and calls for dialog and for churches to work to rectify the situations which make abortion desirable. The paper closes with excerpts from the position statements from several of its member churches.

331.   Nelson, J. Robert. "The Divided Mind of Protestant Christians." In *New Perspectives on Human Abortion,* edited by Thomas W. Hilgers, Dennis J. Horan, and David Mall, 387-404. Frederick, Md.: Aletheia Books, University Publications of America, 1981.

         Shows that Protestant churches, by their very nature, will have different views on abortion. He then outlines the position on abortion taken by the largest Protestant denominations.

332.   ———. "What Does Theology Say About Abortion?" *Christian Century* 90 (1973): 124-128.

         Presents eight beliefs which all Protestant Christians hold in common, regardless of how they apply these to the issue of abortion. Also presents some thoughts on the concept of "sanctity of life."

333.   Newton, Lisa H. "The Irrelevance of Religion in the Abortion Debate." In *Abortion: The Moral Issues,* edited by Edward Batchelor, 3-6. New

York: Pilgrim Press, 1982. Originally published in *Hastings Center Report*, Aug. 1978.

Argues that abortion is not a religious issue, on the grounds that, as she claims, the Bible nowhere mentions the subject.

334. Nicholson, Susan T. *Abortion and the Roman Catholic Church.* JRE Studies in Religious Ethics, 2. Knoxville, Tenn.: Religious Ethics, Inc., 1978.

The author presents a critical analysis of the Catholic Church's position on abortion.

335. ———. "The Roman Catholic Doctrine of Therapeutic Abortion." In *Feminism and Philosophy*, edited by Mary Vetterling-Braggin, Frederick A. Ellison, and Jane English, 385-407. Totowa, N.J.: Littlefield and Adams, 1977.

Analyzes the Roman Catholic doctrine of abortions done in order to preserve the life of the mother. In particular, the author uses the Catholic doctrine of Double Effect in determining why Catholic moralists will allow some therapeutic abortions, but not others.

336. Niederhaus, Patricia A. "A Covenant of Motherhood: A Response to 'Reflecting Theologically.'" In *Affirming Life: Biblical Perspectives on Abortion for the United Church of Christ*, edited by John B. Brown and Robin Fox, 51-58. [S.l.]: United Church of Christ Friends for Life, 1991.

The author presents what she sees as the biblical definition and use of the concept of "covenant," and applies that to the issue of abortion.

337. ———. "The Hard Cases." In *Affirming Life: Biblical Perspectives on Abortion for the United Church of Christ*, edited by John B. Brown and Robin Fox, 63-68. [S.l.]: United Church of Christ Friends for Life, 1991.

Presents arguments against abortion even for the "hard" cases of rape, incest, and fetal deformity, as well as an argument against the concept of "every child a wanted child."

338. Noonan, John T. "Abortion and the Catholic Church: A Summary History." *Natural Law Forum* 12 (1967): 85-131.

Presents a history of the views of the Catholic church on abortion, and then presents his own argument for saying that abortion is morally wrong.

339.   ———. "The Catholic Church and Abortion." *Dublin Review* 241
            (1967): 300-345.

            A history of the teaching on abortion in the New Testament, the early
            church Fathers, representative moral theologians, and authoritative
            statements of popes and councils. He claims that the development in the
            Catholic Church's teaching on abortion has been one of clarification and
            elaboration; there have been no radical shifts in direction.

340.   ———, ed. *The Morality of Abortion: Legal and Historical Perspec-
            tives.* Cambridge, Mass.: Harvard Univ. Press, 1970.

            A collection of articles on abortion from the religious, moral, and legal
            perspectives.

341.   O'Bannon, Robert H. "Some Theological and Biological Considerations
            on the Origin of Human Life." In *Life and Learning: Proceedings of the
            Third University Faculty for Life Conference,* edited by Joseph W.
            Koterski, S.J., 133-150. Washington, D.C.: University Faculty for Life,
            1993.

            Shows that both the Bible and biology give strong support to the pro-life
            cause.

342.   O'Connor, Cardinal John. "Human Lives, Human Rights." *Origins* 14
            (1984): 291-301.

            The Archbishop of New York calls on medical personnel to provide
            medical services without cost when that is needed to save the life of an
            unborn child. He also calls on public officials to oppose abortion on
            demand, and to work for a modification of today's permissive abortion
            laws.

343.   O'Donnell, Thomas J. "A Traditional Catholic's View." In *Abortion and
            Catholicism: The American Debate,* edited by Patricia Beattie Jung and
            Thomas A. Shannon, 44-47. New York: Crossroad, 1988.

            Clarifies two aspects of the traditional Catholic view on abortion: (1) what
            the doctrine of the church has been and is now, and (2) those parts of the
            doctrine which have been most frequently misinterpreted or misunder-
            stood.

344.   O'Mathúna, Dónal P. "Abortion: Biblical Considerations." *Ashland
            Theological Journal* 28 (1996): 60-73.

In responding to two recent books by Christians on abortion, one pro-choice, the other pro-life, the author presents biblical arguments against abortion.

345.   O'Rourke, Joseph. "Is There Life after Birth?" *Church and Society*, March/April 1981, 36-45.

Presents a history and analysis of natural law philosophy, particularly as used by the Roman Catholic community. He presents a new perspective on natural law, which would give a woman the right to choose an abortion. He claims that free choice is the only true anti-abortion moral position.

346.   O'Rourke, Kevin D. "Some Theological and Ethical Perspectives of the Teachings of the Catholic Church in Regard to Abortion." In *Seminar on Abortion: The Proceedings of a Dialogue Between Catholics and Baptists*, edited by Claude U. Broach, 59-68. Charlotte, N.C.: The Ecumenical Press, 1975.

Presents, and defends, the position of the Catholic Church on abortion.

347..   Olson, Mark. "Back to the Bible." *Church and Society*, March/April 1981, 54-66.

An examination to see what, if anything, the Bible teaches on abortion. He concludes that the Bible says nothing specific about the morality or immorality of abortion, though it does have a command against murder. To determine if this command is relevant, he says we must ask whether the Bible considers the fetus to be a human being. Here, again, he says, the Bible does not define the nature of the fetus. Thus, he says, in light of this ambiguity in Scripture, we should be willing to accept a diversity of views on abortion.

348.   Otto, Randall E. "The Relativism of Pro-Choice Ethics." In *Affirming Life: Biblical Perspectives on Abortion for the United Church of Christ*, edited by John B. Brown and Robin Fox, 1-11. [S.l.]: United Church of Christ Friends for Life, 1991.

Shows that the pro-choice position is based on a relativistic view of ethics, and on the autonomy of man to decide what is right and wrong for himself. In contrast, the author shows that biblical theology must inform our ethics, and shows that in the Bible, life is seen as beginning at conception.

349.   Overduin, Daniel Christian. *The Bible Does Speak on Abortion: A Lutheran Appraisal.* Minneapolis, Minn.: ForLIFE, 1978.

An overview of biblical passages dealing with human life, showing that the Bible is opposed to abortion.

350.   ———. "The Ethics of Abortion." In *New Perspectives on Human Abortion,* edited by Thomas W. Hilgers, Dennis J. Horan, and David Mall, 357-386. Frederick, Md.: Aletheia Books, University Publications of America, 1981.

The ethics of abortion depends on the individual's point of departure, or presuppositions. The Humanist begins with the view that man is autonomous, and can make decisions for himself without regard to any supposed absolute norms, as there are no absolute norms. The Christian, however, begins with the recognition that man is a creature of God, and in relation to Him; every act is therefore either an expression of faith or of unbelief. The author begins his discussion of abortion from the latter perspective, but also shows that, because there can be no compromise between these two starting points, there will always be an inevitable collision of views.

351.   Paris, Ginette. *The Sacrament of Abortion.* Translated from the French by Joanna Mott. Dallas, Tex.: Spring Publications, 1992.

Develops the idea that abortion is a sacred act, an expression of maternal responsibility, and not a failure of maternal love. Claims that Judeo-Christian values, which may have seemed necessary two thousand years ago, are now more and more irresponsible, and infinitely more cruel than abortion.

352.   Paris, Peter J. "Is it Moral to Make 'Test-Tube Babies'? A Response." In *The Befuddled Stork: Helping Persons of Faith Debate Beginning-of-Life Issues,* edited by Sally B. Geis and Donald E. Messer, 50-56. Nashville: Abingdon Press, 2000.

The author gives an endorsement of *in vitro* fertilization, provided that it is conjoined with, and not a substitute for, mutual love. Many of the ethical dilemmas involved in the procedure can be resolved if this love of a child, whether it be by heterosexual or homosexual couples, is present.

353.   Patrick, Anne E. "Virtue, Providence, and the Endangered Self: Some Religious Dimensions of the Abortion Debate." In *Abortion and Catholicism: The American Debate,* edited by Patricia Beattie Jung and Thomas A. Shannon, 172-180. New York: Crossroad, 1988.

The author seeks to understand how two equally devout Catholics can reach different conclusions on abortion: the one viewing it as always wrong, the other saying that abortion is a pity whenever it is done, but that there are certain cases when it is justified, and that public policy should not interfere.

354. Paynter, Roger A. "Life in the Tragic Dimension: A Sermon on Abortion." In *The Ethics of Abortion: Pro-Life vs. Pro-Choice.* Rev. ed., edited by Robert M. Baird and Stuart E. Rosenbaum, 187-193. Buffalo: Prometheus Books, 1993.

This sermon, preached at the Lake Shore Baptist Church, Waco, Tex., Jan. 18, 1987, claims that there is no Biblical nor moral mandate against abortion, and so it should remain legal.

355. Perkins, Robert L., ed. *Abortion: Pro and Con.* Issues in Contemporary Ethics. Cambridge, Mass.: Schenkman Pub. Co., 1974.

Essays for and against abortion written from both a religious and a moral perspective.

356. Quinn, James J. "Christianity views Fetal Research." *Linacre Quarterly* 45 (1978): 55-63.

A review of four different views Christians have offered on the subject of fetal research, and offers his own position.

357. Rainey, R. Randall, Gerard Magill, and Kevin D. O'Rourke. "Introduction: Abortion, the Catholic Church, and Public Policy." In *Abortion and Public Policy: An Interdisciplinary Investigation within the Catholic Tradition,* edited by R. Randall Rainey and Gerard Magill, 1-46. Omaha, Neb.: Creighton Univ. Press, 1996.

Presents an historical overview of the Catholic Church's teaching on abortion, as well as its efforts at promoting a public policy against abortion.

358. Ramsey, Paul. "Feticide/Infanticide upon Request." *Religion in Life* 39 (1970): 170-186.

Using a 1969 position statement of the United Methodist Church favoring legalized abortion, the author presents a response to various pro-choice arguments.

359. Roach, Abp. John R., and Cardinal Terence Cooke. "Testimony in Support of the Hatch Amendment." In *Abortion and Catholicism: The American Debate,* edited by Patricia Beattie Jung and Thomas A. Shannon, 10-43. New York: Crossroad, 1988.

In a speech originally given before the United States Senate in support of the Hatch amendment, the authors present, and make a case for the position on abortion taken by the Catholic Church's Magisterium.

360.   Roach, Rev. Richard R., S.J. "Divine Revelation and Abortion." In *Abortion: A New Generation of Catholic Responses,* edited by Stephen J. Heaney, 87-100. Braintree, Mass.: Pope John Center, 1992.

The author claims that abortion is not simply a moral question which can be isolated from the Christian faith; rather it has to do with the very content of the Christian faith. Therefore, he says, two people may not disagree about abortion and yet continue to agee as Christian brothers. If there is such a disagreement between them, he says, they must recognize that they are professing two different faiths. only one of which may be called Christian.

361.   Rudy, Kathy. "Thinking through the Ethics of Abortion." *Theology Today* 51 (1994): 235-248.

Claims that a more consistent and faithful stance to the moral issue of abortion can be developed by the use of casuistry – that is, a case-by-case analysis for determining the moral nature of an action.

362.   Ruether, Rosemary Radford. "Catholics and Abortion: Authority vs. Dissent." *Christian Century* 102 (1985): 859-862.

The author discusses the question of whether, and to what extent, individual Catholics may dissent from the official church teaching on the subject.

363.   Sample, Tex S. "Can 'Partial-Birth' Abortion be a Legitimate Moral Choice? A Response." In *The Befuddled Stork: Helping Persons of Faith Debate Beginning-of-Life Issues,* edited by Sally B. Geis and Donald E. Messer, 139-150. Nashville: Abingdon Press, 2000.

Argues that, on the basis of Christian ethics, there are some tragic circumstances, including the mental health of the mother, when partial-birth abortions are ethically acceptable.

364.   Schaeffer, Francis A., and C. Everett Koop, M.D. *Whatever Happened to the Human Race?* Old Tappan, N.J.: Fleming H. Revell, 1979.

The authors examine abortion, infanticide, and euthanasia, showing that they are a natural consequence of a materialistic, humanistic, world-view. They counteract this with an explanation of the Christian world-view, showing the implications it has for these same life issues.

365.   Schlossberg, Terry. "Abortion Matters: Abortion as a Challenge to Christian Orthodoxy." *Touchstone: A Journal of Ecumenical Orthodoxy* 8, no. 2 (1995): 30-32.

The author claims that while abortion may not be used as a litmus test to separate Christians from non-Christians, it does constitute a test of Christian orthodoxy. She says that those mainline Protestant denominations that favor abortion need to return to the framework of Christian orthodoxy, and then to think about abortion from within that framework. She shows that from a framework of Christian orthodoxy, and faithfulness to the Bible as the Word of God, human beings, both born and unborn, derive their value from God who has made them in his image, and that it is our obligation to protect and care for them and do them no harm.

366.   Schuler, William, Jr., M.D. "The Terrible Infancy of Fetal Cell Transplantation Technology." *Journal of Biblical Ethics in Medicine* 1 (1987): 83-87.

The author expresses his concern that the potential impact of the technology for fetal cell transplantation will be to radically change the face of medicine in such a way that the Bible believing Christian will be in principle excluded from it.

367.   Shannon, Denise. "Outside the Chancery: Catholics Take Issue." In *Guide for Prochoice Catholics: The Church, the State, and Abortion Politics*, 24-28. Washington, D.C.: Catholics for a Free Choice, 1990.

Shows that while the Catholic hierarchy has taken a position that is opposed to abortion, most Catholic lay people are more pro-choice in their opinions.

368.   Shoemaker, Donald P. *Abortion, the Bible, and the Christian.* Grand Rapids, Mich.: Baker Book House, 1976.

Outlines the current abortion controversy, and gives answers from the Bible to several arguments in favor of abortion, as well as giving positive biblical arguments against abortion.

369.   Sider, Ronald J. *Completely Pro-Life: Building a Consistent Stance.* Downers Grove, Ill.: InterVarsity Press, 1987.

On the basis of a biblical definition of life, the author attempts to articulate a consistent pro-life stance on the issues of abortion, poverty, sexuality, and nuclear warfare.

370.   Simmons. Paul D. "Abortion: The Biblical and Human Issues." Chap. 3
          in *Birth and Death: Bioethical Decision-Making.* Philadelphia: Westmin-
          ster Press, 1983.

          Presents the historical and social background to the abortion debate in the
          United States, and then analyzes the biblical teaching on abortion. He
          claims the Bible gives no support to the view that the fetus is a person
          from the moment of conception.

371.   ———. "Personhood. the Bible, and Abortion." In *The Ethics of
          Abortion: Pro-Life vs. Pro-Choice.* Rev. ed., edited by Robert M. Baird
          and Stuart E. Rosenbaum, 170-186. Buffalo: Prometheus Books, 1993.

          A criticism of the common biblical arguments against abortion usually
          propounded by Evangelicals.

372.   ———. "A Theological Response to Fundamentalism on the Abortion
          Issue." *Church and Society,* March/April 1981, 22-35.

          A critique of Fundamentalism and its view on abortion.

373.   Smith, Harmon L. "Abortion–The Theological Tradition." In *Abortion:
          Pro and Con,* edited by Robert L. Perkins, 37-51. Cambridge, Mass.:
          Schenkman Pub. Co., 1974.

          A brief survey of the positions on abortion taken by Judaism and by
          various Christian denominations.

374.   Smith, T. C. "Abortion: A Biblical Perspective." In *Seminar on
          Abortion: The Proceedings of a Dialogue Between Catholics and Baptists,*
          edited by Claude U. Broach, 37-46. Charlotte, N.C.: The Ecumenical
          Institute, 1975.

          A presentation of the teachings on abortion, from the Baptist perspective,
          of the Old Testament, the Talmud, the New Testament, and the Early
          Church Fathers.

375.   Soley, Ginny Earnest. "To Preserve and Protect Life: A Christian Feminist
          Perspective on Abortion." *Sojourners,* Oct. 1986, 34-37.

          A feminist Christian presents an argument against abortion.

376.   Sommers, Mary Catherine. "Living Together: Burdensome Pregnancy
          and the Hospitable Self." In *Abortion: A New Generation of Catholic
          Responses,* edited by Stephen J. Heaney, 243-261. Braintree, Mass.: Pope
          John Center, 1992.

A critique of the theory, advanced by some, that, since childbearing can be burdensome to the mother, then it is also an act of charity, and thus is not a moral obligation.

377.   Sproul, R. C. *Abortion: A Rational Look at an Emotional Issue.* Colorado Springs, Colo.: NavPress, 1990.

Examines the issue of abortion from the perspectives of biblical, civil, and natural law. The author makes the case for saying that abortion is against the law of God, against the laws of nature, and against reason.

378.   Stallsworth, Paul T., ed. *The Church and Abortion: In Search of New Ground for Response.* Nashville: Abingdon Press, 1993.

This book emerges from a conference on the church and abortion held at a United Methodist church   All the papers connect, in some way or another, with the Durham Declaration (see citation # 238), and so all come from a pro-life perspective.

379.   ——— , ed. *The Right Choice: Pro-Life Sermons.* Nashville: Abingdon Press, 1997.

A collection of sermons on abortion by various pastors, all from a Pro-Life perspective.

380.   Steffen, Lloyd, ed. *Abortion: A Reader.* The Pilgrim Library of Ethics. Cleveland: Pilgrim Press, 1996.

A collection of articles on abortion from the religious, moral, and legal perspectives.

381.   Swindoll, Charles R. *Sanctity of Life: The Inescapable Issue.* Foreword by James Dobson. Dallas: Word Publishing, 1990.

Presents a biblical and Christian case against abortion, and encourages Christians to get involved in the anti-abortion movement.

382.   Tauer, Carol A. "The Tradition of Probabilism and the Moral Status of the Early Embryo." *Theological Studies* 45 (1984): 3-33.

The author argues that the Catholic Magisterium, in its position on abortion, inaccurately interprets and applies the traditional methods for resolving moral doubt. As a result, she concludes that their argument is called into question, and that theologians are justified in dissenting from its teaching on abortion.

383.   Templeton, Elizabeth. "Abortion: Our Painful Freedom." In *Abortion in Debate*, 20-29. Edinburgh: Quorum Press, 1987.

         Presents a theological argument in favor of abortion.

384.   Teresa, Mother. "Abortion is a Selfish Choice." In *Abortion: Opposing Viewpoints*, edited by Tamara L. Roleff, 48-52. San Diego: Greenhaven Press, 1997. Reprinted from the March 1994 issue of *Crisis*.

         The text of a speech delivered at the National Prayer Breakfast, Feb. 3, 1994, in which this Catholic Nun portrays abortion as a selfish choice. She claims that abortion destroys one's ability to love, because it is usually done to avoid the hurt that unselfish love would require.

385.   Thielicke, Helmut. "The Interruption of Pregnancy (Problem of Artificial Abortion)." In *Abortion: The Moral Issues*, edited by Edward Batchelor, 129-135. New York: Pilgrim Press, 1982.

         Shows that the question of whether one is ever allowed to destroy innocent life is a complex one, and that theological ethics can only show us what our alternatives are, not answer the question. This is abridged from his *Ethics of Sex* (New York: Harper & Row, 1964), pp. 232-241.

386.   Tickle, Phyllis, ed. *Confessing Conscience: Churched Women on Abortion.* Nashville: Abingdon Press, 1990.

         A collection of essays by women from various Christian traditions who share their thoughts and feelings on the abortion debate.

387.   Vaux, Kenneth L. *Birth Ethics: Religious and Cultural Values in the Genesis of Life.* New York: Crossroad, 1989.

         Presents a history and analysis of the ethical principles involved in the issues of sexual activity, pregnancy, abortion, and newborns with life threatening illnesses.

388.   Walter, James J. "Theological Parameters: Catholic Doctrine on Abortion in a Pluralist Society." In *Abortion and Public Policy: An Interdisciplinary Investigation within the Catholic Tradition*, edited by R. Randall Rainey and Gerard Magill, 91-130. Omaha, Neb.: Creighton Univ. Press, 1996.

         Presents the theological beliefs that underlie the Catholic Church's official moral position on abortion, and at the same time seeks to help politicians, Catholic politicians in particular, to better negotiate the abortion controversy in a pluralist society.

389.   Walters, James W. "Adventist Guidelines on Abortion." In *Abortion: Ethical Issues and Options*, edited by David R. Larson, 173-185. Loma Linda, Calif.: Loma Linda University, Center for Christian Bioethics, 1992.

A Seventh-Day Adventist claims that it is time for his church to reexamine its abortion policy, and he presents his ideas on what shape a set of Adventist guidelines might take.

390.   Wannenwetsch, Bernd. "'Intrinsically Evil Acts': Or, Why Abortion and Euthanasia Cannot Be Justified." In *Ecumenical Ventures in Ethics: Protestants Engage Pope John Paul II's Moral Encyclicals*, edited by Reinhard Hütter and Theodor Dieter, 185-215. Grand Rapids, Mich.: Eerdmans, 1998.

An examination *Veritatis Splendor* and *Evangelium Vitae* from a Protestant perspective. In particular, the author shows how the former's teaching on "intrinsically evil acts" provides the background for the latter's statements on abortion and euthanasia. He then asks the question of whether the pope's use of the concept of "intrinsically evil acts" does justice to the complexity of moral judgements as his theories present it.

391.   Ward, Bernadette Waterman. "Abortion as a Sacrament: Mimetic Desire and Sacrifice in Sexual Politics." In *Life and Learning VIII: Proceedings of the Eighth University Faculty for Life Conference, June 1998, at the University of Toronto*, edited by Joseph W. Koterski, S.J., 305-316. Washington, D.C.: University Faculty for Life, 1999.

Presents the argument that the practice of abortion is itself a sacrament and a sacrifice in its own religion.

392.   Wennberg, Robert N. *Life in the Balance: Exploring the Abortion Controversy*. Grand Rapids, Mich.: Eerdmans, 1985.

An evangelical Christian presents an evaluation of the various arguments, both for and against abortion, and closes with his own reflections.

393.   White, Andrew A.. "Abortion and the Ancient Practice of Child Sacrifice." *Journal of Biblical Ethics in Medicine* 1 (1987): 34-42.

A response to the critique that one cannot take a dogmatic stand against abortion because the Old Testament is silent on the issue. He shows many parallels between the ancient practice of child sacrifice and the current practice of abortion. He concludes that since the Bible is adamantly opposed to the practice of child sacrifice, that likewise, due to the parallels already enumerated, it is also opposed to abortion.

394.   Whitmore, Todd David. "Moral Methodology and Pastoral Responsive-
        ness: The Case of Abortion and the Care of Children." *Theological
        Studies* 54 (1993): 316-338.

        The author analyzes three different Roman Catholic statements on
        abortion, particularly to see how they relate the issues of abortion and the
        care of children.

395.   Willimon, William H. "The Ministry of Hospitality." In *The Church and
        Abortion: In Search of New Ground for Response,* edited by Paul T.
        Stallsworth, 17-24. Nashville: Abingdon Press, 1993.

        Taking one part of the United Methodist baptismal service, where the
        congregation welcomes the newly baptized person, and promises
        hospitality to them as a basis, the author shows that abortion is contrary
        to this promise of hospitality to strangers.

396.   ———. "A Uniquely Christian Stand on Abortion." *Christian Century*
        108 (1991): 220-221.

        A positive review of the Durham Declaration (see citation # 238),
        commending it for presenting a distinctly theological statement on
        abortion, rather than viewing abortion in purely political terms.

397.   Winfrey, Joan Burgess. "Can 'Partial-Birth' Abortion Be a Legitimate
        Moral Choice? A Response." In *The Befuddled Stork: Helping Persons
        of Faith Debate Beginning-of-Life Issues,* edited by Sally B. Geis and
        Donald E. Messer, 151-161. Nashville: Abingdon Press, 2000.

        Presents an argument that partial-birth abortion is both immoral and
        unchristian.

398.   Wogaman, J. Philip, and Harold O. J. Brown. "Abortion: A Protestant
        Debate." *Human Life Review* 1, no. 2 (1975): 22-40.

        Two Protestants debate the issue of abortion. Wogaman first presents his
        position that, while he values human life, he believes that abortion should
        remain legal. Brown then responds.

399.   Young, Curt. *The Least of These.* Chicago: Moody Press, 1983.

        Presents a Christian case against abortion, shows how it is practiced today,
        shows fetal experimentation, infanticide and euthanasia to be legacies of
        abortion, and calls on Christians to become involved in the anti-abortion
        movement.

JEWISH VIEWS

400.   Aaron, Scott. "The Choice in 'Choose Life:' American Judaism and Abortion." *Commonweal,* 28 Feb. 1992, p. 15-18.

Demonstrates why Jews, who celebrate the ethic of "choose life" in Deuteronomy 30:19, can have such disparate views on abortion.

401.   Biale, Rachel. "Abortion in Jewish Law." In *Abortion: A Reader,* edited by Lloyd Steffen, 190-193. Cleveland, Ohio: The Pilgrim Press, 1996.

The author shows what the halacha has to say on abortion. She finds that although it says the fetus is not a person until the moment of birth, most authorities will allow abortion only in cases of grave physical or psychological harm to the mother.

402.   Bleich, Rabbi J. David. "Abortion and Jewish Law." In *New Perspectives on Human Abortion,* edited by Thomas W. Hilgers, Dennis J. Horan, and David Mall, 405-419. Frederick, Md.: Aletheia Books, University Publications of America, 1981.

Based on Halacha, or religious law, as it is found in the Talmud and other Jewish writings, the author attempts to determine the Jewish view towards abortion.

403.   ———. "Pregnancy Reduction." *Tradition* 29, no. 3 (1995): 55-63.

An examination of Talmudic literature to determine the Jewish attitude toward pregnancy reduction in cases where a multiple number of fertilized eggs have been produced – either through fertility drugs or through *in vitro* fertilization.

404.   Davis, Dena S. "Abortion in Jewish Thought: A Study in Casuistry." *Journal of the American Academy of Religion* 60 (1992): 313-324.

The author notes that much of Jewish thought on abortion is based on casuistry, that is, the method of ethical reasoning that focuses on paradigm cases, rather than principles. He then analyzes three such cases, one from the Old Testament, and two from the Talmud.

405.   Feldman, David M. "Abortion: Jewish Perspectives." In *Encyclopedia of Bioethics.* Rev. ed., edited by Warren Thomas Reich. Vol. 1. New York, Macmillan, 1995.

A discussion of Jewish thought on abortion.

406.   ———. "Is Abortion Murder or Not?" *Church and Society*, March/April
            1981, 46-53.

            Shows that, according to Jewish theology, abortion is not considered to be
            murder.

407.   ———. *Jewish Views on Abortion.* New York: American Jewish
            Committee, Institute of Human Relations, [1984].

            A brief survey of Jewish views on abortion. The author takes the position
            that abortion is not equivalent to murder.

408.   ———. *Marital Relations, Birth Control, and Abortion in Jewish Law.*
            New York: Schocken Books, 1974.

            The author surveys the classic texts of Jewish law to outline the Jewish
            teaching on marriage, birth control, and abortion.

409.   Greenberg, Blu. "Abortion: A Challenge to Halachah." *Judaism* 25
            (1976): 201-208.

            An Orthodox Jew argues that the interpretation of the Halachah should be
            broadened to allow for non-therapeutic abortions.

410.   Jakobovits, Immanuel. "Jewish Views on Abortion." *Human Life Review*
            1, no. 1 (1975): 74-84.

            Discusses the view of Jewish law on the abortion issue, describing it as
            being somewhere between the two extremes of the Roman Catholics, who
            oppose all abortions, and the mainline Protestants, who favor a permissive
            attitude toward abortion.

411.   Kraemer, David. "Jewish Ethics and Abortion." *Tikkun* 8, no. 1 (1993):
            55-58, 77-78.

            Shows how a Jewish law (Halacha) approach to issues and an ethicist's
            approach to issues are radically different. Nonetheless, the author
            contends, the ethicist may still use traditional Jewish sources without
            necessarily accepting the ways of Halacha. He shows this by critiquing
            the common halachic approach to abortion, and then illustrating the
            alternative.

412.   Lichtenstein, Aharon. "Abortion: A Halakhic Perspective." Translated
            from the Hebrew by Nathaniel Helfgot. *Tradition* 25, no. 4 (1991): 3-12.

A broad overview of the problems associated with a discussion of abortion, as found in the halachic literature, as well as the decisions reached by the Rabbis, with the author's personal views inserted in the discussion at various points.

413.   Smith, Harmon L. "Abortion–The Theological Tradition." In *Abortion: Pro and Con,* edited by Robert L. Perkins, 37-51. Cambridge, Mass.: Schenkman Pub. Co., 1974.

A brief survey of the positions on abortion taken by Judaism and by various Christian denominations.

BUDDHIST VIEWS

414.   Anderson, Richard W., and Elaine Martin. "Rethinking the Practice of *Mizuko Kuyô* in Contemporary Japan: Interviews with Practitioners at a Buddhist Temple in Tokyo." *Japanese Journal of Religious Studies* 24 (1997): 121-143.

Based on interviews with actual practitioners of the Buddhist abortion rite, *Mizuko Kuyô,* the authors call into question much of the scholarly research on this rite, which is based on practices at temples that practice the rite, but with which the women participants have only an ephemeral connection.

415.   Desmond, Joan Frawley. "Apologizing to the Babies." *First Things,* Oct. 1996, 13-15.

Presents a description of the Buddhist rite of *Mizuko Kuyô* that has arisen in Japan.

416.   Eiki, Hoshino, and Takeda Dōshō. "Indebtedness and Comfort: The Undercurrents of *Mizuko Kuyô* in Contemporary Japan." *Japanese Journal of Religious Studies* 14 (1987): 305-320.

Examines *Mizuko Kuyô,* the Japanese rite for aborted fetuses, and the related memorials for pets, from the perspective of religious studies.

417.   Florida, Robert E. "Abortion in Buddhist Thailand." In *Buddhism and Abortion,* edited by Damien Keown, 11-29. Honolulu: Univ. of Hawaii Press, 1999.

After a brief introduction to Buddhist ethics and its relation to abortion, the author applies this to the practice of abortion in Thailand, where Buddhism is the official religion. He finds that though Buddhism has a great respect for unborn life, many Buddhist leaders in Thailand seem simply unconcerned about the issue, and wind up tolerating abortion, while never actually encouraging it.

418.   ———. "Buddhist Approaches to Abortion." *Asian Philosophy* 1 (1991): 39-50.

The author notes that, while bioethics is widely debated in Western religious and philosophical discourse, Eastern religious leaders have not yet systematically dealt with the problems associated with ever expanding medical techniques. His goal in this article is to further that discussion by presenting some Buddhist responses to the ethical and religious problems raised by abortion.

419.   Gabrielson, Ruth. "A Prayer for the Water Children: *Mizuko Kuyô* in Japan." *Areopagus* 5, no. 5 (1992): 47-50

A description of the Buddhist rite of *Mizuko Kuyô* in Japan.

420.   Green, Ronald M. "The *Mizuko Kuyô* Debate: An Ethical Discussion." *Journal of the American Academy of Religion* 66 (1999): 809-823.

Shows how scholars have dealt with the practice of *Mizuko Kuyô*, a Buddhist rite for stillborn and miscarried babies, as well as aborted fetuses. He claims that scholars have necessarily brought their own ethical judgements to bear on it. He examines the views of several of these scholars.

421.   Hardacre, Helen. *Marketing the Menacing Fetus in Japan.* Twentieth-Century Japan, no. 7. Berkeley, Calif.: Univ. of California Press, 1997.

A discussion of abortion in Buddhist Japan, with particular emphasis on the practice of *Mizuko Kuyô,* a religious ritual for aborted fetuses.

422.   Harrison, Elizabeth. "Strands of Complexity: The Emergence of *Mizuko Kuyô* in postwar Japan." *Journal of the American Academy of Religion* 66 (1999): 769-796.

Discusses the emergence of the practice of *Mizuko Kuyô*, a memorial rite for miscarried and stillborn babies, as well as aborted fetuses, in postwar Japan. She shows that it is a complex phenomenon.

423.   Hughes, James. "Buddhism and Abortion: A Western Approach." In *Buddhism and Abortion,* edited by Damien Keown, 183-198. Honolulu: Univ. of Hawaii Press, 1999.

Shows that the predominant Buddhist attitude has never been to follow their scriptures slavishly, but to continually adapt them to new audiences and new situations. He suggests that abortion may be allowable where the intention is compassionate, and the act achieves the best outcome for all concerned.

424. Keown, Damien. "Buddhism and Abortion: Is There a 'Middle Way'?" In *Buddhism and Abortion,* edited by Damien Keown, 199-218. Honolulu: Univ. of Hawaii Press, 1999.

The author asks whether Buddhism can provide the answer to the abortion debate which so far has eluded the West. He suggests that it can at least provide new insights that can help move the debate forward. He concludes with a possible "middle way" by suggesting that in Buddhist thought, abortion is seen as always being the taking of innocent human life, but that it can be justified when the intentions are compassionate.

425. ———, ed. *Buddhism and Abortion.* Honolulu: Univ. of Hawaii Press, 1999.

A collection of articles which describe the practice of abortion in several Buddhist countries, as well as giving the Buddhist religious response to abortion.

426. LaFleur, William R. "Abortion, Ambiguity, and Exorcism." *Journal of the American Academy of Religion* 66 (1999): 797-808.

A critique of the book, *Marketing the Menacing Fetus in Japan,* by Helen Hardacre. (see citation # 421).

427. ———. *Liquid Life: Abortion and Buddhism in Japan.* Princeton: Princeton Univ. Press, 1992.

A discussion of abortion in relation to Buddhism in Japan. Shows that there is a difference in the position taken on abortion by Buddhists in Japan, and other Japanese who do not hold to the Buddhist religion.

428. Lecso, Phillip A. "A Buddhist View of Abortion." *Journal of Religion and Health* 26 (1987): 214-218.

An examination of the Buddhist view of abortion.

429. McDermott, James P. "Abortion in the Pāli Canon and Early Buddhist Thought." In *Buddhism and Abortion,* edited by Damien Keown, 157-182. Honolulu: Univ. of Hawaii Press, 1999.

Shows that the early Buddhist scriptures treated abortion as gravely wrong, and a breach of the First Principle against taking life.

430.   O'Connor, June. "Ritual Recognition of Abortion: Japanese Buddhist Practices and U.S. Jewish and Christian Proposals." In *Embodiment, Morality, and Medicine,* edited by Lisa Sowle Cahill and Margaret A. Farley, 93-111. Dordrecht: Kluwer Academic Publishers, 1995.

Examines the Japanese Buddhist practice of *Mizuko Kuyô,* a ritual performed for aborted and miscarried fetuses, particularly asking whether this rite is something that arose to fit the peculiar needs of one culture, or whether it accords with more general human needs.

431.   Smith, Bardwell. "Buddhism and Abortion in Contemporary Japan: *Mizuko Kuyô* and the Confrontation with Death." *Japanese Journal of Religious Studies* 15 (1998): 3-24.

An analysis of *Mizuko Kuyô,* the Buddhist rite for aborted and stillborn fetuses, putting it into a broader socio-religious background, and into the context of other research.

432.   Stott, David. "Buddhadharma and Contemporary Ethics: Some Notes on the Attitude of Tibetan Buddhism to Abortion and Related Procedures." *Religion* 22 (1992): 171-182.

Presents an analysis of traditional Tibetan Buddhist views on abortion, together with their doctrinal basis, and the implications of these attitudes for the successful transmission of the religion to the west.

433.   Tworkov, Helen. "Anti-Abortion/Pro-Choice: Taking Both Sides." *Tricycle: The Buddhist Review* 1, no. 3 (1992): 60-69.

Explains how Buddhists, due to their concepts of life and death, can be both pro-choice and anti-abortion at the same time.

434.   Underwood, Meredith. "Strategies of Survival: Women, Abortion, and Popular Religion in Contemporary Japan." *Journal of the American Academy of Religion* 66 (1999): 739-768.

An examination of the Buddhist ritual of *Mizuko Kuyô,* a memorial rite for miscarried and stillborn babies, as well as aborted fetuses.

435.   Werblowsky, R. J. Zwi. "*Mizuko Kuyô*: Notulae on the Most Important 'New Religion' of Japan." *Japanese Journal of Religious Studies* 18 (1991): 295-354.

Presents an analysis of *Mizuko Kuyô*, the Buddhist abortion rite, as well as abortion as practiced in Japan.

HINDU VIEWS

436.　　Lipner, Julius L. "The Classical Hindu View on Abortion and the Moral Status of the Unborn." Chap. 2 in *Hindu Ethics: Purity, Abortion, and Euthanasia*, by Harold G. Coward, Julius J. Lipner, and Katherine K. Young. Albany: State University of New York Press, 1989.

The author describes the classic Hindu view that abortion is a morally intolerable act, and gives reasons for this traditional view.

ISLAMIC VIEWS

437.　　Bakar, Osman. "Abortion: Islamic Perspectives." In *Encyclopedia of Bioethics*. Rev. ed., edited by Warren Thomas Reich. Vol. 1. New York: Macmillan, 1995.

A discussion of Islamic teaching on abortion.

438.　　Rahman, Fazlur. "Birth and Abortion in Islam." In *Abortion: A Reader*, edited by Lloyd Steffen, 202-209. Cleveland: The Pilgrim Press, 1996.

A presentation of the Islamic view of abortion, birth, and contraception, based on statements in the Koran and other Islamic writings.

439.　　Rispler-Chaim, Vardit. "The Right Not to Be Born: Abortion of the Disadvantaged Fetus in Contemporary Fatwas." *Muslim World* 89 (1999): 130-143.

A discussion of abortion in the case of fetal deformity as found in contemporary Islamic writings.

440.　　Rogers, Therisa. "The Islamic Ethics of Abortion in the Traditional Islamic Sources. *Muslim World* 89 (1999): 122-129.

A survey of the Koran's discussion of topics related to abortion, as well as some legal interpretations.

3 THE CHRISTIAN CHURCH IN THE ABORTION CONTROVERSY

THE CHURCH'S INVOLVEMENT IN THE ABORTION CONTROVERSY

441.   Bernardin, Cardinal Joseph. "Abortion: Catholics must change hearts as well as laws." *U.S. Catholic* 54 (1989): 31-33

A call by a well known Catholic cardinal for Catholics to be involved in other areas of the abortion controversy besides the legal. They must, he says, also educate people as to what abortion entails.

442.   Blanchard, Dallas A. *The Anti-Abortion Movement and the Rise of the Religious Right: From Polite to Fiery Protest.* Social Movements Past and Present. New York: Twayne Publishers, 1994.

Presents a history and analysis of the anti-abortion movement in the United States, and examines the role that the religious right has played in that movement.

443.   Bohrer, Dick. "Abortion's Incredible History." *Moody Monthly,* May 1980, 30-32.

Gives a brief history of the abortion issue in the United States, and then shows how Evangelicals can and should fit into that picture. He gives suggestions on how they can become involved in the Pro-Life movement.

444.   Brown, Harold O. J. "The Abortion Issue and the Integrity of the Church." *Presbyterian Communique,* Sept.-Oct. 1979, 14-15.

Showing how the courts, and other secular voices and institutions, have already begun to try to shut the church out of any legitimate role in shaping public policy, the author urges the church to speak out against abortion while it can.

445.   Byrnes, Timothy A. "How 'Seamless' a Garment? The Catholic Bishops and the Politics of Abortion." *Journal of Church and State* 33 (1991): 17-35.

Examines the activity of the National Council of Catholic Bishops in the abortion controversy, and compares that with the "consistent ethic of life" position first articulated by Cardinal Joseph Bernardin, and endorsed by the Bishops. He claims that while Bernardin's consistent ethic calls for putting equal emphasis on all the life issues, the Church, for various reasons, has always put more emphasis on abortion than it has other issues, such as nuclear war and capital punishment.

446.   "Catholics and Abortion." Editorial. *Commonweal* 100 (1974): 299-300.

Encourages Catholic leaders to drop their efforts to obtain a legal ban on abortion, and to work with others who would also oppose abortion, except for the most severe cases.

447.   Cuneo, Michael W. *Catholics Against the Church: Anti-Abortion Protest in Toronto, 1969-1985.* Toronto: University of Toronto Press, 1989.

Discusses the Pro-Life Movement among Catholics in Canada, as well as the reaction of the Canadian Catholic hierarchy to it.

448.   ———. "Keepers of the Faith: Lay Militants, Abortion, and the Battle for Canadian Catholicism." In *Sociological Studies in Roman Catholicism: Historical and Contemporary Perspectives,* edited by Roger O'Toole, 127-142. Lewiston, N.Y.: Edwin Mellen Press, 1989.

Presents a history of the Pro-Life movement in Canada, showing that, while it is largely composed of lay Catholics, the relation of the movement to the Catholic hierarchy in Canada has been one of defiance, as the Canadian bishops have refused to take a strong stand against abortion.

449.   Eidum, Charles D. "Voices for the Voiceless." Editorial. *The Evangel,* Jan.-Feb. 1997, 13.

The editor of this newsletter of the American Association of Lutheran Churches calls on all Lutherans to stand up and use their voices in defense of the unborn.

450.   Ferraro, Barbara, and Patricia Hussey. *No Turning Back: Two Nuns'*
         Battle with the Vatican over Women's Right to Choose. With Jane
         O'Reilley. New York: Poseidon Press, 1990.

         The story of two Catholic nuns who actively opposed the Roman Catholic
         Church's official position against abortion.

451.   Foreman, Joseph Lapsley. *Shattering the Darkness: The Crisis of the*
         Cross in the Church Today. Preface by Ruth Bell Graham. Foreword by
         George Grant. Montreat, N.C.: Cooling Spring Press, 1992.

         A call to Christians to become active in the anti-abortion movement, and
         especially in Rescue efforts, claiming that such activity is part and parcel
         of the Christian's endeavor to take up his cross and follow Christ.

452.   Fournier, Keith A. *In Defense of Life.* With William D. Watkins.
         Virginia Beach, Va.: Liberty, Life, and Family Publications, 1994.

         Presents information on both abortion and euthanasia, showing them to be
         immoral, and showing how they have contributed to a culture of death in
         the United States. He calls on Christians to help lead the country back
         from this culture of death to a culture which values life, and gives them
         suggestions for how to go about it.

453.   George, Robert P., and Ramesh Ponnuru. "The New Abortion Debate."
         First Things, April 1996, 10-12.

         Some Pro-Life advocates have claimed that the Pro-Life movement should
         not push for the legal prohibition of abortion, but should rather seek to
         lower the abortion rate by changing the culture. The authors of this article
         disagree with that sentiment.

454.   *Guide for Prochoice Catholics: The Church, the State, and Abortion*
         Politics. Washington, D.C.: Catholics for a Free Choice, 1990.

         A collection of articles prepared as a guide for Catholics who are pro-
         choice.

455.   Hehir, J. Bryan. "The Church and Abortion in the 1990's: The Role of
         Institutional Leadership." In *Abortion and Public Policy: An Interdisci-*
         plinary Investigation within the Catholic Tradition, edited by R. Randall
         Rainey and Gerard Magill, 203-228. Omaha, Neb.: Creighton Univ.
         Press, 1996.

         Examines how the Catholic Church has used its institutional leadership in
         the abortion controversy in the past, and evaluates how that institutional

role should be exercised, and whether the Church should change either its strategy or its tactics.

456.   Hitchcock, James. "The Catholic Church and Abortion." *Human Life Review* 12, no. 1 (1986): 59-78.

Outlines and examines how the Catholic Church has dealt with people in its own communion who have come out with public statements in support of keeping abortion legal.

457.   Hofman, Brenda D. "Political Theology: The Role of Organized Religion in the Anti-Abortion Movement." *Journal of Church and State* 28 (1986): 225-247.

Presents a history of how religious groups have gotten involved in the anti-abortion movement, showing that it has grown into a highly organized political effort.

458.   Kelly, James R. "Learning and Teaching Consistency: Catholics and the Right-to-Life Movement." In *The Catholic Church and the Politics of Abortion: A View from the States,* edited by Timothy A. Byrnes and Mary C. Segers, 152-168. Boulder, Colo.: Westview Press, 1992.

An analysis of the relationship of the Catholic Church with, and its influence upon, the Right to Life Movement as a whole.

459.   Kissling, Frances, and Liz Seaton. "Church Law and Abortion: Deciphering the Code." In *Guide for Prochoice Catholics: The Church, the State, and Abortion Politics,* 20-23. Washington, D.C.: Catholics for a Free Choice, 1990.

Analyzes what the Catholic Church's Canon Law says about excommunication, and gives suggestions on the basis of that to individual Catholics who speak out in favor of abortion, and to Catholic women who have had abortions, but are afraid of being excommunicated.

460.   Maestri, Rev. William F. "The Abortion Debate after *Webster:* The Catholic-American Moment." *Linacre Quarterly* 57, no.1 (1990): 46-57.

In the wake of the Supreme Court's *Webster v. Reproductive Health Services* decision (1989), the author calls Catholics to (1) engage in civil discourse, (2) respect the rights and liberties of all citizens, and (3) take the lead in working for the elimination of those sinful social structures which dehumanize the human person.

461.   Martin, Michele D. "Abortion: Is Abortion Just Another Social Issue?" *The Baptist Bulletin*, June 1988, 6-7, 17.

A call for Christians to become active in the anti-abortion movement, claiming that abortion is the most crucial social issue we face today.

462.   McKenzie, Michael. "When Good Men Do Nothing: Reflections From a Modern-Day *Bürgermeister.*" In *The Silent Subject: Reflections on the Unborn in American Culture*, edited by Brad Stetson, 151-167. Westport, Conn.: Praeger, 1996.

The author criticizes many Christians for sitting idly by while millions of children are aborted. He then examines some of the reasons for this inaction, and concludes by presenting a call for the future.

463.   Mills, Samuel A. "Abortion and Religious Freedom: The Religious Coalition for Abortion Rights (RCAR) and the Pro-Choice Movement, 1973-1989." *Journal of Church and State* 33 (1991): 569-594.

Shows how the Religious Coalition for Abortion Rights RCAR), formed by religious organizations which favored abortion rights, has pursued a strategy to help preserve the abortion freedoms created by *Roe v. Wade*, and has, at the same time, provided the Pro-Choice movement with a religious dimension. The author analyzes the history of the RCAR, along with its successes and its failures.

464.   Morecraft, Joe III. "How to Stop Abortion in America." *Counsel of Chalcedon*, December 1988, 9-11, 14-18.

The author describes what he sees as the current failure of the Pro-Life movement, and the reasons for that failure. He then gives biblical strategies for stopping abortion. He calls into question the usefulness of, and the biblical warrant for, direct action campaigns, such as those of Operation Rescue.

465.   O'Bannon, Robert H. "The Chattanooga Story: How One City Reduced its Abortion Rate." In *Life and Learning V: Proceedings of the Fifth University Faculty for Life Conference, June 1995, at Marquette University*, edited by Joseph W. Koterski, S.J., 69-86. Washington, D.C.: University Faculty for Life, 1996.

After outlining the conflict which led to the elimination of all abortion clinics in Chattanooga, Tenn., the author draws some principles and conclusions to help religious pro-life people close abortion clinics in their communities.

466.   Perry, Frances Johnson. "Convergence of Support for Issues by the Antiabortion Movement and the Religious New Right: An Examination of Social Movement Newsletters." Ph.D. diss., Bowling Green State University, 1985.

This study explores the connections between the single issue anti-abortion movement, as represented by the National Right to Life Committee, and the multi-issue religious New Right political movement, as represented by the Moral Majority.

467.   Segers, Mary C. "The Loyal Opposition: Catholics for a Free Choice." In *The Catholic Church and the Politics of Abortion: A View from the States,* edited by Timothy A. Byrnes and Mary C. Segers, 169-184. Boulder, Colo.: Westview Press, 1992.

The official position of the Catholic Church is that all or nearly all, abortions are immoral. However, there have always been people and groups in the Catholic Church who have disagreed with that official teaching. This article presents a history and description of one such organization, Catholics for a Free Choice.

468.   Simmons, Paul D. "Dogma and Discord: Religious Liberty and the Abortion Debate." *Church and State* 43, no. 1 (1990): 17-21.

Shows how religious people have gotten involved in the abortion debate, on both sides of the issue, and how some of these people have gone too far. Also spends time discussing the implications of the Supreme Court's *Webster v. Reproductive Health Services* decision.

469.   ———. "Religious Liberty and the Abortion Debate." *Journal of Church and State* 32 (1990): 567-584.

The author contends that religious groups who are working for the restoration of laws against abortion are at the same time sacrificing the religious liberty they hold so dear.

470.   Sinclair-Faulkner, Tom. "Canadian Catholics: At Odds on Abortion." *Christian Century* 98 (1981): 870-871.

Shows that the Catholic Church in Canada, while being pro-life, is seriously divided as to how far, and how fast, to press for legislation against abortion.

471.   Terian, Sara Kärkkäinen. "Communicating Grace: The Church's Role in the Abortion Controversy." In *Abortion: Ethical Issues and Options,*

edited by David R. Larson, 205-220. Loma Linda, Calif.: Loma Linda University, Center for Christian Bioethics, 1992.

A Seventh-Day Adventist comments that the role of the church in society is to communicate God's grace and to inspire people to extend that grace to others, with the goal of changing the world from within. The church is to serve as the moral compass of society. She comments that the Seventh-Day Adventist church has been inconsistent in this respect with regard to the abortion issue. She calls on her church to take on its prophetic mission in the abortion controversy, and to critique contemporary culture, offer a better alternative, and let Christ transform the culture.

472.   Wolfe, Christopher. "Abortion and Political Compromise." In *Life and Learning V: Proceedings of the Fifth University Faculty for Life Conference, June 1995, at Marquette University*, edited by Joseph W. Koterski, S.J., 42-68. Washington, D.C.: University Faculty for Life, 1996.

Presents thoughts on what pro-life people can and ought to do in regards to the legality of abortion in the United States. He shows that compromise will be necessary.

THE CHURCH'S ROLE IN INFLUENCING PUBLIC POLICY

473.   Bernardin, Cardinal Joseph. "Remaining a Vigorous Voice for Life in Society." *Origins* 26 (1996): 237-242.

An address delivered September 9, 1996 at Georgetown University in Washington D.C., in which this Catholic cardinal advocates a broad role for religious institutions in shaping public life.

474.   Borrelli, Mary Anne. "The Consistent Life Ethic in State Politics: Joseph Cardinal Bernardin and the Abortion Issue in Illinois." In *The Catholic Church and the Politics of Abortion: A View from the States*, edited by Timothy A. Byrnes and Mary C. Segers, 71-86. Boulder, Colo.: Westview Press, 1992.

Examines the influence of Joseph Cardinal Bernardin, Archbishop of Chicago, in Illinois politics, especially in regard to his consistent life ethic, which calls for the valuing of all human life, from conception to natural death.

475.   Byrnes, Timothy A. "The Cardinal and the Governor: The Politics of Abortion in New York State." In *The Catholic Church and the Politics of Abortion: A View from the States*, edited by Timothy A. Byrnes and Mary C. Segers, 137-151. Boulder, Colo.: Westview Press, 1992.

Examines the issue of abortion in New York State politics, laying particular emphasis on the relationship of John Cardinal O'Connor, Archbishop of New York City, and New York's then Catholic governor, Mario Cuomo.

476.   ————. "The Politics of Abortion: The Catholic Bishops." In *The Catholic Church and the Politics of Abortion: A View from the States,* edited by Timothy A. Byrnes and Mary C. Segers, 14-26. Boulder, Colo.: Westview Press, 1992.

Examines how the Supreme Court's decision in *Webster v. Reproductive Health Services* (July 1989) has affected the Catholic bishops' approach to abortion as a legal and political issue.

477.   Byrnes, Timothy A., and Mary C. Segers, eds. *The Catholic Church and the Politics of Abortion: A View from the States.* Boulder, Colo.: Westview Press, 1992.

A collection of articles which analyze the efforts of the Catholic Church to shape public policy on the issue of abortion.

478.   Canavan, Francis. "Simple-Minded Separationism." *Human Life Review* 3, no. 4 (1977): 36-46.

Accuses those who claim that Christians have no right to influence public policy on abortion because their views are "theological," and thus violate the separation of church and state, as being guilty of a simple-minded separationism. He shows that, though there is no necessary connection between law and morality, most important legal questions have a moral dimension, and therefore moral views on what the law should be cannot be excluded from the debate merely because they are moral.

479.   Clapp, Spencer McCoy. "Leading the Nation after *Webster:* Connecticut's Abortion Law." In *The Catholic Church and the Politics of Abortion: A View from the States,* edited by Timothy A. Byrnes and Mary C. Segers, 118-136. Boulder, Colo.: Westview Press, 1992.

In 1990, Connecticut became the first and only state to guarantee a woman's right to an abortion as a matter of law. This article examines the role played by the Catholic Church in helping to get some important restrictions to that right included in the final legislation.

480.   Curran, Charles E. "Civil Law and Christian Morality: Abortion and the Churches." In *Abortion: The Moral Issues,* edited by Edward Batchelor, 143-165. New York: Pilgrim Press, 1982. Originally published in *Conversations,* Spring 1975.

Presents the typical view of the Catholic Church on civil law and the relationship of church and state. He then presents a call for a new attitude towards civil law, and applies it to the abortion question.

481.   Day, Christine. "Abortion and Religious Coalitions: The Case of Louisiana." In *The Catholic Church and the Politics of Abortion: A View from the States*, edited by Timothy A. Byrnes and Mary C. Segers, 105-117. Boulder, Colo.: Westview Press, 1992.

Examines the influence of the Catholic Church in Louisiana politics, particularly in the aftermath of the Supreme Court's decision in *Webster v. Reproductive Health Services.*

482.   De Valk, Alphonse. *Morality and Law in Canadian Politics: The Abortion Controversy.* Montreal: Palm Publishers, 1974.

Examines the history behind the change of the Canadian abortion law in 1969, as well as the moral and religious influences on that history.

483.   Destro, Robert A. "Religion: Establishment, Free Exercise, and Abortion." In *New Perspectives on Human Abortion*, edited by Thomas W. Hilgers, Dennis J. Horan, and David Mall, 236-256. Frederick, Md.: Aletheia Books, University Publications of America, 1981.

Discusses the role that religion plays in the formulation and reevaluation of abortion related social policy.

484.   Evans, Nancy H., and Denise Shannon. "BishopSpeak: A Chronology of the U.S. Catholic Clergy's Involvement in Abortion Politics, November 1989 - June 1990." In *Guide for Prochoice Catholics: The Church, the State, and Abortion Politics*, 30-36. Washington, D.C.: Catholics for a Free Choice, 1990.

A chronological listing of news reports, showing the involvement of bishops and other representatives of the Catholic Church in the abortion politics of the United States.

485.   Fimian, Charles. "The Effects of Religion on Abortion Policy-Making: A Study of Voting Behavior in the U.S. Congress, 1976-1980." Ph.D. diss., Arizona State University, 1983.

This study examines the effects of religion on the votes cast by members of the United States Congress on abortion-funding legislation during the period 1976-1980.

486.   Gaffney, Edward McGlynn. "The *Abortion Rights Mobilization* Case:
        Political Advocacy and Tax Exemption of Churches." In *The Role of
        Religion in the Making of Public Policy*, edited by James E. Wood, Jr. and
        Derek Davis, 127-157. Waco, Tex.: J. M. Dawson Institute of Church-
        State Studies, 1991.

        The author uses the *Abortion Rights Mobilization* (ARM) case as a means
        of discussing the larger issue of the proper role of the church in helping
        shape public policy. The ARM was a case in which several parties
        unsuccessfully sought to revoke the tax-exempt status of the Roman
        Catholic Church, alleging that the Church had violated the ban on political
        activity by tax exempt religious organizations because of its activity in the
        abortion issue.

487.   O'Connor, Robert E., and Michael B. Berkman. "Religious Determinants
        of State Abortion Policy." *Social Science Quarterly* 76 (1995): 447-459.

        The authors show that Roman Catholics and conservative Protestants
        impact state abortion policy in different ways. They suggest that the
        structural differences – the Catholic Church is one, with a unified
        leadership, whereas there are many conservative Protestant churches with
        no unified leadership – account for these differences.

488.   O'Hara, Thomas J. "The Abortion Control Act of 1989: The Pennsylvania
        Catholics." In *The Catholic Church and the Politics of Abortion: A View
        from the States,* edited by Timothy A. Byrnes and Mary C. Segers, 87-104.
        Boulder, Colo.: Westview Press, 1992.

        Discusses the passage in November 1989 in Pennsylvania, of what was
        then the most restrictive abortion law in the nation, and the role of the
        Catholic Church in supporting it.

489.   Peach, Lucinda Joy. "Legislating Morality: Problems of Religious
        Identity, Gender, and Pluralism in Abortion Lawmaking." Ph.D. diss.,
        Indiana University, 1995.

        This study examines the question of what influence religion should have
        on public lawmaking in a religiously pluralistic society. In particular, it
        examines how the religious convictions of U.S. lawmakers influence their
        official decision making. It also examines the effect that religious, gender,
        and other differences between lawmakers and their constituents should
        have on these questions.

490.   Rainey, R. Randall, and Gerard Magill, eds. *Abortion and Public Policy:
        An Interdisciplinary Investigation within the Catholic Tradition.* Omaha,
        Neb.: Creighton Univ. Press, 1996.

A collection of essays originally delivered at a conference held at St. Louis University, March 11-13, 1993.

491.   Rainey, R. Randall, Gerard Magill, and Kevin D. O'Rourke. "Introduction: Abortion, the Catholic Church, and Public Policy." In *Abortion and Public Policy: An Interdisciplinary Investigation within the Catholic Tradition*, edited by R. Randall Rainey and Gerard Magill, 1-46. Omaha, Neb.: Creighton Univ. Press, 1996.

Presents an historical overview of the Catholic Church's teaching on abortion, as well as its efforts at promoting a public policy against abortion.

492.   Salokar, Rebecca M. "The First Test of *Webster's* effect: The Florida Church." In *The Catholic Church and the Politics of Abortion: A View from the States*, edited by Timothy A. Byrnes and Mary C. Segers, 48-70. Boulder, Colo.: Westview Press, 1992.

Examines the role played by the Catholic Church in Florida's electoral process in the two years after the Supreme Court's ruling in *Webster v. Reproductive Health Services*.

493.   Saucedo, Michael Angelo. "Abortion and Public Policy." In *Abortion: Ethical Issues and Options*, edited by David R. Larson, 221-235. Loma Linda, Calif.: Loma Linda University, Center for Christian Bioethics, 1992.

A Seventh-Day Adventist offers suggestions to his church on what methods are most effective in helping shape public policy in the abortion debate.

494.   Segers, Mary C. "Abortion Politics Post-*Webster*: The New Jersey Bishops." In *The Catholic Church and the Politics of Abortion: A View from the States*, edited by Timothy A. Byrnes and Mary C. Segers, 27-47. Boulder, Colo.: Westview Press, 1992.

Examines the role played by Catholic bishops in New Jersey, in that state's 1989 elections, shortly after the Supreme Court's ruling in *Webster v. Reproductive Health Services*.

495.   ———. "American Catholicism: The Search for a Public Voice in a Pluralistic Society." In *Guide for Prochoice Catholics: The Church, the State, and American Politics*, 4-9. Washington, D.C.: Catholics for a Free Choice, 1990.

Presents a history of the relationship between the Catholic church and the rest of American society, shows how this applies to the controversy over abortion, and offers suggestions for Catholic legislators.

496.   ———. "The Bishops, Birth Control, and Abortion Policy: 1950-1985." In *Church Polity and American Politics: Issues in Contemporary American Catholicism*, edited by Mary C. Segers, 215-231. New York: Garland, 1990.

Examines the history of the American Catholic bishops' policies on both birth control and abortion from 1950 to 1985. She notes that while they acquiesced to the legalization of birth control in the 1960's, they militantly opposed the legalization of abortion in the 1970's. She examines the two issues to see why they had different reactions to them, and makes predictions on how they will treat these two issues in the future.

497.   ———. "The Catholic Church as a Political Actor." In *Perspectives on the Politics of Abortion*, edited by Ted G. Jelen, 87-130. Westport, Conn.: Praeger, 1995.

Examines the role of the Catholic Church in political efforts to shape public policy on abortion. In particular, the article examines several questions regarding the church's role as a political lobby.

498.   Shannon, Thomas A. "Abortion: A Review of Ethical Aspects of Public Policy." *Annual of the Society of Christian Ethics* (1982): 71-98.

The author shows the inter-relation of the ethical and political issues in abortion – how ethical views shape pb lic policy, as well as the ethical problems raised by some policy questions. He then presents conclusions based on this.

499.   Walter, James J. "Theological Parameters: Catholic Doctrine on Abortion in a Pluralist Society." In *Abortion and Public Policy: An Interdisciplinary Investigation within the Catholic Tradition*, edited by R. Randall Rainey and Gerard Magill, 91-130. Omaha, Neb.: Creighton Univ. Press, 1996.

Presents the theological beliefs that underlie the Catholic Church's official moral position on abortion, and at the same time seeks to help politicians, Catholic politicians in particular, to better negotiate the abortion controversy in a pluralist society.

500.   Walters, Leroy. "The Fetus in Ethical and Public Policy Discussion from 1973 to the Present." In *Abortion and the Status of the Fetus*, edited by

William B. Bondeson, H. Tristram Engelhardt, Jr., Stuart F. Spicker, and Daniel H. Winship, 15-30. Dordrecht: D. Reidel Pub. Co., 2000.

An examination of the ethical and public policy views regarding the fetus found in three different public policy documents published in the United States between 1973 and 1979.

501.   Welch, Michael R., David C. Leege, and Robert Woodberry. "Pro-Life Catholics and Support for Political Lobbying by Religious Organizations." *Social Science Quarterly* 79 (1998): 649-663.

An examination of the relationship between individual Catholic parishioners' attitudes toward abortion and their support for political lobbying by religious groups. Results show that those who take a Pro-Life position are more likely to support political lobbying by religious groups than those who hold a pro-choice view.

THE RELATIONSHIP BETWEEN LAW AND MORALITY

502.   Brody, Baruch A. "Abortion and the Law." *Journal of Philosophy* 68 (1971): 357-369.

The author demonstrates that it is impossible to hold the following two views simultaneously: 1) That abortion is immoral because it is the taking of an innocent human life, and 2) that it is wrong for me to impose my morality on others, and so abortion should be legal for those who want it. Thus the author shows that it is totally inconsistent for a person who believes abortion to be immoral to also believe that it should remain legal for those who want it.

503.   Callahan, Joan C. "The Fetus and Fundamental Rights." *Commonweal* 112 (1986): 203-209

Attempts to show that being personally opposed to abortion on moral grounds, yet not favoring a public policy banning it, is a justifiable position, because the case for the unborn's right to life is not very compelling.

504.   Canavan, Francis. "On Being Personally Opposed." *Human Life Review* 9, no. 4 (1983): 21-24.

A critique of the view that one can be personally opposed to abortion, yet at the same time favor keeping it legal, especially for those who can't afford one.

505.   Crosby, John F. "The Human Person Exists in Freedom under the Truth."
         In *Life and Learning VII: Proceedings of the Seventh University Faculty
         for Life Conference, June 1997 at Loyola College*, edited by Joseph W.
         Koterski, S.J., 54-64. Washington, D.C.: University Faculty for Life,
         1998.

         Answers the argument made by many on the pro-choice side, that the very
         freedom of persons demands that all truth and value be relative to persons,
         and thus that it is wrong for the pro-life person to impose his morality on
         others.

506.   Cuomo, Mario. "Abortion and the Law." *Origins* 14 (1984): 301-303.

         An address, delivered Oct. 3, 1984 at St. Francis College, Brooklyn, New
         York, in which the former governor of New York clarifies and extends the
         remarks he made at the University of Notre Dame. (see citation # 507).

507.   ———. "Religious Belief and Public Morality." *Origins* 14 (1984): 234-
         240.

         A speech delivered at the University of Notre Dame, September 13, 1984,
         In which the former governor of New York explains how he can agree
         with the Catholic Church that abortion is wrong, yet at the same time
         believe that, as a matter of public policy, it ought to remain legal.

508.   Gentles, Ian. "The Unborn Citizen: Do We Need a Law against Abor-
         tion?" In *The Right to Birth: Some Christian Views on Abortion*, edited
         by Eugene Fairweather and Ian Gentles, 13-24. Toronto: The Anglican
         Book Centre, 1976.

         Many have said, since we live in a pluralistic society, and there are many
         different views on the morality of abortion, that Christians should not
         force their views on others by working to make abortion illegal. The
         author argues that this argument is flawed, and that Christians should not
         be ashamed to support legislation that gives legal protection to the unborn
         child.

509.   Grib, Philip J., S.J. "Catholic Teaching in the United States on the
         Appropriate Relationship between Civil Law and Morality in a Democrat-
         ic, Pluralist Society: A Jurisprudential Focus on Abortion Laws." Chap.
         3 in *Divorce Laws and Morality: A New Catholic Jurisprudence*.
         Lanham, Md.: Univ. Press of America, 1985.

         A history of Catholic teaching on abortion, with particular emphasis on
         how the church has responded to the critique that it is foisting its religious
         and moral beliefs on a democratic, pluralistic society.

510.   Hittinger, Russell. "Resolving Conflicting Normative Claims in Public Policy." In *Abortion and Public Policy: An Interdisciplinary Investigation within the Catholic Tradition*, edited by R. Randall Rainey and Gerard Magill, 72-90. Omaha, Neb.: Creighton Univ. Press, 1996.

Shows through legal and philosophical reasoning that those who say they are personally opposed to abortion, but favor a public policy allowing it, are holding an impossible position.

511.   Hubbard, Bp. Howard. "A Response to Gov. Cuomo." *Origins* 14 (1984): 304.

A critique of Gov. Mario's address at the Univ. of Notre Dame (see citation # 507) in which he argued for a separation of public policy from private beliefs on abortion.

512.   Kalpakgian, Mitchell. "The Right to Life and the Natural Law." In *Life and Learning IX: Proceedings of the Ninth University Faculty for Life Conference, June 1999, at Trinity International University, Deerfield, Ill.*, edited by Joseph W. Koterski, S.J., 101-114. Washington, D.C.: University Faculty for Life, 2000.

Shows that the right to life position is based on natural law, that is, on timeless principles that nearly all cultures have recognized. Thus, he claims, arguments that pro-life people should not impose their morality on others are totally mistaken, because the pro-life position is more than just a private opinion.

513.   Lawler, Peter Augustine. "The Bishops vs. Mario Cuomo." In *Church Polity and American Politics: Issues in Contemporary American Catholicism*, edited by Mary C. Segers, 175-193. New York: Garland, 1990.

The author outlines the debate between Mario Cuomo, who, as a Catholic, personally opposed abortion, but in public policy did not favor making it illegal, and the American bishops who criticized him for this inconsistent view, and said that the legitimate diversity of views among Catholics did not extend to the opinion that abortion falls outside of public policy. He concludes that the bishops have a good case against Cuomo.

514.   Luce, Claire Boothe. "The 'Kilpatrick Position.'" *Human Life Review* 3, no. 1 (1977): 6-13.

Using the published views of the journalist Jack Kilpatrick as a starting point, the author critiques the view that Christians who oppose abortion should not impose their morality on the rest of society.

515. McConnell, Terrance. "Permissive Abortion Laws, Religion, and Moral Compromise." *Public Affairs Quarterly* 1, no. 1 (1987): 95-109.

Some public officials have supported permissive abortion laws while at the same time maintaining that their religious convictions lead them to personally oppose abortion. They have been criticized for taking such a position. This article examines this criticism to see if it is legitimate. By examining several possible responses the public official might to this criticism, and finding them flawed, the author finds the criticisms to be legitimate.

516. McInerny, Dennis Q. "What's in an Assertion?" In *Abortion: A New Generation of Catholic Responses,* edited by Stephen J. Heaney, 299-312. Braintree, Mass.: Pope John Center, 1992.

Many people have made an assertion to the following effect: "I am personally opposed to abortion, but I honor a woman's right to have an abortion." The author of this article presents the argument that this assertion, based on a correct understanding of its meaning, is incoherent.

517. Mills, Samuel A. "Parochiaid and the Abortion Decisions: Supreme Court Justice William J. Brennan, Jr. versus the U.S. Catholic Hierarchy." *Journal of Church and State* 34 (1992): 751-773.

Supreme Court Justice William J. Brennan, Jr. is a Catholic, who was supported by the U.S. Catholic hierarchy when he was first nominated by President Eisenhower. The author shows, however, through two prominent cases, that of government aid to parochial schools and of abortion, that justice Brennan consistently went contrary to his religion and to the wishes of the Catholic Church.

518. Segers, Mary C. "Moral Consistency and Public Policy: Cuomo and Califano on Abortion." In *Church Polity and American Politics: Issues in Contemporary American Catholicism,* edited by Mary C. Segers, 157-173. New York: Garland, 1990.

Using Joseph Califano and Mario Cuomo as examples of Catholic public officials who have privately opposed abortion, but publicly favored keeping it legal, the author asks whether a Catholic lawmaker should work toward the reinstatement of restrictive abortion laws. She concludes that Catholic lawmakers are not morally required to challenge the legality of abortion.

519. Shinn, Robert L. "Personal Decisions and Social Policies in a Pluralist Society." *Perkins Journal* 27, no. 1 (1973): 58-63.

Demonstrates that in some, but not all, cases, it is possible to legislate morality. He then asks the question "what is it possible to legislate?" Throughout, he applies this to the issue of abortion.

THE CONFLICT OF CONSCIENCE AND DUTY

520. Cannold, Leslie. "Consequences for Patients of Health Care Professionals' Conscientious Actions: The Ban on Abortions in South Australia." *Journal of Medical Ethics* 20 (1994): 80-86.

Uses the refusal of nurses in South Australia, on the grounds of conscience, to participate in second trimester abortions, as a test case for determining whether such refusal is morally permissible.

521. Conley, John J., S.J. "Problems of Cooperation in an Abortive Culture." In *Life and Learning VI: Proceedings of the Sixth University Faculty for Life Conference, June 1996 at Georgetown University,* edited by Joseph W. Koterski, S.J., 103-115. Washington, D.C.: University Faculty for Life, 1997.

Examines the dilemma faced by an individual who is firmly opposed to abortion and wants to refuse any sanction for it, but who also lives in a society which actively promotes abortion and increasingly tries to get people to compromise their beliefs. He examines such issues as having to pay taxes and insurance premiums, some of which are used to fund abortions, being asked to at least refer for an abortion, etc.

522. Moylan, Joseph W. "No Law Can Give Me the Right to do What is Wrong." In *Life and Learning V: Proceedings of the Fifth University Faculty for Life Conference, June 1995, at Marquette University,* edited by Joseph W. Koterski, S.J., 234-242. Washington, D.C.: University Faculty for Life, 1996.

A judge describes how he resigned from the bench rather than sign an order allowing a minor to procure an abortion. He did so because he felt that no law could force him to do what was wrong.

THE CHRISTIAN AND CIVIL DISOBEDIENCE

523. Belz, Mark. *Suffer the Little Children: Christians, Abortion, and Civil Disobedience.* Westchester, Ill.: Crossway Books, 1989.

The author, a Christian attorney, defends his position that peaceful, non-violent, civil disobedience, in an effort to save the unborn, is morally and biblically justified.

524.   Blanchard, Dallas A., and Terry J. Prewitt. *Religious Violence and Abortion: The Gideon Project.* Gainesville, Fla.: University of Florida Press, 1993.

Examines the bombing of three Pensacola abortion clinics on Christmas day, 1984 as a case study of the social context in which both religious fundamentalism and the anti-abortion movement operate, and what causes some of its members to become violent.

525.   Dixon, Nicholas. "The Morality of Anti-Abortion Civil Disobedience." *Public Affairs Quarterly* 11 (1997): 21-38.

An examination of whether anti-abortion protestors are justified in committing civil disobedience. He compares civil disobedience practiced by pro-life forces with the civil disobedience practiced by civil rights advocates. While he finds many points of similarity, he finds enough differences to say that the civil disobedience practiced by pro-life forces to be morally problematic, and deserving of substantial punishment.

526.   Hanink, James G. "Abortion: A Catholic Case for Nonviolent Intervention." In *Abortion: A New Generation of Catholic Responses,* edited by Stephen J. Heaney, 347-359. Braintree, Mass.: Pope John Center, 1992.

The author claims that it is morally permissible for Catholics, and others who similarly reject abortion, to engage in nonviolent direct action to prevent abortions.

527.   Holly, James L. *A Matter of Life and Death.* Foreword by John F. MacArthur, Jr. Nashville: Broadman & Holman, 1995.

Outlines how some pro-life activists have resorted to violence, such as the killing of abortionists and the bombing of abortion clinics. He then presents a biblical critique of such violence, condemning it as being both un-Christian, as well as counter-productive.

528.   McGoldrick, James Edward. *God or Caesar? Life or Death?* Grand Rapids, Mich.: Baptists for Life, n.d.

Gives advice and counsel to Christians on how to balance the competing demands of obedience to God's law and obedience to the civil law in the issue of abortion. He gives advice on how far they may go in protesting abortion.

529. Polter, Julie. "Seeking Common Ground on Abortion Clinic Activism." *Sojourners,* May-June 1999, 11-12.

A call for people on both sides of the abortion issue to seek common ground on the issue of protests at abortion clinics.

530. Tollefsen, Christopher. "Donagan, Abortion, and Civil Rebellion." *Public Affairs Quarterly* 11 (1997): 303-312.

Presents a case for saying that, in common morality, violence against abortion providers and clinics is an unjustified form of revolutionary activity.

531. Waldron, Samuel E. *We Must Obey God: The Biblical Doctrine of Conscientious Disobedience to Human Authority, With Special Reference to Operation Rescue.* Avinger, Tex.: Simpson Pub. Co., 1992.

Outlines the biblical doctrine of human authority, and when disobedience to that authority is permitted, paying special attention to the actions of Operation Rescue.

OPERATION RESCUE

532. Alcorn, Randy C. *Is Rescuing Right? Breaking the Law to Save the Unborn.* Downers Grove, Ill.: InterVarsity Press, 1990.

A defense of peaceful, non-violent civil disobedience in order to save the unborn.

533. Beckwith, Francis J., and John Feinberg. "Operation Rescue: Debating the Ethics of Civil Disobedience." *Christian Research Journal,* Spring 1995, 32-41.

Two pro-life advocates present differing opinions on the legitimacy of Christians engaging in civil disobedience in the abortion controversy.

534. Brenton, Paul. "Casualties of the Abortion Wars." *Christianity Today,* 26 October 1992, 22-24.

A pastor, who is also a dedicated pro-life advocate, nevertheless expresses doubts about Operation Rescue.

535. Cash, Richard. "Saved from Slaughter: A Biblical Evaluation of Operation Rescue." M.A. thesis, Gordon-Conwell Theological Seminary, 1990.

Presents a biblical theology of rescue actions and civil disobedience as a means of evaluating whether Operation Rescue is a permissible form of Christian activism, or to what extent it might be obligatory in nature.

536.   Cassidy, Keith. "Pro-Life Direct Action Campaign: A Survey of Scholarly and Media Interpretations." In *Life and Learning VI: Proceedings of the Sixth University Faculty for Life Conference, June 1996 at Georgetown University*, edited by Joseph W. Koterski, S.J., 235-244. Washington, D.C.: University Faculty for Life, 1997.

A brief survey of the scholarly literature on direct action campaigns of the Pro-Life movement, such as those of Operation Rescue.

537.   Frame, Randy. "Rescue Theology." *Christianity Today*, 17 Nov. 1989, 46-48.

Though the rescue movement has been popular among some pro-life groups, many have serious concerns about its biblical basis.

538.   Ginsburg, Faye. "Saving America's Souls: Operation Rescue's Crusade against Abortion." In *Fundamentalisms and the State: Remaking Polities, Economies, and Militance*, edited by Martin E. Marty and R. Scott Appleby, 557-588. Chicago: Univ. of Chicago Press, 1993.

A presentation of the history, and Fundamentalist origin, of Operation Rescue.

539.   Gunn, Grover E., III. "Operation Rescue: An Ethical Evaluation." *Counsel of Chalcedon*, December 1988, 22-24.

A critique of the tactics of Operation Rescue, saying that there is no biblical mandate for Christians to participate in civil disobedience in the abortion issue, and that their time would be better served helping a crisis pregnancy center.

540.   Lawler, Philip F. *Operation Rescue: A Challenge to the Nation's Conscience.* Huntington, Ind.: Our Sunday Visitor, 1992.

A description of the history, tactics, and the Christian background, of Operation Rescue.

541.   Leber, Gary. "We Must Rescue Them." *Hastings Center Report* 19, no. 6 (1989): 26-27.

A biblical and religious defense of the nonviolent rescue missions performed by Operation Rescue.

542.   Meyers. Jeffrey J. "An Open Letter to Pro-Lifers about Rescue Opera-
         tions." *Counsel of Chalcedon,* December 1988, 20-21, 25-27.

         The author explains to fellow Pro-Life people, why he could not, in good
         faith, participate in a rescue operation. He doubts that they will be
         effective, and he questions the biblical warrant for such action.

543.   North, Gary. *Trespassing for Dear Life: What about Operation Rescue?*
         Fort Worth, Tex.: Dominion Press, 1989.

         Presents a basic biblical defense of Operation Rescue as a legitimate form
         of civil disobedience, but he does wish that Operation Rescue would issue
         a statement decrying the use of violence.

544.   Reuter, Jonathan M. "Not So Quiet on the Western Front: Operation
         Rescue and Civil Disobedience." M.A. thesis, Kent State University,
         1994.

         A claim that Operation Rescue's use of violence in its anti-abortion efforts
         has put into question its claim that its tactics are simply examples of civil
         disobedience.

545.   Rice, Charles E. "Operation Rescue." In *Abortion: A New Generation of
         Catholic Responses,* edited by Stephen J. Heaney, 325-345. Braintree,
         Mass.: Pope John Center, 1992.

         A defense of the activities of Operation Rescue.

546.   Rogers, Wayne. "Operation Rescue." *Counsel of Chalcedon,* December
         1988, 19, 40.

         A criticism of the tactics of Operation Rescue based on Peter's use of the
         sword in John 18:10-11.

547.   Steiner, Mark Allan. "The Rhetoric of Operation Rescue: Representation
         and Evangelical Social Protest in the Abortion Controversy." Ph. D. diss.,
         Indiana University, 1999.

         Examines the rhetoric of Operation Rescue, and claims that it constructs
         simplistic representations of the Christian faith which reproduce an anti-
         intellectualism and an impulse to hegemony, and which also promote a
         simplistic understanding of truth. These representations also make the
         move to violence easier. The author then focuses on what correctives
         can be made for these deficiencies.

548.   Terry, Randall A. *Operation Rescue.* Springdale, Pa.: Whitaker House, 1988.

Presents a history of Operation Rescue, and a defense of its peaceful tactics.

549.   Whitchurch, Joseph B. "Is the Civil Disobedience of the 'Operation Rescue Phenomenon' an Ethically or Theologically Legitimate Evangelical Option?" M.A. thesis, Trinity Evangelical Divinity School, 1990.

Presents a defense of the ethical, theological, and prudential legitimacy of the civil disobedience that characterizes the rescue movement, as a useful vehicle for evangelical protest of abortion on demand.

THE CHURCH'S MINISTRY IN THE AREA OF ABORTION

550.   Achtemeier, Elizabeth. "Speaking the Unspeakable: A Demonstration." *Preaching* 11, no. 4 (1996): 17-18, 20-21.

Presents guidance to the preacher on how to go about preaching a sermon on the controversial topic of abortion – texts to use, theological reasoning, methodology, and what to do after the sermon.

551.   Allison, Lorain. *Finding Peace After Abortion: Accepting the Grace and Healing of Forgiveness.* St. Meinrad, Ind.: Abbey Press, 1990.

The author describes how she found peace and forgiveness from God after having had an abortion, and reaches out with empathy to other victimized women, offering them the same peace and forgiveness.

552.   Banks, Bill, and Sue Banks. *Ministering to Abortion's Aftermath.* Kirkwood, Mo.: Impact Books, 1982.

Using several case studies, the authors show that women who have had abortions can achieve freedom from the guilt and depression that result from it. They show how true freedom can be found in Jesus Christ.

553.   Blocher, Mark B. "Alternatives to Abortion: Accepting the Responsibility to Love." *The Baptist Bulletin,* January 1986, 13-14.

Using the parable of the Good Samaritan as a basis, the author shows the need for pro-life Baptists to present women caught in crisis pregnancies with real alternatives to abortion.

554. Brown, Ruth S. "The Ministry of a Crisis Pregnancy Center." In *The Church and Abortion: In Search of New Ground for Response,* edited by Paul T. Stallsworth, 67-82. Nashville: Abingdon Press, 1993.

The author shows how both individual Christians and local churches can, and should, become involved in the ministry of crisis pregnancy centers.

555. Cahill, Lisa Sowle. "Catholic Commitment and Public Responsibility." In *Abortion and Public Policy: An Interdisciplinary Investigation within the Catholic Tradition,* edited by R. Randall Rainey and Gerard Magill, 131-162. Omaha, Neb.: Creighton Univ. Press, 1996.

A call for viewing abortion as being anchored in Catholic social ethics, which would draw on the social justice tradition of Catholicism in order to develop a more supportive approach to women and their families. She argues that the "right" social solution to abortion may not be easy to devise or recognize.

556. Condon, Guy M. "Fatherhood Aborted: The Hidden Trauma of Men and Abortion and what the Church Can Do about it." *Christianity Today,* 9 Dec. 1996, p. 36-39.

The author points out that abortion can have serious emotional and spiritual consequences on the fathers of aborted children, and gives suggestions on how the church can minister to these men.

557. Forsyth, Diane. "Abortion and the 'Corporate Conscience' of the Church." In *Abortion: Ethical Issues and Options,* edited by David R. Larson, 187-203. Loma Linda, Calif.: Loma Linda University, Center for Christian Bioethics, 1992.

A Seventh-Day Adventist offers six ethical guidelines for how the church should respond to abortion, and to those caught in crisis pregnancies.

558. Jeffrey, Karen. "Helping Women with Post-Abortion." *Journal of Biblical Counseling* 17, no. 3 (1999): 27-29.

Gives guidance to the Christian counselor on helping women who have had an abortion and are experiencing guilt and grief over it.

559. Mannion, Michael T. *Abortion and Healing: A Cry to be Whole.* 2nd. ed., rev. and enl. Kansas City, Mo.: Sheed & Ward, 1992.

Describes how women who have had abortions can achieve spiritual and psychological healing.

560.   Massé, Sydna, and Joan Phillips. *Her Choice to Heal: Finding Spiritual and Emotional Peace after Abortion.* Colorado Springs, Colo.: Chariot Victor Publishing, 1998.

Two women who have had abortions, and experienced first hand the effects of it, give guidance to other women struggling with post-abortion trauma on how to obtain spiritual and emotional healing.

561.   Matthewes-Green, Frederica. "The Dilemma of a Pro-Life Pastor: How Churches Should Handle the Delicate Issue of Abortion when nearly One-Fifth of Women Who Get Abortions Are Sitting in our Pews." *Christianity Today,* 7 April 1997, 27-29, 31.

Delineates the problems pro-life pastors face in their ministries, especially considering that many of the women who have abortions come from evangelical congregations.

562.   Picchioni, Anthony, and Joe Barnhart. "The Abortion Question and Pastoral Counseling." *American Journal of Pastoral Counseling* 1, no. 2 (1998): 3-21.

In order to aid the pastoral counselor when counseling people faced with the dilemma of abortion, the authors provide information and facts pertinent to the abortion debate, and present different ways of looking at the issue.

563.   Pohl, Christine D. "Abortion: Responsibility and Moral Betrayal." In *Bioethics and the Future of Medicine: A Christian Appraisal,* edited by John F. Kilner, Nigel M. de S. Cameron, and David L. Schiedermayer, 212-223. Grand Rapids: Eerdmans Pub. Co., 1995.

Presents the accounts of many different women who had abortions, describing their reasons for having one, and their feelings at the time, and since. She then uses these accounts as a springboard for presenting five practical applications for pro-life Christians who deal with women in crisis pregnancies.

564.   Schlossberg, Terry A., and Elizabeth Achtemeier. *Not My Own: Abortion and the Marks of the Church.* Grand Rapids, Mich.: Eerdmans, 1995.

Using the marks of the true church as a basis – the proper preaching of the Word, the proper administration of the sacraments, and church discipline – the authors examine how the church can respond to the moral crisis of abortion in American life. Based on a consultation on the Church and Abortion held at Princeton Theological Seminary in 1992.

565.   Selby, Terry. *The Mourning After: Help for Postabortion Syndrome.*
         With Marc Bockmon. Grand Rapids, Mich.: Baker Book House, 1990.

         Gives psychological and religious tips and techniques for dealing with
         post-abortion syndrome (PAS).

566.   Sher, George. "Subsidized Abortion: Moral Rights and Moral Compro-
         mise." *Philosophy and Public Affairs* 10 (1981): 361-372.

         The author argues that no moral reason can be brought forward to justify
         society providing welfare funds for purely elective abortions.   He
         maintains that liberals should concede this to the conservatives and cease
         fighting for such welfare funds. Instead, they should attend to the needs
         of the poor in other ways.

567.   Speckhard, Anne. *Post-Abortion Counseling: A Manual for Christian
         Counselors.* Falls Church, Va.: PACE, 1987

         Designed as a training tool with practical applications for post-abortion
         counseling done by trained practitioners in crisis pregnancy centers.

568.   Vought, Jeannette. *Post-Abortion Trauma: 9 Steps to Recovery.* Grand
         Rapids, Mich.: Zondervan, 1991.

         Outlines the complexity of the abortion problem, and the church's
         response to it; describes who is affected by abortion, as well as how they
         are affected, physically, emotionally, and spiritually. It then outlines nine
         steps for emotional and spiritual recovery from abortion.

569.   Weisheit, Eldon. *Abortion?: Resources for Pastoral Counseling.* St.
         Louis: Concordia Publishing House, 1976.

         Consists of two parts: the first part is designed for the woman contempla-
         ting an abortion. It gives her things to think about, without taking a
         position. The second part is designed for the counselor, enabling him to
         gain further perspective into the abortion decision.

570.   Winslow, Gerald R. "Abortion Policies in Adventist Hospitals." In
         Abortion: Ethical Issues and Options, edited by David R. Larson, 237-
         250. Loma Linda, Calif.: Loma Linda University, Center for Christian
         Bioethics, 1992.

         The author analyzes the results of a survey of Seventh-Day Adventist
         hospitals on the matter of abortion policies, and offers reflections on the
         shape that hospital policy should take in Adventist hospitals.

571.   Wisnefske, Ned. "Abortion and Creation: A Response for Communities
        of Faith." *Word and World* 11 (1991): 199-207.

        The author maintains that, while Christians may legitimately disagree over
        the legality of abortion, they should all find practical ways to help, both
        materially and spiritually, women who find themselves in problem
        pregnancies.

4 INFLUENCE OF RELIGION ON ATTITUDES TOWARD ABORTION

572.   Cochran, John K., Mitchell B. Chamlin, Leonard Beeghley, Angela
         Harnden, and Brenda Sims Blackwell. "Religious Stability, Endogamy,
         and the Effects of Personal Religiosity on Attitudes toward Abortion."
         Sociology of Religion 56 (1996): 291-309.

         Extends the current literature on the influence of religion on attitudes
         toward abortion by examining the effect of personal religiosity on attitudes
         toward abortion across faith groups and across contexts of religious
         stability/change and endogamy/exogamy.   Results show that the
         religiosity-abortion attitude relationship does indeed vary across faith
         groups, but that the influence of religious stability/change and endog-
         amy/exogamy on this relationship is not as pronounced as anticipated.

573.   Cook, Elizabeth Adell, Ted G. Jelen, and Clyde Wilcox. "Catholicism
         and Abortion Attitudes in the American States: A Contextual Analysis."
         Journal for the Scientific Study of Religion 32 (1993): 223-230.

         Using state exit data from 1990, the authors examine how the Roman
         Catholic Church affects abortion attitudes both within its own members
         and in the community at large.   The results suggest that the Catholic
         church is rather effective in teaching anti-abortion sentiment to its own
         members, but that its effect on people outside the church is a negative one.

574.   D'Antonio, William V., and Steven Stack. "Religion, Ideal Family Size,
         and Abortion: Extending Renzi's Hypothesis." *Journal for the Scientific
         Study of Religion* 19 (1980): 397-408.

         Previous research by Renzi had noted a negative relationship between
         ideal family size and pro-abortion attitudes. This study furthers that study
         by adding the variable of religious affiliation. The study finds that while

Renzi's hypothesis generally holds true when the variable of religious affiliation is added, there are numerous exceptions, particularly among denominations with strong pro-abortion attitudes.

575.   Ebaugh, Helen Rose Fuchs, and C. Allen Haney. "Church Attendance and Attitudes toward Abortion: Differentials in Liberal and Conservative Churches." *Journal for the Scientific Study of Religion* 17 (1978): 407-413.

The study shows that frequency of church attendance is positively related to a disapproval of legalized abortion among members of conservative churches. On the other hand, it finds no relationship between frequency of church attendance and attitudes toward abortion among members of liberal churches.

576.   Emerson, Michael O. "Through Tinted Glasses: Religion, Worldviews, and Abortion Attitudes." *Journal for the Scientific Study of Religion* 35 (1996): 41-55.

The author claims that we lack knowledge of the factors intervening between religion and abortion attitudes. He tests the plausibility that world-view dimensions serve as intervening factors.

577.   Felling, Albert, Jan Lammers, and Leo Spruit. "Church-Membership, Religion and Attitude towards Abortion in the Netherlands." *Journal of Empirical Theology* 5, no. 1 (1992): 53-69.

Examines the relationship of church membership or non-membership in the Netherlands to one's attitude toward abortion. Results show that church membership seems to be an important factor in one's acceptance or rejection of abortion.

578.   Finlay, Barbara. "Gender Differences in Attitudes toward Abortion among Protestant Seminarians." *Review of Religious Research* 37 (1996): 354-360.

Presents the results of a survey of 81 Master of Divinity students, both male and female, at a Presbyterian seminary. Results showed that the male students were more conservative on abortion than the general public, whereas the female students were more liberal than the average.

579.   Granberg, Donald. "Conformity to Religious Norms regarding Abortion." *Sociological Quarterly* 32 (1991): 267-275.

Examines the attitude toward abortion as a function of religion at age 16, spouse's religion, and current religion.

580. Granger, Bruce. "Religiosity and Abortion Attitudes among Couples in the Early Stage of the Family Formation Process." Ph.D. diss., Bowling Green State University, 1980.

The author's purpose in this dissertation is to (1) determine the strength of the relationship between religiosity and abortion attitudes, (2) test for the convergence among various subgroups in the population on abortion attitudes, and (3) test the predictability of abortion attitudes by religiosity when controlling for other social variables.

581. Harris, Richard J., and Edgar W. Mills. "Religion, Values and Attitudes toward Abortion. *Journal for the Scientific Study of Religion* 24 (1985): 137-154.

Noting that there is a wide disparity between support for abortion for *physical* reasons (life of the mother, rape, etc.), and support for abortion for *social* reasons (not wanting more children, not able to afford more children, etc.), the authors speculate that the disparity is due to conflicting values. They further suggest that religion, since it emphasizes an ethic of responsibility, produces a negative correlation between religiosity and support for abortion, particularly for social reasons.

582. Jelen, Ted G. "Respect for Life, Sexual Morality and Opposition to Abortion." *Review of Religious Research* 25 (1984): 220-231.

Examines the relative importance of respect for human life and sexual conservatism in explaining opposition to abortion.

583. Jelen, Ted G., John O'Donnell, and Clyde Wilcox. "A Contextual Analysis of Catholicism and Abortion Attitudes in Western Europe." *Sociology of Religion* 54 (1993): 375-383.

Analyzes the effects of the Roman Catholic Church on abortion attitudes in Western Europe, both at the individual level and at the country level. Results show that at the individual level, the Church is effective in producing negative attitudes toward abortion, whereas the contextual effects of Catholicism run in the opposite direction. Thus non-Catholic individuals in largely Catholic countries will be more likely to favor abortion than non-Catholics living in largely Protestant Countries. The author then discusses the implications of this study for Catholic political activism.

584. Kelley, Jonathan, M. D. R. Evans, and Bruce Headey. "Moral Reasoning and Political Conflict: The Abortion Controversy. *The British Journal of Sociology* 44 (1993): 589-612.

Argues that the abortion controversy has one major source – religion, and two minor ones – attitudes toward sexual permissiveness and women's employment. Using a large national sample from Australia, the authors test their hypothesis that religious belief, anti-feminism, sexual permissiveness, and attitudes toward abortion serve as four distinct factors, rather than as all being aspects on one conservatism factor. They find that deductive reasoning from Christian belief is the most important source of opposition to abortion. Contrary to received wisdom, however, they find that views on women's employment matter only a little.

585.   Kelly, James R. "Ecumenism and Abortion: A Case Study of Pluralism, Privatization and the Public Conscience." *Review of Religious Research* 30 (1989): 225-235.

Uses various churches' responses to abortion as a measure of the internalization of ecumenism.

586.   Krishnan, Vijaya. "Abortion in Canada: Religious and Ideological Dimensions of Women's Attitudes." *Social Biology* 38 (1991): 249-257.

Using data from the Canadian Fertility Survey of 1984, the author examines a number of demographic and socio-cultural factors as predictors of women's attitudes toward abortion. Results show that women's attitudes toward abortion are to a great extent based on their ideological positions. In particular, religiosity and sex role ideology were found to be the two strongest predictors of abortion attitudes, with high religiosity and a conservative view of sex role generally pre-disposing one to an anti-abortion stance.

587.   Luker, Kristin. *Abortion and the Politics of Motherhood.* Berkeley, Calif.: Univ. of California Press, 1984.

Examines the history of the abortion debate, and asks how people come to differ in their opinions on the rightness or wrongness of abortion. She shows that the reason the abortion debate has been so emotional is that the two sides share almost no common premises, and very little common language.

588.   ———. *Taking Chances: Abortion and the Decision Not to Contracept.* Berkeley, Calif.: Univ. of California Press, 1975.

Shows how our values on sexuality, contraception, and abortion have helped create the social realities we now find ourselves in. Thus, she claims that many of our opinions on these matters has been shaped, not by facts, but by our value judgements.

589.   Massagli, Michael P. *Polarization and Convergence: Religion, Politics, and Attitudes toward Abortion in the United States, 1972-1985.* Working Paper no. 1988-27. University Park, Pa.: Population Issues Research Center, 1988.

Examines the General Social Surveys of 1972 and 1985 for trends in liberalism toward abortion, focusing on the effects of religious group membership, church attendance, and participation in presidential elections.

590.   McIntosh, William Alex, Letitia T. Alston, and Jon P. Alston. "The Differential Impact of Religious Preference and Church Attendance on Attitudes toward Abortion." *Review of Religious Research* 20 (1979): 195-213.

The relationship among religious preference, church attendance and the consequences of religion are explored in terms of the acceptance/rejection of the legalization of abortion. The findings indicate that frequent church attenders tend to be anti-abortion, regardless of the degree of liberal ideologies normally associated with certain churches.

591.   Petersen, Larry R., and Armand L. Mauss. "Religion and the 'Right to Life:' Correlates of the Opposition to Abortion." *Sociological Analysis* 36 (1976): 243-254.

From the fact that opposition to abortion is associated with political conservatism, and from the fact that religious and political conservatism/liberalism are highly correlated, the authors hypothesize that more conservative churches will tend to oppose abortion, while the more liberal churches will tend to favor it.

592.   Pett, Mark Edward. "Religion and the Abortion Patient: A Study of Anxiety as a Function of Religious Belief and Participation and the Decision-Making Process." Ph.D. diss., University of Iowa, 1975.

Given the opposition of conservative religious groups to abortion, this study examines how women who adhere to such religious beliefs would react when they had the procedure. Was their anxiety level higher than with those who did not have such conservative religious beliefs? It also examines what factors contributed to their decision to have an abortion.

593.   Rhodes, A. Lewis. "Religion and Opposition to Abortion Reconsidered." *Review of Religious Research* 26 (1985): 158-168.

In this article, the author reports on a research study comparing opposition to abortion with religious preference in a sample of 18,004 new college freshmen. The results indicate that the relationship between religion and opposition to abortion may be more complicated than previous research had indicated.

594.   Smetana, Judith G. *Concepts of Self and Morality: Women's Reasoning about Abortion.* New York: Praeger, 1982.

Examines women's decision-making process on the issue of abortion, and how this relates to social reasoning and social concepts. With regard to abortion, the author finds two categories of social judgement – the moral and the personal. Her research shows that women used both types , but that they differed in whether they treated abortion itself as a moral or as a personal issue.

595.   Sullins, D. Paul. "Catholic/Protestant Trends on Abortion: Convergence and Polarity." *Journal for the Scientific Study of Religion* 38 (1999): 354-369.

Using data from 1972-1996 General Social Surveys, the author finds no significant difference between Catholics and Protestants, in the most recent five year period (1992-1996), in the proportion holding either a pro-life or a pro-choice position. He also presents the sociological factors that were found to contribute to this convergence.

596.   Tamney, Joseph B., Stephen D. Johnson, and Ronald Burton. "The Abortion Controversy: Conflicting Beliefs and Values in American Society." *Journal for the Scientific Study of Religion* 31 (1992): 32-46.

Based on data from a random survey done in 1989, this study shows that the strongest effects on abortion attitudes were a belief that life begins at conception, a belief in privacy rights, and religion. Among Protestants, social traditionalism was also found to be important, and among Catholics, a general regard to avoid taking one's life was found important. It also found that attending pro-life churches increased one's likelihood of using abortion in voting decisions.

597.   Wall, Sally N., Irene Hanson Frieze, Anuška Ferligoj, Eva Jarošová, Daniela Pauknerová, Jasna Horvat, and Nataša Šarlija. "Gender Role and Religion as Predictors of Attitude toward Abortion in Croatia, Slovenia, the Czech Republic, and the United States." *Journal of Cross-Cultural Psychology* 30 (1999): 443-468.

Examines the importance of religious identification, degree of religious participation, desired number of children, and gender role as predictors of approval of abortion for reasons of personal choice, and compares and contrasts the results as found in the United States with the results as found in Central and East European nations.

598. Welch, Michael R., David C. Leege, and James C. Cavendish. "Attitudes toward Abortion among U.S. Catholics: Another Case of Symbolic Politics?" *Social Science Quarterly* 76 (1995): 142-157.

Based on survey data from a representative sample of Catholic parishioners, the authors conclude that Catholics who oppose abortion are most likely to be shaped by sexual and religious orientations.

599. Wilcox, Clyde. "Race, Religion, Region and Abortion Attitudes." *Sociological Analysis* 52 (1992): 97-103.

Some studies have shown that African Americans are typically less supportive of legal abortion than are whites. This study demonstrates that religious variables play an important role in this difference. The study shows that religiosity and doctrinal orthodoxy are important predictors of abortion attitudes among both blacks and whites, and explain much of the racial differences in attitude toward abortion.

600. Wilcox, Clyde, and Leopoldo Gomez. "The Christian Right and the Pro-Life Movement: An Analysis of the Sources of Political Support." *Review of Religious Research* 31 (1990): 380-389.

Only a fraction of pro-life supporters have also supported the Christian Right; and likewise, only a portion of Christian Right supporters have also supported the Pro-Life movement. This authors report on a study which shows that religious differences, even among evangelicals, are quite important in distinguishing between the supporters of the two groups. They lay out the religious variables involved and show which groups of evangelicals support both, and which support one or the other.

601. Williams, Dorie Giles. "Religion, Beliefs about Human Life, and the Abortion Discussion." *Review of Religious Research* 24 (1982): 40-48.

Examines how religious factors and beliefs about human life, among women with problem pregnancies, influence their decision on whether to seek an abortion.

602. Woodrum, Eric, and Beth L. Davison. "Reexamination of Religious Influences of Abortion Attitudes." *Review of Religious Research* 32 (1992): 229-243.

Addresses the question of why religious variables are so influential on abortion attitudes. Examines the influence of several factors, including religion, on abortion attitudes.

5 OFFICIAL DOCUMENTS OF THE CATHOLIC CHURCH

603.   "Abortion and Catholic Public Officials." *Origins* 6 (1977): 136-138.

604.   Bernardin, Cardinal Joseph. "Abortion and Euthanasia: Violation of the Right to Life." *L'Osservatore Romano* (English ed.), 15 Dec. 1977, 8-9.

An address delivered Aug. 16, 1977.

605.   ———. "Cardinal Bernardin's Call for a Consistent Ethic of Life." *Origins* 13 (1983): 491-494.

606.   ———. "The Consistent Ethic of Life and Health Care Reform." *Origins* 24 (1994): 60-64.

607.   ———. "The Defense of Human Life." *Origins* 6 (1976): 341, 343-345.

Address opening the annual meeting of the National Conference of Catholic Bishops, Nov. 8-11, 1976.

608.   ———. "Enlarging the Dialogue on a Consistent Ethic of Life." *Origins* 13 (1984): 705, 707-709.

609.   ———. "A Fundamental Right which must Take Precedence." *Origins* 4 (1975): 573-574.

Homily delivered Jan. 22, 1975, in support of sanctity of life throughout all of life.

610.   ———. "Science and the Creation of Life." *Origins* 17 (1987): 21, 23-26.

An address given in support of the Vatican Doctrinal Congregation's "Instruction on Respect for Human Life in its Origin and on the Dignity of Procreation." (see citation # 736).

611. ———. "The Value of the Consistent-Ethic Approach." *Origins* 14 (1984): 397-398.

A report to the U.S. Catholic Bishops by the chairman of that body's Committee for Pro-Life Activities.

612. Bernardin, Cardinal Joseph., and Cardinal Terence Cooke. "Pastoral Plan for Pro-Life Activities." *L'Osservatore Romano* (English ed.), 1 Jan. 1976, 3-4.

613. Bishops' Conferences of England and Wales, Scotland and Ireland. Joint Committee on Bioethical Issues. "Use of the 'Morning-After Pill' in Cases of Rape." *Origins* 15 (1986): 633, 635-638.

A statement in which the bishops advocate the use of the morning after pill in cases of rape, but only when ovulation has not yet occurred. If ovulation has occurred, then its use is rejected. They also reject the use of the Intra-Uterine Device (IUD) in cases of rape.

614. ———. "Use of the Morning-After Pill in Cases of Rape." *Origins* 16 (1986): 237-238.

A clarification of the committee's earlier statement (see citation # 118)

615. Bishops of Maine, New Hampshire, Vermont and Massachusetts. "Not a Single-Issue Church, Bishops Say." *Origins* 14 (1984): 217-218.

Text of a statement in which the bishops reject the charge that the Catholic Church is only concerned with the abortion issue.

616. Bruns, Sr. Margaret Mary, "Approaches to Abortion Questions." *Origins* 2 (1973): 269, 284.

617. Bryce, Fr. Edward. "Reconciliation: Missing Piece in Abortion Picture." *Origins* 11 (1981): 181-184.

618. Burghardt, Walter, S.J. "Crossing the Credibility Gap." *Origins* 3 (1973): 89-95.

An address before the Catholic Health Assembly, June 3-7, 1973, on the sanctity of life.

619.   Byron, William. "Abortion Debate: How Intellectuals and Moral Leaders Can Help Politicians." *Origins* 22 (1992): 81, 83-87.

A Catholic priest, and the outgoing president of the Catholic University of America, describes how Catholic academics and moralists can help the politician shape public policy on abortion.

620.   Canadian Conference of Catholic Bishops. "The Right to Life." Sect. 2 in "The Medico-Moral Guide of Canadian Bishops." *Origins* 1 (1971): 427-428.

621.   ———. "Statement on Abortion." *L'Osservatore Romano* (English ed.), 29 Oct. 1970, 5.

622.   Catholic Bishops of Massachusetts. "In Defense of Unborn Human Life." *L'Osservatore Romano* (English ed.), 6 May 1971, 5.

623.   Catholic Bishops of Missouri. "Missouri Catholic Bishops' Statement on Abortion." *L'Osservatore Romano* (English ed.), 22 July 1971, 11.

624.   Catholic Bishops of New Jersey. "In God's Image: A Statement on the Sanctity of Human Life." *Origins* 14 (1984): 151-153

625.   Catholic Bishops of New Jersey. "Pastoral on Abortion." *Catholic Mind,* June 1970, 9-10.

626.   Catholic Bishops of Pennsylvania. "The Church, Public Policy and Abortion." *Origins* 20 (1990): 14-15.

627.   Catholic Bishops of Pennsylvania. "In Defense of Human Life." *Catholic Mind,* Jan. 1971, 9-11.

628.   Catholic Hospital Association. "Serving Public Notice." *Origins* 2 (1973): 553.

Press release issued Feb. 1, 1973 in response to the Supreme Court's *Roe v. Wade* decision.

629.   Cody, Cardinal John. "The Court's Criteria." *Origins* 2 (1974): 606.

Address before the Senate Subcommittee on Constitutional Amendments, March 7, 1974, in favor of a human life amendment.

630.   Colorado Bishops. "Colorado Bishops Endorse Amendment no. 3." *Origins* 14 (1984): 223-224.

A statement in which the Bishops endorse a state constitutional amendment to prohibit the use of state funds for elective abortions.

631.   College of Cardinals. "Communique: College of Cardinals Meeting." *Origins* 20 (1991): 745, 747-748.

A statement in which the world's cardinals ask Pope John Paul II to develop a major church document, preferably an encyclical, on the value of human life.

632.   Cooke, Cardinal Terence. "The Impact of Abortion." *Origins* 10 (1980): 283-285.

An address delivered to the 1980 International Synod of Bishops on the impact of abortion on marriage and family life.

633.   ———. "Will Church Institutions be Forced to Make Medical Payments for Abortions?" *Origins* 6 (1978): 577, 579.

Report to the Administrative Committee of the National Conference of Catholic Bishops.

634.   Curtiss, Abp. Elden. "Abortion: Moral Blight, National Scandal." *Origins* 30 (2000): 303-304.

635.   Daughters of St. Paul. "Abortion." In *Pro-Life Catechism: Abortion, Genetics, Euthanasia, Suicide, Child Abuse,* 3-47. Boston: Daughters of St. Paul, 1984.

636.   Doerflinger, Richard. "Destructive Stem-Cell Research on Human Embryos." *Origins* 28 (1999): 769, 771-773.

The Assistant Director of the National Conference of Catholic Bishops' Office for Pro-Life Activities presents testimony, April 16, 1999, before the National Bioethics Advisory Commission created by President Clinton.

637.   ———. "New Embryonic Stem-Cell Research Guidelines Criticized." *Origins* 30 (2000): 193, 195.

A statement issued August 23, 2000, in response to new guidelines for embryonic stem cell research issued by the National Institutes of Health.

638.   ———. "Public Policy and Reproductive Technology." *Origins* 17 (1987): 143-144

The Assistant Director of the National Conference of Catholic Bishops' Office for Pro-Life Activities presents testimony before the House Select Committee on Children, Youth and Families in opposition to *in vitro* fertilization.

639.   Firenza, Bp. Joseph. "On Federal Funding for Embryonic Stem Cell Research." *Origins* 31 (2001): 169-170.

A letter from the president of the United States Catholic Conference to President George W. Bush, urging him not to support federal funding for embryonic stem cell research where human embryos would be destroyed.

640.   Gelineau, Bp. Louis. "The Dignity of Human Life & Love." *Origins* 8 (1978): 513, 515-516.

Pastoral letter reaffirming Catholic teaching on human sexuality and family life.

641.   Gouldrick, John. "Aborted Fetal Tissue Use in Experimental Transplants Opposed." *Origins* 18 (1989): 495-496.

A statement by the Director of the National Conference of Catholic Bishops' Office for Pro-Life Activities.

642.   Hickey, Cardinal James. "Birthing and Abortion Healing Programs Announced." *Origins* 21 (1991): 105, 107-108.

Cardinal Hickey of Washington announces two new archdiocesan programs; one a pastoral care outreach program for women in crisis pregnancies who cannot afford the cost of delivering a baby, and the second, a counseling and healing ministry for women who have had abortions.

643.   Hubbard, Bp. Howard. "After 'Webster': Bishops and Catholic Office-holders." *Origins* 19 (1989): 474-476.

644.   Hume, Cardinal George Basil. "The Ethics of Experiments on Human Embryos." *Origins* 14 (1984): 145, 147.

A statement delivered July 20, 1984, on behalf of the Bishops' Conference of England and Wales.

645.   Hurley, Bp. Mark. "Basic Human Values in a Radically Different Age." *Origins* 6 (1976): 405, 407-410.

Address, Dec. 1, 1976, to the First General Session of the Value Life Project, sponsored by the Texas Conference of Churches.

646.   Indiana Catholic Conference. "Abortion." In "How to Confront Current Moral Issues." *Origins* 2 (1973): 462.

647.   John Paul II, Pope. "Abortion, Euthanasia, Genetic Manipulations are Grave Dangers of Deviation for the Doctor." *L'Osservatore Romano* (English ed.), 16 July 1984, 10-11.

An address to the faculty of medicine at the Sacred Heart University, Milan, Italy.

648.   ———. "Abortion is immoral." In *Abortion: Opposing Viewpoints*, edited by Tamara L. Roleff, 17-22. San Diego: Greenhaven Press, 1997.

An excerpt from his encyclical, *Evangelium Vitae.*

649.   ———. "Building a Culture of Life." *Origins* 28 (1998): 314-316.

An address, October 2, 1998, to the bishops of California, Nevada, and Hawaii during their *ad limina* visit.

650.   ———. "A Celebration of Life." *Origins* 23 (1993): 177, 179-180.

An address to participants in the eighth World Youth Day, held in Denver, calling on them to celebrate life, and to fight against the "culture of death" so prevalent in society today.

651.   ———. "The Christian Must React Against Abortion." *L'Osservatore Romano* (English ed.), 18-26 Dec. 1989, 8.

An address to a French pro-life group, Nov. 10, 1989.

652.   ———. "Christians and the Moral Order." *The Pope Speaks* 38 (1993): 193-200.

An address to the Bishops of South Western Germany during their *ad limina* visit, speaking of many aspects of church and political life in Germany, including abortion and euthanasia.

653.   ———. "A Clear Moral Evil is Involved." *National Catholic Reporter*, 4 Nov. 1994, 2.

An excerpt from his book, *Crossing the Threshold of Hope.*

654.   ———. *Evangelical Letter* Evangelium Vitae *addressed by the Supreme Pontiff John Paul II to the Bishops, Priests and Deacons, Men and Women Religious, Lay Faithful, and All People of Good Will on the Value and Inviolability of Human Life.* Publication no. 316-7. Washington, D.C.: United States Catholic Conference, n.d.

655.   ———. "How to Build the Culture of Life." *Origins* 30 (2001): 651-652.

An address delivered March 3, 2001, to the Pontifical Academy for Life.

656.   ———. "Human Life is Inviolable." *The Pope Speaks* 34 (1989): 289-292.

An address to the pro-life congress sponsored by the Italian Episcopal Conference, delivered April 6, 1989.

657.   ———. "Letter on Combatting [sic] Abortion and Euthanasia." *Origins* 21 (1991): 136.

A papal letter to Catholic Bishops.

658.   ———. "Seek Full Legal Protection for Unborn Life." *L'Osservatore Romano* (English ed.), 28 Jan. 1998, 16.

A message sent to Cardinal Law for a gathering in Washington, D.C., on Jan. 22, 1998, marking the 25th anniversary of *Roe v. Wade.*

659.   ———. "'Stand up' for Human Life." *Origins* 9 (1979): 277, 279-280.

Homily, Oct. 7, 1979, on the Capitol Mall, Washington, D.C.

660.   ———. "The State as Executioner." *The Pope Speaks* 31 (1986): 128-130.

An address in audience with members of the Italian Pro-Life movement, regarding state financed abortions, Jan. 25, 1986.

661.   ———. "An Unambiguous Witness to Human Life." *L'Osservatore Romano* (English ed.), 30 June 1999, 2.

A letter sent to the German bishops asking them to ensure that pregnant women in crisis situations who receive church related counseling not be given the possibility of obtaining an abortion in accordance with German law.

662.   Katenkamp, Jane Blank. *Respecting Life: An Activity Guide.* Washington, D.C.: Office of Publishing and Promotion Services, United States Catholic Conference, 1985.

663.   Krol, Cardinal John. "The Ills of our Society." *Origins* 2 (1973): 337, 339-341, 351.

        Address opening the fourteenth general meeting of the National Conference of Catholic Bishops, Nov. 12-16, 1973.

664.   ————. "Unique Human Life." *Origins* 2 (1974): 601, 603-604.

        Address before the Senate Subcommittee on Constitutional Amendments, March 7, 1974, in favor of a human life amendment.

665.   Law, Cardinal Bernard. "Letter to the Senate: Partial-Birth Abortions." *Origins* 27 (1997): 24-25.

        A letter from the chairman of the Committee for Pro-Life Activities to members of the U.S. Senate, asking them to support the partial-birth abortion ban act, then being considered by the Senate.

666.   ————. "Moratorium Asked on Clinic Pro-Life Demonstrations." *Origins* 24 (1995): 515-516.

        In light of violence at abortion clinics, the Cardinal of Boston calls for a moratorium on pro-life demonstrations at abortion clinics.

667.   ————. "Moratorium Lifted for Individuals: Action at Clinics." *Origins* 25 (1995): 100-101.

        The cardinal of Boston lifts the moratorium he had previously placed on pro-life demonstrations at abortion clinics. He calls for all pro-life activity at abortion clinics to be non-violent.

668.   Leadership Conference of Women Religious. "Choose Life: The Value & Quality of Life." *Origins* 6 (1977): 161, 163-167.

669.   "Letter to the President." *Origins* 26 (1997): 639.

        A letter from seven Catholic cardinals in the United States, and the president of the National Conference of Catholic Bishops to President Clinton, asking him to publically proclaim that he now supports a ban on partial-birth abortions, and will sign such a ban into law.

670.   Lipscomb, Abp. Oscar. "Violence and Homicide Rejected in Pro-Life Cause." *Origins* 24 (1994): 273, 275-278.

       An address to Catholic pro-life leaders in Florida, rebuking the killing of abortionists and other forms of violence in the pro-life cause.

671.   Louisiana Bishops. "On Supporting Imperfect Bills." *Origins* 20 (1991): 728.

       The bishops call on the Louisiana legislature to pass anti-abortion legislation, even if these bills have to include exceptions for rape and incest, which the Catholic church opposes.

672.   Lynch, Msgr. Robert. "The Bishops' Pro-Life Public Relations Campaign. *Origins* 20 (1990): 189-192.

       In an address to the Knights of Columbus convention, the General Secretary of the National Council of Catholic Bishops outlines the goals of a pro-life public relations campaign initiated by the U.S. Bishops.

673.   Mahony, Cardinal Roger. "Delivering the Pro-Life Message without Violence." *Origins* 24 (1995): 551-554.

       An address to the National Prayer Vigil for Life, in which he says that if the pro-life message is to be heard, it must be "delivered without violence, either in thought, speech, or deed."

674.   ———. "A Time to Galvanize Pro-Life Americans." *Origins* 22 (1992): 471-472.

       A Catholic Cardinal from Los Angeles, and the chairman of the National Conference of Catholic Bishops' Committee on Pro-Life Activities, in light of the election of Bill Clinton as President of the United States, calls on all pro-life people to put aside their differences and pull together to stop the Freedom of Choice bill.

675.   Manning, Cardinal Timothy. "All Human Rights." *Origins* 2 (1974): 604-605.

       Address before the Senate Subcommittee on Constitutional Amendments, March 7, 1974, in favor of a human life amendment.

676.   McHugh, Bp. James. "Abortion and the Officeholder." *Origins* 20 (1990): 40-42.

An address to the New Jersey Knights of Columbus convention, in which he states that Catholic agencies should not bestow public honors or privileges on Catholic public officials who are pro-choice.

677.   ———. "Guidelines: Pro-Life Activity at Abortion Clinics." *Origins* 24 (1995): 516-517.

The Bishop of Camden, New Jersey issues guidelines for pro-life demonstrations at abortion clinics.

678.   ———. "Political Responsibility and Respect for Life." *Origins* 19 (1989): 460-461.

A letter written for parish bulletins in his diocese.

679.   McHugh, Msgr. James T. "Experiments and the Fetus: Why the Opposition?" *Origins* 2 (1973): 268.

Letter to the chairman of the House Subcommittee on Health and Environment, in opposition to experiments on aborted fetuses, Oct. 4, 1973.

680.   McHugh, Msgr. James T., Charles E. Curran, and J. Philip Wogaman. "Civil Law and Christian Morality: The Churches and Abortion." *Origins* 4 (1975): 564-573

Addresses by three Catholic prelates at a Conference held Feb. 4-5, 1975, in New York.

681.   Medeiros, Cardinal Humberto. "Abortion and the Elections." *Origins* 10 (1980): 239.

Pastoral letter urging Catholics not to vote for legislators who support legalized abortion.

682.   ———. "Shaping an Amendment." *Origins* 2 (1974): 605.

Address before the Senate Subcommittee on Constitutional Amendments, March 7, 1974, in favor of a human life amendment.

683.   Meehan, Francis X. *Pro-Life Work and Social Justice.* Washington, D.C.: National Conference of Catholic Bishops, Committee for Pro-Life Activities, 1980.

684.   Montana Bishops. "Catholic Officeholders and Abortion." *Origins* 19 (1989): 457-459.

685.   "Moral Evaluation and the Spectrum of Life Issues." *Origins* 14 (1984): 311.

A statement signed by 23 U.S. Catholic Bishops encouraging a concern for all life issues, not just abortion.

686.   Myers. Bp. John J. "The Obligations of Catholics and the Rights of Unborn Children: A Pastoral Statement." *Linacre Quarterly* 56 (Aug. 1990): 15-26.

687.   National Conference of Catholic Bishops. "Abortion and the Supreme Court: Advancing the Culture of Death." *Origins* 30 (2000): 405. 407.

A statement by the U.S. bishops, in which they re-commit themselves to the task of reversing both *Roe v. Wade,* and *Stenberg v. Carhart.*

688.   ———. "Bishops meet Carter." *Origins* 6 (1976): 207.

Letter read to presidential candidate Jimmy Carter, in support of a constitutional amendment to ban abortion, Aug. 31, 1976.

689.   ———. *Documentation on Abortion and the Right to Life II.* Washington, D.C.: Publications Office, United States Catholic Conference, 1976.

A compilation of source documents on abortion by several Catholic prelates and Catholic bodies.

690.   ———. *Documentation on the Right to Life and Abortion.* Washington, D.C.: Publications Office, United States Catholic Conference, 1974.

A compilation of source documents on abortion by several different Catholic prelates and Catholic bodies.

691.   ———. *Faithful for Life: A Moral Reflection.* Publication no. 5-019. Washington, D.C.: United States Catholic Conference, 1995.

692.   ———. "Human Dignity and the Value of Life." *Origins* 6 (1977): 287.

Address given at the First World Synod of Bishops in 1977.

693.   ———. "Issues in Care for the Beginning of life." Part 4 of "Ethical and Religious Directives for Catholic Health Care Services." *Origins* 31 (2001): 159-160.

694.   ———. "Life's Dignity: Issue Binding other Social Concerns." *Origins* 6 (1976): 216.

Letter read to presidential candidate Gerald Ford. Sept. 10, 1976.

695.   ———. "Living the Gospel of Life: A Challenge to American Catholics."
Origins 28 (1998): 429, 431-437.

A statement, adopted November 18, 1998.

696.   ———. "The Nation 25 Years after *Roe v. Wade.*" *Origins* 27 (1997):
410-411.

697.   ———. *Pastoral Plan for Pro-Life Activities.* Washington, D.C.: United
States Catholic Conference, 1975.

698.   ———. *Pastoral Plan for Pro-Life Activities: A Reaffirmation.*
Publication no. 980. Washington, D.C.: United States Catholic Conference, 1985.

699.   ———. "Personhood." *Origins* 6 (1976): 314-317.

Resolutions on personhood given at the "Call to Action" conference, Oct.
21-23, 1976.

700.   ———. "Resolution on Abortion." *Origins* 19 (1989): 395-396.

701.   ———. *Respect Life.* Respect Life Program, 1989-1990. Washington,
D.C.: United States Catholic Conference, 1989.

702.   ———. "Rockefeller and Abortion." *Origins* 4 (1974): 374.

Letter to the Senate Committee on Rules and Administration, raising
questions about the nomination of Nelson Rockefeller as Vice President
of the United States, due to his pro-choice position.

703.   ———. "Statement on Partial-Birth Abortion Ban Veto." *Origins* 26
(1996): 110.

704.   ———. *Statements of National Conference of Catholic Bishops and
United States Catholic Conference in Response to Supreme Court
Decision on Abortion.* Washington, D.C.: Publications Office, United
States Catholic Conference, 1973

705.   ———. "Towards a Pro-Life Amendment." *Origins* 2 (1973): 360.

706.   ———. "We Reject This Decision of the Court." *Origins* 2 (1973): 553-
555.

707.   National Conference of Catholic Bishops. Ad hoc Committee on Pro-Life
        Activities. *Pastoral Guidelines for the Catholic Hospital and Catholic
        Health Care Personnel.* Washington, D.C.: Publications Office, United
        States Catholic Conference, 1973.

708.   National Conference of Catholic Bishops. Committee for Pro-Life
        Activities. "No Alternative Teaching on Abortion." *Origins* 15 (1985):
        312.

        A statement asserting that dissent from the Church's teaching on abortion
        cannot be seen as legitimate moral teaching.

709.   ———. *Respect Life!* Respect Life Program, 1978/1979. Washington,
        D.C.: National Conference of Catholic Bishops, 1978.

710.   ———. "'Webster': Opportunity to Defend Life." *Origins* 19 (1989):
        215-216.

        A response to the Supreme Court's ruling in *Webster v. Reproductive
        Health Services.*

711.   National Conference of Catholic Bishops. Committee on Doctrine.
        "Moral Principles concerning Infants with Anencephaly." *Origins* 26
        (1996): 276.

        A statement in which the bishops oppose abortion in cases where the fetus
        is anencephalic.

712.   National Federation of Priests' Councils. "A Letter on Approaches to the
        Abortion Issue." *Catholic Mind,* March 1977, 9-10.

        Resolution calling for the passage of a human life amendment.

713.   ———. "NFPC Board on Abortion Strategy." *Origins* 6 (1976): 235.

        Letter to the National Conference of Catholic Bishops Committee for Pro-
        Life Activities.

714.   New York State Catholic Bishops. "Abortion: the Role of Public
        Officials." *Origins* 13 (1984): 759-760.

715.   O'Boyle, Cardinal Patrick. "Legality vs. Morality." *Origins* 2 (1973):
        267, 269.

        Address at a special mass, Oct. 8, 1973, at the National Shrine of the
        Immaculate Conception.

716.   O'Connor, Cardinal John. "Abortion: Questions and Answers." *Origins*
         20 (1990): 97, 99-115.

         A statement presenting questions and answers on abortion, public policy,
         and the proper role of the Catholic Church in effecting that public policy
         on abortion.

717.   ———. "The AFL-CIO and the Abortion Issue." *Origins* 19 (1990): 581,
         583.

         A statement made upon hearing that the AFL-CIO was considering
         passing a pro-choice resolution.

718.   ———. "Peaceful, Non-Violent Prayer Vigils." *Origins* 24 (1995): 517-
         520.

         A rejection of the use of violence at abortion clinics, and a support for
         Cardinal Law's call for a moratorium on pro-life demonstrations at
         abortion clinics (see citation # ?).

719.   Ohio Bishops. "Statement on Abortion and Political Life." *Origins* 19
         (1989): 499-500.

720.   "Override Urged of Partial-Birth Abortion Ban Veto." *Origins* 26 (1996):
         213, 215.

         A letter from eight Cardinals in the United States and the president of the
         National Conference of Catholic Bishops to members of Congress,
         encouraging them to override President Clinton's veto of the partial-birth
         abortion ban.

721.   Owen, Mary Jane. "Recomputing the Quality-of-Life Equations."
         Origins 29 (2000): 572-573.

         An address by the executive director of the National Catholic Office for
         Persons with Disabilities, February 7, 2000, in which she opposes the use
         of embryonic stem cells for research.

722.   "The Partial-Birth Abortion Ban Veto." *Origins* 25 (1996): 753, 755-756.

         A letter from eight Cardinals in the United States and the president of the
         National Conference of Catholic Bishops to president Clinton, criticizing
         his veto of a ban on partial-birth abortions. President Clinton's letter in
         response is also included.

723. Paul VI, Pope. "Abortion and Euthanasia are Murder." *L'Osservatore Romano* (English ed.), 11 Feb. 1971, 2.

An address broadcast on French television, Jan. 27, 1970.

724. ———. *Encyclical Letter of His Holiness Pope Paul VI on the Regulation of Birth: to the Venerable Patriarchs, Archbishops and Bishops, and other Local Ordinaries in Peace and Communion with the Apostolic See, to Priests, the Faithful, and to all Men of Good Will.* [Vatican City]: Tipografia, Poliglotta Vaticana, 1968?

The pope's encyclical, *Humanae Vitae.*

725. ———. "Let Responsibility Keep Pace with your Knowledge." *L'Osservatore Romano* (English ed.), 5 May 1977, 9.

An address to a group of Catholic doctors from Flanders, April 23, 1977, on the necessity to embrace the pro-life position, even as they increase their medical knowledge.

726. ———. "The Right to Be Born." *The Pope Speaks* 17 (1973): 333-335.

An address to the Society of Italian Catholic Jurists, Dec. 9, 1972.

727. ———. "Pope Praises U.S. Bishops for Pro-Life Efforts." *Origins* 8 (1978): 41-42.

Statement to bishops from Ohio, Michigan, and Minnesota, praising the U.S. Bishops for their pro-life activities.

728. Pontifical Academy for Life. "When Human Life Begins." *Origins* 26 (1997): 662-663.

A statement released February 20, 1997, in which they say that fertilization is, both scientifically and morally, the most logical place to draw the line between what is and is not human life.

729. Pontifical Council for the Family. *In the Service of Life (Instrumentum Laboris).* Vatican City, 1991; distributed by the United States Catholic Conference.

730. Quinn, Abp. John. "Taking up the Role of Prophets." *Origins* 6 (1978): 524-526.

Statement condemning the Supreme Court's *Roe v. Wade* decision.

731.   Ratzinger, Cardinal Joseph. "Doctrinal Document on Threats to Life Proposed." *Origins* 20 (1991): 755-759.

         Calls on the College of Cardinals to develop a doctrinal statement on the defense of human life, and outlines the features such a statement might have.

732.   Roach, Abp. John R. "Letter to Two Catholic Politicians on Pro-Choice Position." *Origins* 22 (1992): 187-188.

         The archbishop of Minneapolis and St. Paul, Minnesota writes an open letter to two Catholic Minnesota politicians asking them to re-consider their switch away from a pro-life position. The responses of the two politicians are also included.

733.   Roach, Abp. John R., and Terence Cardinal Cooke. "Bishops Support Hatch Amendment." *Origins* 11 (1981): 357, 359-372.

         Testimony before Congress of the president of the National Conference of Catholic Bishops and the chairman of that body's Committee for Pro-Life Activities in favor of a human life amendment, Nov. 5, 1981.

734.   Sacred Congregation for the Doctrine of the Faith. *Declaration on Abortion: November 18, 1974.* Washington, D.C.: United States Catholic Conference, 1974.

735.   ———. "Declaration on Procured Abortion." *Linacre Quarterly* 42 (1975): 133-147.

736.   ———. "Instruction on Respect for Human Life in its Origin and on the Dignity of Procreation." *Origins* 16 (1987): 697, 699-711.

737.   Schnurr, Msgr. Dennis. "Harvesting Embryonic Stem Cells for Research: Responses to NIH Draft Guidelines." *Origins* 29 (2000): 566-571.

         A statement by the General Secretary of the United States Catholic Conference, in response to NIH draft guidelines which had advocated the use of embryonic stem cells for research purposes.

738.   Sullivan, Bp. Walter. "Abortion Strategy." *Origins* 20 (1990): 87-88.

         A statement saying that the challenge of the Church is not what to communicate regarding abortion, but how to communicate it.

739.   United States Catholic Conference. "Abortion: An Affirmative Public Good?" *Origins* 9 (1980): 534-535.

A Friend of the Court Brief filed with the U.S. Supreme Court when they agreed to hear a case regarding the Hyde Amendment, *Harris v. McRae.*

740. ———. "Convictions about Human Dignity." *Origins* 5 (1976): 661, 663-667.

Written testimony submitted to a House subcommittee conducting hearings on a proposed constitutional amendment to restrict abortion.

741. ———. "The Inalienable Right to Life." *Origins* 2 (1974): 620-627.

Excerpts from a lengthy statement delivered to the Senate Subcommittee on Constitutional Amendments, in favor of a human life amendment.

742. ———. *Living the Gospel of Life: A Challenge to American Catholics.* Publication no. 5-300. Washington, D.C.: United States Catholic Conference, 1998.

743. ———. "Missouri Abortion Case before Supreme Court." *Origins* 18 (1989): 645, 647-653.

A friend of the court brief filed with the Supreme Court in association with *Webster v. Reproductive Health Services.*

744. ———. "Parents and a Minor's Abortion Decision." *Origins* 16 (1987): 537, 539-546.

A friend of the court brief filed with the Supreme Court while it was reviewing the Illinois Parental Notice of Abortion Act.

745. ———. "State's Partial-Birth Abortion Ban Supported." *Origins* 29 (2000): 617-623.

The text of a friend of the court brief to the U.S. Supreme Court, in conjunction of its review of a Nebraska law prohibiting partial birth abortions.

746. ———. "U.S. Bishops' Conferences File Suit on Abortion Benefits." *Origins* 9 (1979): 97, 99-103.

Statement explaining and defending the class action law suit filed by the United States Catholic Conference and the National Conference of Catholic Bishops against the U.S. Department of Justice and the Equal Employment Opportunity Commission, asking for relief from the legal obligation of many employers to pay abortion related fringe benefits.

747. ———. "USCC Brief in Pennsylvania Abortion Law Case." *Origins* 15 (1985): 193, 195-201.

An *Amicus Curiae* brief filed with the U.S. Supreme Court in association with *Thornburgh v. American College of Obstetricians and Gynecologists*.

748. ———. "USCC Statements on Abortion Brief." *Origins* 15 (1985): 201-203.

The Catholic bishops defend their *Amicus Curiae* brief (see citation # ?) against criticisms.

749. Vatican. "RU-486: The 'Abortion Pill.'" *Origins* 21 (1991): 28-33.

A letter sent to bishops' conferences throughout the world, calling the abortion pill, RU-486, "a new serious threat to human life."

750. Vatican. "The Vatican's Summary of *Evangelium Vitae*." *Origins* 24 (1995): 728-730.

751. Villot, Cardinal Jean. "The Physician and Protection of Life." *The Pope Speaks* 15 (1970): 208-210.

An address of the Vatican Secretary of State to the International Federation of Catholic Medical Associations, held in Washington, D.C., Oct. 11-14, 1970.

752. Wisconsin Bishops. "A Consistent Ethic of Life." *Origins* 19 (1989): 461-465.

753. Wuerl, Bp. Donald. "Post-Abortion Reconciliation and Healing." *Origins* 30 (2000): 14-15.

6 OFFICIAL DOCUMENTS OF PROTESTANT RELIGIOUS GROUPS

PRO-CHOICE

754.   American Lutheran Church. "Abortion, Christian Counsel, and the Law." *Reports and Actions of the General Convention of the American Lutheran Church* 5th (1970): 904-907.

755.   ———. "A Statement on Abortion." *Reports and Actions of the General Convention of the American Lutheran Church* 8th (1976): 1042-1055.

756.   National Spiritualist Association of Churches. *Social Policy Statements.* Brochure. Lily Dale, N.Y.: The Stow Memorial Foundation, Bureau of Public Relations, [1992]; distributed by the National Spiritualist Association of Churches.

757.   Presbyterian Church in the United States. "Abortion." *Minutes of the General Assembly* 110th (1970): pt. 1:124-126.

758.   ———. "Abortion." *Minutes of the General Assembly* 113th (1973): Pt. 1: 133-144.

759.   ———. "Resolution to the Standing Committee on Justice & Human Development." *Minutes of the General Assembly* 118th (1978): Pt. 1: 91, 193.

760.   ———. "A Resolution on the Abortion Rights Crisis." *Minutes of the General Assembly* 119th (1979): Pt. 1: 236-238.

761.   ———. "The Nature and Value of Human Life." A Study paper prepared by the Council on Theology and Culture. *Minutes of the General Assembly* 121st (1981): Pt. 1: 286-304.

762.   Presbyterian Church (U.S.A.). *Abortion: All Materials Related to how the Following Church Bodies Have Struggled with the Issue of Abortion from 1969-1989: The United Presbyterian Church in the United States of America, The Presbyterian Church in the United States, The Presbyterian Church (U.S.A.).* Compiled by Alex W. Williams. Athens, Ga: Presbyterian Campus Ministry, 1990.

763.   ———. "Abortion." Web page, November 1997. Available at http://www.pcusa.org/pcusa/info/abortion.htm.

764.   ———. "Commissioner's Resolution regarding Support for the Freedom of Access to Clinic Entrances (FACE) Act." *Minutes* 205th General Assembly (1993): Pt. 1: 945-946.

765.   ———. "Covenant and Creation: Theological Reflections on Contraception and Abortion." *Minutes* 195th General Assembly (1983): Pt. 1: 367-370.

766.   ———. "The Covenant of Life and the Caring Community: What Are We To Do as Responsible People of Faith?" *Minutes* 195th General Assembly (1983): Pt. 1: 363-367.

767.   ———. "Do Justice, Love Mercy, Walk Humbly." Report of the Special Committee on Problem Pregnancies and Abortion. *Minutes* 204th General Assembly (1992): pt.1: 357-377

768.   ———. "National Dialogue on Abortion Perspectives." *Church and Society*, January/February 1990.

769.   ———. "Overture on Speaking against Violence against Staff, Clients, and Facilities of Women's Health Clinics." *Minutes* 207th General Assembly (1995): Pt. 1: 708.

770.   ———. "Recommendation in Support of Choice in Abortion." *Minutes* 198th General Assembly (1986): Pt. 1: 641-642.

771.   ———. *Reproductive Rights and Responsibilities Resource Manual.* Louisville: Women's Ministry Unit, Presbyterian Church (U.S.A.), 1988.

772.   ———. "Resolution in Support of Operation Respect." *Minutes* 201st General Assembly (1989): Pt. 1: 500-501.

773.   ———. "Resolution on Reproductive Rights." *Minutes* 199th General Assembly (1987): Pt. 1: 580-581.

774.   Presbyterians Affirming Reproductive Options. *Abortion in Good Faith: A Reformed Approach to Reproductive Options.* Written by Gloria H. Albrecht. [n.p.]: Presbyterians Affirming Reproductive Options, [1995?].

775.   United Church of Christ. "Freedom of Choice." *Minutes* 9th General Synod (1973): 78.

776.   ———. "Freedom of Choice Concerning Abortion." *Minutes* 8th General Synod (1971): 121-133.

777.   ———. "Pregnancy and Choice." *Minutes* 18th General Synod (1991): 79.

778.   ———. "Reaffirmation of United Church of Christ Support for Freedom of Choice." *Minutes* 17th General Synod (1989): 52-53.

779.   ———. "Resolution on Freedom of Choice." *Minutes* 13th General Synod (1981): 71.

780.   ———. "Resolution on Reaffirmation of Freedom of Choice Regarding Abortion." *Minutes* 12th General Synod (1979): 89-90.

781.   ———. "Sexuality and Abortion: A Faithful Response." *Minutes* 16th General Synod (1987): 82-83.

782.   United Methodist Church. "Abortion." In *The Book of Discipline of the United Methodist Church, 1980,* paragraph 71g. Nashville: United Methodist Publishing House, 1980.

783.   ———. "Abortion." In *The Book of Discipline of the United Methodist Church, 1984,* paragraph 71g. Nashville: United Methodist Publishing House, 1984.

784.   ———. "Abortion." In *The Book of Discipline of the United Methodist Church, 1988,* paragraph 71g. Nashville: United Methodist Publishing House, 1988

785.   ———. "Abortion." In *The Book of Discipline of the United Methodist Church, 1992,* paragraph 71h. Nashville: United Methodist Publishing House, 1992.

786.   ———. "Abortion." In *The Book of Discipline of the United Methodist Church, 1996,* paragraph 65j. Nashville: United Methodist Publishing House, 1996.

787.   ———. "Birth and Death." In *The Book of Discipline of the United Methodist Church, 1972,* paragraph 72d. Nashville: United Methodist Publishing House, 1973.

788.   ———. "Responsible Parenthood." In *The Book of Resolutions of the United Methodist Church,* 126-128. Nashville: United Methodist Pub. House, 1996.

789.   United Presbyterian Church in the U.S.A. "Abortion." *Minutes of the General Assembly* 182nd (1970): 910-914.

790.   ———. "Freedom of Personal Choice in Problem Pregnancies." *Minutes of the General Assembly* 184th (1972): Pt. 1: 265-267.

791.   ———. *Problem Pregnancies: Toward a Responsible Position.* New York: Office of the General Assembly, [1976]. A paper approved by the General Assembly for study and distribution to all local churches.

792.   ———. "Resolution on Abortion." *Minutes of the General Assembly* 192nd (1980): Pt. 1: 68, Sect.K.

793.   ———. "Resolution on Freedom of Choice." *Minutes of the General Assembly* 190th (1978): Pt. 1: 67, Sect. EEE.

794.   ———. "Resolution on the Abortion Rights Crisis." A Joint Resolution of the Council on Women and the Church, and the Advisory Council on Church and Society. *Minutes of the General Assembly* 191st (1979): Pt. 1: 433-435. [Also see pt. 1:82, Sect. J for the disposition of this resolution].

MODERATE

795.   Anglican Church of Canada. *Abortion: An Issue for Conscience.* [Toronto]: Anglican Book Centre, 1974.

796.   ———. *Abortion in a New Perspective: Report of the Task Force on Abortion.* Toronto: Anglican Book Centre, 1989.

797.   ———. *The Abortion Question.* Toronto: Anglican Book Centre, 1983.

798.   Episcopal Church. "Abortion and Birth Control." In *The Social Policies of the Episcopal Church,* Revised January 1998.

799.   ———. "Adopt a Statement on Childbirth and Abortion." *Journal of the General Convention of the Episcopal Church* (1988): 683.

800.   ———. "Oppose Certain Legislation Requiring Parental Consent for Termination of Pregnancy." *Journal of the General Convention of the Episcopal Church* (1991): 839.

801.   ———. "Reaffirm Church's Guidelines on the Termination of Pregnancy." *Journal of the General Convention of the Episcopal Church* (1982): C-156.

802.   ———. "Reaffirm General Convention Statement on Childbirth and Abortion." *Journal of the General Convention of the Episcopal Church* (1994): 323-325

803.   ———. "Resolution on Partial Birth Abortions." *Journal of the General Convention of the Episcopal Church* (1995): 270.

804.   Evangelical Lutheran Church in America. "Social Teaching Statement on Abortion." *Reports and Records* (1991): Vol. 2: 554-562.

805.   Evangelical Lutheran Church in Canada. *Stewards of Creation: Respect for Human Life.* Winnipeg: Division for Church and Society, Evangelical Lutheran Church in Canada, 1991.

806.   Lutheran Church in America. *The Problem of Abortion after the Supreme Court Decision.* Written by Franklin E. Sherman. Studies in Man Medicine and Theology series. New York: Division for Mission in North America, Department for Church and Society, Lutheran Church in America, 1974.

807.   ———. *A Resource Book on the Statement on Sex, Marriage, and Family.* N.p.: Board of Social Ministry, Lutheran Church in America, 1972.

808.   ———. "Sex, Marriage, and Family." *Minutes* 5th Biennial Convention (1970): 655-658.

809.   Reformed Church in America. *Abortion: Seeking Common Ground.* [Grand Rapids, Mich.]: Reformed Church Press, 1996.

810.   ———. "Report of the Commission on Theology." *Minutes of the General Synod* (1984): 248.

811.   ———. "Report of the Task Force on Abortion/Unwanted Pregnancies." *Minutes of the General Synod* (1990).

812.   ———. "Statement on Abortion." *Minutes of the General Synod* (1973): 106.

813.   Roman Catholic/Presbyterian-Reformed Consultation. "A Statement on Abortion." In *Ethics and the Search for Christian Unity: Two Statements by the Roman Catholic/Presbyterian-Reformed Consultation.* Washington, D.C.: Publications Office of the United States Catholic Conference, 1981.

814.   Seventh-Day Adventist Church. "Abortion Guidelines." *Ministry*, March 1971, 10-11.

815.   ———. "The Church on Abortion: Current Suggested Guidelines." *Adventist Review*, 25 Sept. 1986, 14-15.

816.   ———. "Guidelines on Abortion." In *Statements, Guidelines & Other Documents: A Compilation*, 68-71.   Silver Spring, Md.: Seventh-Day Adventist Church, 1996.

817.   United Church of Canada. *Contraception and Abortion: A Statement of the Twenty-Eighth General Council of the United Church of Canada, August, 1980.* [Etobicoke, Ont.]: United Church of Canada, 1982.

PRO-LIFE

818.   American Association of Lutheran Churches.   "The Sanctity of Human Life." *The Evangel*, Jan.-Feb. 1996, 16.

819.   Antiochian Orthodox Christian Archdiocese of North America. "Challenging "Roe v. Wade.": The Amicus Curiae (Friend of the Court) Brief." Web page, February 1989. Available at http://www.christianity.com/CC/article/0.,PTID3863|CHID102308|CIID172368,00.html.

820.   Assemblies of God. *A Biblical Perspective on Abortion.* Springfield Mo.: Assemblies of God Gospel Publishing House, 1985.

821.   Baptist General Conference. "Abortion." In *BGC Resolutions.* June 17, 1991, p. 3. Resolution adopted by the General Conference, 1971.

822.   ———. "Abortion." In *BGC Resolutions.* June 17, 1991, p. 9. Resolution adopted by the General Conference, 1981.

823.   Brethren in Christ Church. *Abortion.* Brethren in Christ Accents and Issues, no.5. Upland Calif.: Brethren in Christ Board of Administration, 1986. Brochure

824. ———. "Statement on Abortion." *General Conference Minutes* (1986): 98-99.

825. Christian Reformed Church. "Abortion." *Acts of Synod* (1972): 479-483.

826. ———. Overture supporting a human life amendment. *Acts of Synod* (1976): 63-64.

827. ———. "Overture 13: Reaffirm Commitment to the Sanctity of Life. *Agenda for Synod* (1997): 443. [Also see the *Acts of Synod* (1997): 607-608 for the disposition of this overture.]

828. ———. "Overture 3: Challenge North Americans to Recognize the Holocaust of Abortion and to Oppose it Boldly; Urge Councils to Respond Publicly." *Agenda for Synod* (1998): 208-210. [Also see the *Acts of Synod* (1998): 442-443 for the disposition of this overture.]

829. Church of England. Board for Social Responsibility. *Abortion: An Ethical Discussion.* [London]: Church Information Office, 1965.

830. Church of God (Cleveland, Tenn.). "Resolution on Abortion." In *Celebrating our Heritage: A Century of Holy Spirit Revival, 1896-1996,* 15-17.

831. Church of the Lutheran Brethren. *What about Abortion?* Brochure. Fergus Falls, Minn.: Church of the Lutheran Brethren, [n.d.].

832. Church of the Nazarene. "Abortion." Sect. 36 in *Manual, 1993-97, Church of the Nazarene.* Kansas City, Mo.: Nazarene Publ. House, 1993.

833. Churches of God, General Conference. "Abortion." In *Pressing toward the Mark: Partial Report of the Committee on Resolutions,* 1. Forty-Fifth Session, Churches of God, General Conference, June 9-13, 1986.

834. Conservative Congregational Christian Conference. "Statement on Abortion." Web page, 1998. Available at http://www.ccccusa.org/4cabortion.htm.

835. Evangelical Mennonite Church. "Position Paper on Abortion." In *Manual of Faith, Practice, and Organization,* 95-97. Fort Wayne, Ind.: Evangelical Mennonite Church, [1990].

836. Evangelical Presbyterian Church. "Abortion." *Minutes of the General Assembly* 4th (1984): 213-216.

837.   ———. "Position Paper on Abortion." *Minutes of the General Assembly* 6th (1986): 136.

838.   ———. "The Value and Respect for Human Life." *Minutes of the General Assembly* 4th (1984): 204-208.

839.   Free Methodist Church of North America. "The Sanctity of Human Life." Par. A/331 in *The Book of Discipline, 1995.*

840.   General Association of Regular Baptist Churches. "Abortion and Fetal Tissue Research." Resolution adopted at the Annual Conference, 1992. *The Baptist Bulletin,* July/August 1992, 24-25.

841.   ———. "Concerning Chemical Abortifacients." Resolution adopted at the Annual Conference, 1990. *The Baptist Bulletin,* October 1990, 34.

842.   ———. "Partial-Birth Abortion." Resolution adopted at the Annual Conference, 1996. *The Baptist Bulletin,* August/September 1996, 18-19.

843.   ———. "Sanctity of Life." Resolution adopted at the Annual Conference, 1985. *The Baptist Bulletin,* July/August 1985, 29.

844.   Greek Orthodox Archdiocese of North and South America. "A Statement on Abortion." In *Abortion: A Reader,* edited by Lloyd Steffen, 162-163. Cleveland, Ohio: The Pilgrim Press, 1996.

845.   Lutheran Church—Missouri Synod. "Abortion: The Challenge." Web page, November 1993. Available at http://www.lcms.org/president/stabort.html.

846.   ———. *Abortion: Theological, Legal, and Medical Aspects: A report of the Commission on Theology and Church Relations.* N.p.: Lutheran Church–Missouri Synod, [1971].

847.   ———. *Abortion in Perspective: A Report of the Commission on Theology and Church Relations of the Lutheran Church—Missouri Synod as Prepared by its Social Concerns Committee.* St. Louis: The Commission, 1984.

848.   ———. "Resolution 2-39: To State Position on Abortion." *Proceedings of the 49th Regular Convention of the Lutheran Church—Missouri Synod* (1971): 126.

849.   ———. "Resolution 3-02: To Implement Pro-Life Programs." *Convention Proceedings* (1981): 155-156.

850.   ———. "Resolution 3-02A: To State Position on Abortion." *Convention Proceedings* (1979): 117.

851.   ———. "Resolution 3-04B: To Reaffirm and Implement the Synod's Pro-Life Position." *Convention Proceedings* (1983): 154-155.

852.   ———. "Resolution 3-08C: To Support Efforts to Protect the Living but Unborn." *Convention Proceedings* (1977): 130-131.

853.   ———. "Resolution 3-09A: To Address Recent Developments and Continued Concerns on Pro-Life Issues." *Convention Proceedings* (1989): 115-116.

854.   ———. "Resolution 3-10: To Promote Greater Activity in Support of Scripture's Pro-Life Position." *Convention Proceedings* (1992): 116.

855.   ———. "Resolution 7-09A: To Support Lutherans for Life." *Convention Proceedings* (1986): 212.

856.   ———. "That They May Have Life." *First Things*, Aug.-Sept. 1997, 47-50.

857.   ———. *What about ... Abortion.* St. Louis: Office of the President, Lutheran Church—Missouri Synod, 1999.

858.   ———. "What has the Lutheran Church—Missouri Synod Done about Abortion?" Web page. Available at http:www.ogi.lcms.org/OGI/HTML/Documents/LCMSonabortion.html.

859.   National Association of Evangelicals. "Abortion." In *NAE Resolutions: Selected Resolutions Adopted by the National Association of Evangelicals during the Past Four Decades.*

860.   National Association of Free Will Baptists. "Abortion." In *Reports: Temperance Committee, Resolutions Committee, 1935-1992*, p. 66. Antioch, Tenn.: Executive Office of the National Association of Free Will Baptists, [1992].

861.   ———. "Abortion." In *Reports: Temperance Committee, Resolutions Committee, 1935-1992*, p. 79. Antioch, Tenn.: Executive Office of the National Association of Free Will Baptists, [1992].

862.   ———. "Abortion." In *Reports: Temperance Committee, Resolutions Committee, 1935-1992*, p. 104. Antioch, Tenn.: Executive Office of the National Association of Free Will Baptists, [1992].

863.   Orthodox Church in America. "On the Sanctity of Life: Ninth All-American Council of the Orthodox Church in America." In *Abortion: A Reader*, edited by Lloyd Steffen, 164-165. Cleveland, Ohio: The Pilgrim Press, 1996.

864.   Orthodox Presbyterian Church. "Report of the Committee to Study the Matter of Abortion." *Minutes of the General Assembly* 38th (1971): 135-156.

865.   ———. "Statement on Abortion." *Minutes of the General Assembly* 39th (1972): 17-18.

866.   Presbyterian Church in America. "Report of the Ad Interim Committee on Abortion." *Minutes of the General Assembly* 6th (1978): 270-285.

867.   ———. "Report of the Committee of Commissioners on Bills and Overtures." *Minutes of the General Assembly* 7th (1979): Sect. 7-37, III-3 (p. 97-98).

868.   ———. "Overture 12." *Minutes of the General Assembly* 8th (1980): 97-98

869.   ———. "Personal Resolution 3: Humble Petition Concerning Partial Birth Abortion." *Minutes of the General Assembly* 24th (1996): 315.

870.   Reformed Presbyterian Church, Evangelical Synod. "Abortion: The Disruption of Continuity." Report of the Study Committee on Abortion. *Minutes of the General Synod* 153rd (1975): 98-108.

871.   ———. "Resolution on Abortion." *Minutes of the General Synod* 156th (1978): 200.

872.   Reformed Presbyterian Church of North America. "Report of the Committee to Handle Paper 81-8." A letter to a subcommittee of the U.S. Sanate Judiciary Committee, advocating passage of a human life amendment. *Minutes of the Synod* 152nd (1981): 116-117.

873.   ———. "Resolution concerning Abortion." *Minutes of the Synod* 154th (1983): 146.

874.   ———. "Resolution concerning Abortion." *Minutes of the Synod* 156th (1985): 83.

875.   ———. "Resolution on Abortion." *Minutes of the Synod* 153rd (1982): 121-122

876. ————. "Resolution regarding Abortion." *Minutes of the Synod* 149th (1978): 104-105.

877. ————. "Special Resolution on Abortion from the St. Lawrence Presbytery." *Minutes of the Synod* 157th (1986): 24-26.

878. Seventh Day Baptist General Conference. "Resolution on Abortion." *Year Book Business Minutes* (1990): A46.

879. Southern Baptist Convention. "Recommendation on Fetal Tissue Experimentation." *Annual of the Southern Baptist Convention* (1992): 92-93.

880. ————. "Resolution on Abortion." *Annual of the Southern Baptist Convention* (1971): 72

881. ————. "Resolution on Abortion and Sanctity of Human Life." *Annual of the Southern Baptist Convention* (1974): 76

882. ————. "Resolution on Abortion." *Annual of the Southern Baptist Convention* (1976): 57-58.

883. ————. "Resolution on Abortion." *Annual of the Southern Baptist Convention* (1977): 53

884. ————. "Resolution on Abortion." *Annual of the Southern Baptist Convention* (1979): 50-51.

885. ————. "Resolution on Abortion." *Annual of the Southern Baptist Convention* (1980): 48-49.

886. ————. "Resolution on Abortion." *Annual of the Southern Baptist Convention* (1984): 66.

887. ————. "Resolution on Abortion." *Annual of the Southern Baptist Convention* (1987): 65-66.

888. ————. "Resolution on Abortion and Infanticide." *Annual of the Southern Baptist Convention* (1982): 65.

889. ————. "Resolution on Encouraging Laws Regulating Abortion." *Annual of the Southern Baptist Convention* (1989): 53-54.

890. ————. "Resolution on Human Fetal Tissue Trafficking." *Annual of the Southern Baptist Convention* (2000): 80-81.

891.   ———. "Resolution on Pro-Life Activities of SBC Agencies." *Annual of the Southern Baptist Convention* (1988): 72-73.

892.   ———. "Resolution on RU-486, the French Abortion Pill." *Annual of the Southern Baptist Convention* (1994): 101-102.

893.   ———. "Resolution on Sanctity of Human Life." *Annual of the Southern Baptist Convention* (1991): 74.

894.   ———. "Resolution on Support of the Danforth Amendment." *Annual of the Southern Baptist Convention* (1987): 66.

895.   ———. "Resolution on the Freedom of Choice Act, Hyde Amendment and Other Abortion Policies." *Annual of the Southern Baptist Convention* (1993): 99-100.

896.   ———. "Resolution on the Partial-Birth Abortion Ban." *Annual of the Southern Baptist Convention* (1996): 86-87.

897.   ———. "Resolution Requesting All Political Parties to Include a Pro-Life Platform." *Annual of the Southern Baptist Convention* (1996): 91.

898.   WELS Lutherans for Life. *Examining Life Issues: Biblical Principles that Guide Us.* Brochure. Milwaukee: WELS Lutherans for Life, 1998.

899.   ———. *Position Statement on Abortion.* Milwaukee: WELS Lutherans for Life, n.d.

900.   Wisconsin Evangelical Lutheran Synod. "Resolution on Abortion." In *Doctrinal Statements of the WELS.* Prepared by the Commission on Inter-Church Relations of the Wisconsin Evangelical Lutheran Synod, 1997, 53-56. Milwaukee: Northwestern Publishing House, [1997].

7 ABORTION IN MORAL AND PHILOSOPHICAL THOUGHT

GENERAL DISCUSSIONS

901.   Abernathy, Virginia. "Children, Personhood, and a Pluralistic Society." In *Abortion: Understanding Differences,* edited by Sidney Callahan and Daniel Callahan, 117-135. New York: Plenum Press, 1984.

Argues that our attitudes toward children and child-rearing validate a pluralist position toward abortion.

902.   Agich, George J. "Science, Policy, and the Fetus: Comments on Walters and Biggers." In *Abortion and the Status of the Fetus,* edited by William B. Bondeson, H. Tristram Engelhardt, Jr., Stuart F. Spicker, and Daniel H. Winship, 55-66. Dordrecht: D. Reidel Pub. Co., 1983.

Presents positive and negative comments on articles by Leroy Walters (see citation #), and John D. Biggers (see citation #).

903.   Alcorn, Randy. *Pro Life Answers to Pro Choice Arguments.* Portland, Ore.: Multnomah, 1992

Takes 39 pro-choice arguments normally given for allowing abortion, and answers them from a pro-life perspective.

904.   Anderson, Susan Leigh. "Criticisms of Liberal/Feminist Views on Abortion." *Public Affairs Quarterly* 1, no. 2 (1987): 83-96.

A critique of the various liberal/feminist arguments usually given in favor of abortion on demand.

905.   Armstrong, Robert. "The Right to Life." *Journal of Social Philosophy* 8,
          no. 1 (1977): 13-19.

          Examines what is meant by a "right to life." He maintains that fetuses
          have a right to life only when they possess a real or serious potentiality.

906.   Atkinson, Gary M. "The Church's Condemnation of Procured Abortion:
          A Philosophical Defense." In *Abortion: A New Generation of Catholic
          Responses,* edited by Stephen J. Heaney, 101-119. Braintree, Mass.: Pope
          John Center, 1992.

          The author presents a philosophical defense of the Catholic Church's
          position against abortion. His main thesis is that the right to life is
          possessed by all members of the human species.

907.   ———. "The Morality of Abortion." *IPQ, International Philosophical
          Quarterly* 14 (1974): 347-362.

          The author claims that the arguments commonly given in support of
          abortion either fail to meet the conditions of good reason, or else also
          serve to justify infanticide and involuntary euthanasia. He claims that
          nothing but specious and arbitrary distinctions can be drawn between
          abortion, infanticide, and euthanasia as moral issues.

908.   Baird, Robert M., and Stuart E. Rosenbaum, eds. *The Ethics of Abortion:
          Pro-Life vs. Pro-Choice.* Rev. ed. Contemporary Issues. Buffalo:
          Prometheus, 1993.

          A collection of articles on the morality of abortion, from all points of
          view.

909.   Bardon, Adrian. "Abortion, Property Rights, and the Welfare State."
          Public Affairs Quarterly 12 (1998): 369-381.

          Claims that liberals who favor abortion rights should be careful about
          accepting Judith Thomson's argument (see citation # 1082) uncritically.
          Thomson's natural rights view, the author says, is inconsistent with a
          common argument in favor of the welfare state. The author also casts
          doubt on the possibility of there being any consistent natural rights
          position which supports both abortion and welfare.

910.   Barry, Rev. Robert P., O.P. "Thomson and Abortion." In *Abortion: A
          New Generation of Catholic Responses,* edited by Stephen J. Heaney, 163-
          176. Braintree, Mass.: Pope John Center, 1992.

A critique of Thomson's article, "A Defense of Abortion." (see citation # 1082).

911.   Batchelor, Edward, ed. *Abortion: The Moral Issues.* New York: Pilgrim Press, 1982.

A collection of articles by leading religious ethicists which survey the present debate over abortion.

912.   Beckwith, Francis J. "Abortion and Public Policy: A Response to Some Arguments." *Journal of the Evangelical Theological Society* 32 (1989): 503-518.

Presents a pro-life response to the most popular arguments in favor of abortion rights.

913.   ———. "Answering the Arguments for Abortion Rights," parts 1-4. *Christian Research Journal,* Fall 1990, 20-26; Winter 1991, 27-32; Spring 1991, 8-13, 34; Summer 1991, 28-33.

Presents pro-life answers to many popular arguments for abortion rights.

914.   ———. *Politically Correct Death: Answering the Arguments for Abortion Rights.* Grand Rapids, Mich.: Baker Books, 1993.

Begins with an introduction to moral reasoning, then answers many arguments commonly given in favor of abortion, by showing that many of them violate at least one of the rules of moral reasoning. In particular, he shows that many of them begin by assuming what they want to prove. The author closes by making a positive argument for a pro-life position.

915.   Beckwith, Francis J. and Norman L. Geisler. *Matters of Life and Death: Calm Answers to Tough Questions About Abortion and Euthanasia.* Grand Rapids: Baker Book House, 1991.

The authors present pro-life answers to various medical, legal, moral, and social questions on abortion, infanticide and euthanasia.

916.   Belshaw, Christopher. "Abortion, Value and the Sanctity of Life." *Bioethics* 11 (1997): 130-150.

A critique of Ronald Dworkin's book, *Life's Dominion* (see citation # 955). The article criticizes Dworkin's contentions that (1) both sides of the abortion debate agree that life is sacred and (2) the issue of personhood is not central to the debate.

917.   Benson, Iain T. "What's Wrong with 'Choice.'" In *A Time to Choose Life: Women, Abortion and Human Rights,* edited by Ian Gentles, 24-46. Toronto: Stoddart, 1990.

A critique of several pro-choice arguments, as well as the terminology they use, such as "freedom of choice," "potential life," and "The woman's right to control her own body."

918.   Bentley, G. B. "A Moral–Theological Approach." In *Abortion and the Sanctity of Human Life,* edited by J. H. Channer, 54-73. Exeter, Eng.: Paternoster Press, 1985.

After a discussion of some basic ethical principles, the author presents an argument that abortion is morally and ethically wrong.

919.   Blumenfeld, Jean Beer. "Abortion and the Human Brain." *Philosophical Studies* 32 (1977): 251-268.

The author first addresses the issue of whether intentionally killing an innocent human being is always morally wrong. He concludes that at least some form of that statement is valid. He then addresses the issue of whether intentionally killing a zygote, embryo, or fetus is always morally wrong, and concludes that it is not.

920.   Bok, Sissela. "Ethical Problems of Abortion." *Hastings Center Studies* 2, no. 1 (1974): 33-52

The author examines several ethical issues such as: (1) Is abortion always killing, or can it sometimes be seen as the withdrawal of bodily support? (2) Is the fetus a human being, and at what point does it achieve that status? (3) What are our reasons for protecting life? She then concludes that abortion in the early stages should be allowed on demand. After viability, however, abortion should be allowed only for very substantial reasons.

921.   ———. "Who Shall Count as a Human Being? A Treacherous Question in the Abortion Discussion." In *Abortion: Pro and Con,* edited by Robert L. Perkins, 91-105. Cambridge, Mass.: Schenkman Pub. Co., 1974.

The author claims that efforts to decide when human life begins are deceptive at best, and do not help us solve the abortion debate. She says that we should rather decide what are the common principles we have for the protection of life; why do we consider life to be sacred? She lists several reasons for protecting life, and claims that these reasons do not apply to a fetus in the early stages of pregnancy.

922.   Bolton, Martha Brandt. "Responsible Women and Abortion Decisions."
         In *Having Children: Philosophical and Legal Reflections on Parenthood,*
         edited by Onora O'Neill and William Ruddick, 40-51. New York: Oxford
         Univ. Press, 1979.

         The author argues against two positions: 1. The position that in general,
         perhaps with a few exceptions, abortion is morally wrong. 2. The position
         that abortion has no moral significance. That it is a personal and private
         decision with no moral consequences.

923.   Boonin-Vail, David. "Death Comes for the Violinist: On Two Objections
         to Thomson's 'Defense of Abortion.'" *Social Theory and Practice* 22
         (1997): 329-364.

         Defends Thomson's article "A Defense of Abortion," (see citation # 1082)
         by criticizing two common objections to her thesis.

924.   ———. "A Defense of 'A Defense of Abortion': On the Responsibility
         Objection to Thomson's Argument." *Ethics* 106 (1997): 286-313.

         Many people have criticized Judith Jarvis Thomson's contention (see
         citation # 1082) that even if the fetus is a person with a right to life, the
         woman can still abort it, because she has not voluntarily accepted the
         obligation of the pregnancy. They say that, at least in non-rape cases, the
         woman, by voluntarily having sexual intercourse, has given her consent
         to the pregnancy. The author of this article refutes that critique, thus
         arguing in favor of Thomson's thesis.

925.   Borchert, Donald M., and J. Phillip Jones. "Abortion: Morally Right or
         Wrong?" *Listening* 22 (1987): 22-35.

         The authors suggest a strategy for coming to a moral decision about
         abortion. They identify some of the morally relevant issues that must be
         considered.

926.   Bork, Robert H. "Inconvenient Lives." *First Things,* December 1996, 9-
         13.

         The author presents his own reasons for rejecting abortion. He also shows
         that statistically, most abortions are done for reasons of convenience,
         rather than for medical reasons.

927.   Brandt, R. B. "The Morality of Abortion." In *Abortion: Pro and Con,*
         edited by Robert L. Perkins, 151-169. Cambridge, Mass.: Schenkman
         Pub. Co., 1974.

The author asks the question whether it is *prima facie* morally wrong to perform an abortion, that is, is there anything morally objectionable to abortion for no other reason than the mother wants it. He concludes that there is no such *prima facie* obligation not to cause an abortion. This paper is a revision of one of the same title published in *The Monist* 56 (1972): 504-526.

928.   Bringsjord, Selmer. *Abortion: A Dialogue.* Indianapolis: Hackett Publishing, 1997.

Using the form of a dialog among a pro-life person, a pro-choice person, and an agnostic on the issue, the author presents the issues involved in the abortion controversy.

929.   Brody, Baruch A. *Abortion and the Sanctity of Human Life: A Philosophical View.* Cambridge, Mass.: MIT Press, 1975.

Presents a philosophical argument that abortion, except to save the life of the mother, is morally wrong.

930.   ———. "Thomson on Abortion." *Philosophy and Public Affairs* 1 (1972): 335-340.

Criticizes the article by Judith Jarvis Thomson (see citation # 1082) on the basis that she does not take into account the distinction between our duty to save a life, and our duty not to take that life.

931.   Cahill, Lisa Sowle. "Abortion." In *The Westminster Dictionary of Christian Ethics,* edited by James F. Childress and John Macquarrie, 1-5. Philadelphia: The Westminster Press, 1986.

A review of the teaching on abortion from the vantage point of Christian ethics and Christian theology.

932.   Callahan, Daniel. *Abortion: Law, Choice and Morality.* New York: Macmillan Pub. Co., 1970.

States that the issue surrounding abortion is a complex one, allowing no easy answers. He criticizes both the extreme pro-life view that the preservation of all life, even potential life, is the single overriding criterion, as well as the extreme pro-choice view that the only value at stake is the woman's right to an abortion if she wants one. He argues for a middle ground, which states that abortion is neither always right, nor always wrong, nor are there any automatic grounds either for abortion or against abortion.

933.　　──────. "Abortion: Some Ethical Issues." In *Abortion, Medicine, and the Law*, 4th ed., completely revised, edited by J. Douglas Butler and David F. Walbert, 694-702. New York: Facts on File, 1992.

The author takes nine arguments advanced, by both pro-life and pro-choice leaders, and shows them to be weak arguments, and closes with some conclusions of his own.

934.　　──────. "Abortion: Thinking and Experiencing." *Christianity and Crisis* 32 (1973): 295-298.

Describes abortion as a choice that is often a necessary choice, which in the best of all possible worlds would not have to be made, but which can be made when it must be.

935.　　Callahan, Joan C. "Ensuring a Stillborn: The Ethics of Lethal Injection in Late Abortion." In *Reproduction, Ethics, and the Law: Feminist Perspectives*, edited by Joan C. Callahan, 266-283. Bloomington, Ind.: Indiana Univ. Press, 1995.

Argues in favor of using a lethal injection to insure the death of a late term, healthy fetus. She claims that a late-term abortion is not morally problematic.

936.　　Callahan, Sidney. "Value Choices in Abortion." In *Abortion: Understanding Differences*, edited by Sidney Callahan and Daniel Callahan, 285-301. New York: Plenum Press, 1984.

The author demonstrates that abortion remains a troubling and intractable issue because it is closely linked with our personal world-views. She presents the various values and world-views that undergird the different positions in the abortion debate.

937.　　Callahan, Sidney, and Daniel Callahan, eds. *Abortion: Understanding Differences*. New York: Plenum Press, 1984.

A collection of essays, both for and against abortion. Each essay is followed with a response by a proponent of the opposite position.

938.　　Cannold, Leslie. *The Abortion Myth: Feminism, Morality, and the Hard Choices Women Make*. Hanover, N.H.: The University Press of New England, 2000.

Using interviews conducted with many women, both pro-choice and pro-life, the author shows that all women view abortion as a moral question, regardless of their particular position on it, and that women do have to make hard choices, regardless of whether they choose to abort or not.

939.   Carrier, L. S. "Abortion and the Right to Life." *Social Theory and Practice* 3 (1975): 381-401.

The author sets out to prove the assertion that there is some nonarbitrary point between conception and birth, before which it is morally permissible to abort a fetus, and after which point, it is no longer morally permissible.

940.   Claire, Miriam. *The Abortion Dilemma: Personal Views on a Public Issue.* New York: Plenum Press, 1995.

In non-technical language, and through many personal interviews, the author expresses her view that abortion is an intensely personal decision, and that it can be a moral choice. She endeavors to show that it is an extremely complex issue that allows no easy solution. She believes that women may make, and should be allowed to make, a decision to abort if they feel that it is in their best interest.

941.   Clark, Lorenne M. G. "Reply to Professor Sumner." *Canadian Journal of Philosophy* 4 (1974): 183-190.

While criticizing some of Sumner's points in his article, "Toward a Credible View of Abortion" (see citation # 1079) the author agrees with many of his conclusions.

942.   Cohen, Howard. "Abortion and the Quality of Life." In *Feminism and Philosophy,* edited by Mary Vetterling-Braggin, Frederick A. Elliston, and Jane English, 429-440. Totowa, N.J.: Littlefield, Adams, 1977.

Comments that most philosophical arguments about abortion do not address the quality of life concerns of women who are faced with the decision whether or not to bring a fetus to term. The author suggests that quality of life issues should be given equal weight, and he argues that many times they are sufficient by themselves to justify an abortion.

943.   Conley, John J., S.J. "Distortions of the Will." In *Life and Learning: Proceedings of the Third University Faculty for Life Conference,* edited by Joseph W. Koterski, S.J., 105-114. Washington, D.C.: University Faculty for Life, 1993.

The author claims that the reduction of the abortion question to a matter of sovereign choice involves a distortion of what the will really is. The will, he claims, is not autonomous, but is shaped by evidence regarding the act of abortion, especially that act's status as a sub-set of unjustified homicide.

944.   Conn, Christopher Hughes. "Female Genital Mutilation and the Moral Status of Abortion." *Public Affairs Quarterly* 15 (2001): 1-15.

Many girls and women in Africa, Asia, and the Middle East have been forced to go through various forms of female genital mutilation. He gives reasons for saying that such a practice is immoral. He then shows that abortion is wrong for the very same reasons that female genital mutilation is wrong, and that abortion is significantly more wrong.

945.   Connell, Richard J. "The Abortifacient RU 486." In *Abortion: A New Generation of Catholic Responses*, edited by Stephen J. Heaney, 133-149. Braintree, Mass.: Pope John Center, 1992.

The author presents a philosophical argument which states that RU 486 violates a fundamental moral principle that is accepted by the medical profession in its treatment of disease, a principle that is also accepted by those who seek to preserve the natural environment from pollutants. Thus, he claims, that to be consistent, environmentalists must also be anti-abortion.

946.   Crosby, John F. "Max Scheler's Principle of Moral Solidarity and its Implications for the Pro-Life Movement." In *Life and Learning V: Proceedings of the Fifth University Faculty for Life Conference, June 1995, at Marquette University*, edited by Joseph W. Koterski, S.J., 384-397. Washington, D.C.: University Faculty for Life, 1996.

Outlines the philosophy of Max Scheler (1874-1928) which, using World War I as an example, stated that in one sense of the word, everyone bore some guilt for the war, in that they helped create the moral milieu in which the war was possible in the first place. The author then compares that to the abortion controversy today, and says that even pro-life advocates (whom he supports), bear some responsibility for the moral and cultural milieu which makes abortion possible.

947.   Crum, Gary, and Thelma McCormack. *Abortion: Pro-Choice or Pro-Life?* The American University Press Public Policy Series. Washington, D.C.: The American University Press, 1992.

Two authors, active in the abortion controversy, debate the issue. Crum presents the argument that abortion at any time in the life of the fetus, and under any circumstances, is abhorrent. McCormack presents the view that abortion should be allowed, except in cases where the pregnancy has extended past the second trimester, or in cases where the only motivation for the abortion is sex selection.

948.   Cudd, Ann E. "Sensationalized Abortion: A Reply to Marquis' 'Why Abortion is Immoral.'" *Journal of Philosophy* 86 (1990): 262-264.

A critique of the article "Why is Abortion Immoral," by Marquis (see citation # 1011) by rebutting Marquis' initial assumption that the morality of abortion stands or falls on the question of the moral status of the fetus.

949.   Davis, Michael. "Foetuses, Famous Violinists, and the Right to Continued Aid." *Philosophical Quarterly* 32 (1983): 259-278.

A critique of Judith Jarvis Thompson's article, "A Defense of Abortion." (see citation # 1082). In particular, he argues that (1) the analogy between violinist and fetus does not establish the moral permissibility of abortion to end a pregnancy due to rape, and (2) that there is probably no way to save Thomson's defense without first confronting the metaphysics of personhood.

950.   Degnan, Daniel A. "Laws, Morals, and Abortion." *Commonweal* 100 (1974): 305-308.

The author points out the distinction between law and morality, and shows that calls for a constitutional amendment to ban abortion will fail. At the same time, however, he calls for a more moderate approach, which will recognize abortion to be a grave moral issue, but will allow abortions in the early months and for the life of the mother, rape, incest, and severe fetal deformity.

951.   DeMarco, Donald. "Abortion: Fear of the Actual and Preference for the Possible." In *New Perspectives on Human Abortion,* edited by Thomas W. Hilgers, Dennis J. Horan, and David Mall, 440-449. Frederick, Md.: Aletheia Books, University Publications of America, 1981.

The author argues that the pro-abortion position is based on a view which gives greater weight and credence to that which is *possible* than it does to the *actual.* He illustrates this in several ways, and claims that it is precisely this kind of thinking which will bring an end to the pro-abortion position.

952.   ———. "Abortion: Legal and Philosophical Considerations." *American Ecclesiastical Review* 168 (1974): 251-267.

Examines the philosophical roots of the pro-abortion position.

953.   Devine, Philip E. "'Conservative' Views of Abortion." In *New Essays on Abortion and Bioethics,* edited by Rem B. Edwards, 183-202. Greenwich, Conn.: JAI Press, 1997.

The author presents, and then defends what he terms the "Conservative" view on abortion – that is, that abortion, except to save the life of the mother, is wrong.

954.   Dombrowski, Daniel A. "Asymmetrical Relations, Identity, and Abortion." *Journal of Applied Philosophy* 9 (1992): 161-170.

Using the theory of asymmetrical relations, i.e., that one is internally related to one's past, yet externally related to the future, the author presents an argument that abortion in the early stages is morally permissible.

955.   Dworkin, Ronald. *Life's Dominion: An Argument about Abortion, Euthanasia, and Individual Freedom.* New York: Alfred A. Knopf, 1993.

A review of the various positions taken on abortion, from the conservative to the liberal, and claims that the difference between them is due, not to different views on the personhood of the fetus, but rather to different ways of viewing the intrinsic value, or sanctity, of human life.

956.   Edwards, Rem B., ed. *New Essays on Abortion and Bioethics.* Advances in Bioethics, vol. 2, 1997. Greenwich, Conn.: JAI Press, 1997.

A collection of essays discussing abortion from the bioethical point of view. The views expressed range from the liberal to the conservative.

957.   Elshtain, Jean Bethke. "Reflections on Abortion, Values, and the Family." In *Abortion: Understanding Differences,* edited by Sidney Callahan and Daniel Callahan, 47-72. New York: Plenum Press, 1984.

The author demonstrates that our positions on abortion are shaped by our views on human community and the nature and good of that community. She then offers some reflections on the dangers she believes we will face if our society remains tied to a utilitarian ethic that absolutizes choice at the expense of obligation.

958.   Engelhardt, H. Tristram, Jr. "Viability and the Use of the Fetus." In *Abortion and the Status of the Fetus,* edited by William B. Bondeson, H. Tristram Engelhardt, Jr., Stuart F. Spicker, and Daniel H. Winship, 183-208. Dordrecht: D. Reidel Pub. Co., 1983.

Examines the extent to which the stage of viability can have moral implications for the decision on abortion or fetal research. Also suggests some public policy implications of this analysis.

959.   Feezell, Randolph M. "Potentiality, Death, and Abortion." *Southern Journal of Philosophy* 25 (1987): 39-48.

Commenting that he finds both the extreme conservative and the extreme liberal views on abortion implausible, the author seeks to find a common sense, moderate position. The results of his investigation, he says, give some moral direction, without the precision found in the extreme positions.

960.   Feinberg, Joel, ed. *The Problem of Abortion*. Basic Problems in Philosophy Series. Belmont, Calif.: Wadsworth Pub. Co., 1973.

Essays on abortion, from various perspectives.

961.   ———, ed. *The Problem of Abortion*. 2nd. ed. Belmont, Calif.: Wadsworth Pub. Co., 1984.

Essays on abortion, from various perspectives.

962.   Feinberg, Paul D. "The Morality of Abortion." In *Thou Shalt not Kill: The Christian Case against Abortion*, edited by Richard L. Ganz, 127-149. New Rochelle, N.Y.: Arlington House, 1978.

The author presents ethical arguments against abortion.

963.   Finnis, John. "The Rights and Wrongs of Abortion: A Reply to Judith Thomson." *Philosophy and Public Affairs* 2 (1973): 117-145.

A critique of the article by Judith Jarvis Thomson (see citation 1082) on the grounds that her defense of abortion on the basis of "rights" needlessly complicates and confuses the issue.

964.   Fletcher, David B., and Albert J. Smith. "Abortion, Bioethics, and the Evangelical." In *Abortion: A Christian Understanding and Response*, edited by James K. Hoffmeier, 115-126. Grand Rapids, Mich.: Baker Book House, 1987.

A review of the discipline of bioethics, of five different ethical positions on abortion, the issues involved in reaching an ethical judgement on abortion, and how evangelical Christians relate to the bioethical debate about abortion.

965.   Foot, Philippa. "Killing and Letting Die." In *Abortion: Moral and Legal Perspectives*, edited by Jay L. Garfield and Patricia Hennessey, 177-185. Amherst, Mass.: Univ. of Massachusetts Press, 1984.

The author presents an argument for saying that there is a moral difference between killing someone, and letting him die. She then examines the implications of that thesis on the issue of abortion.

966.   Francke, Linda Bird. *The Ambivalence of Abortion.* New York: Random House, 1978.

The author presents both her own story, as well as the stories of many other women who chose to have abortions. She examines their reasons for doing so, as well as their feelings after the abortion.

967.   Frohock, Fred M. *Abortion: A Case Study in Law and Morals.* Contributions in Political Science, no. 102. Westport, Conn.: Greenwood Press, 1983.

The author explains the intricate structure of beliefs on both sides of the abortion debate, and combines this theoretical discussion with interviews from activists on both sides of the debate. He discusses the legal, political, and moral aspects of abortion, and presents some possible resolutions to the controversy.

968.   Frost, Norman, David Chudwin, and Daniel I. Wikler. "The Limited Moral Significance of Fetal Viability." *Hastings Center Report* 10, no. 6 (1980): 10-13

Fetal viability has been used as a criterion for the regulating of abortion and for the care of newborns. The authors survey past definitions of viability, and propose their own more comprehensive definition. In the process, they question the validity of using viability as a criterion for abortion, though they admit it does have some usefulness for the care of newborns.

969.   Gahringer, Robert E. "Observations on the Categorical Proscription of Abortion." In *Abortion: Pro and Con*, edited by Robert L. Perkins, 53-67. Cambridge, Mass.: Schenkman Pub. Co., 1974.

The author examines the arguments usually given for prohibiting abortion in all cases, and finds them weak. He argues for a policy of allowing abortions in cases where the child is unwanted.

970.   Gensler, Harry J. "A Kantian Argument against Abortion." *Philosophical Studies* 49 (1986): 83-98.

The author criticizes some anti-abortion and some pro-abortion arguments, and then appeals for a Kantian consistency (a form of the Golden Rule). He argues that if we take this consistent approach, and phrase the question correctly, we will come to an anti-abortion position.

971.   Gillespie, Norman C. "Abortion and Human Rights." *Ethics* 86 (1977): 237-243.

Argues against the notion that (a) there is a point between conception and adulthood that defines when a person begins and (b) that the morality of abortion depends on finding that point. He claims that there are morally significant differences between early and late abortions, but that this does not mean that there is some demarcation line which determines whether an abortion is permissible or not.

972.   Gordon, Doris. "Abortion and Rights: Applying Libertarian Principles Correctly." *Studies in Prolife Feminism* 1 (1995): 121-140.

Most Libertarians, on the grounds that a woman has the right to control her own body, support legalized abortion. The author contends, however, that the right to control one's body prohibits the choice to kill or to abandon one's child. Since abortion kills, and therefore violates the rights of the unborn child, the author contends that Libertarians, of all people, should not want the state to defend and protect it.

973.   Grisez, Germain. *Abortion: The Myths, the Realities, and the Arguments.* New York: Corpus Books, 1970.

After presenting facts developed from the fields of medicine, sociology, religion, and law, the author presents an ethical argument against abortion based on these facts, and also presents a proposal for a sound public policy.

974.   Hanegraaff, Hank. "Annihilating Abortion Arguments." *Christian Research Journal,* Winter 1997, 28-34.

Presents pro-life answers to common arguments in favor of abortion.

975.   Hare, R. M. "Abortion and the Golden Rule." *Philosophy and Public Affairs* 4 (1975): 201-222.

Using the Christian Golden Rule, the author argues that by this principle, abortion is morally wrong unless sufficient countervailing reasons can be found. He says also, however, that sufficient countervailing reasons are easy to find.

976.   Hauerwas, Stanley. "Abortion: The Agent's Perspective." *Amerian Ecclesiastical Review* 167 (1973): 102-120.

First examines two questions: (1) When does life begin? and (2) When can life be taken legitimately? His response to these questions leads him to conclude that abortion should not be allowed, except in a very limited number of cases. He then asks a third question: What does the woman understand to be happening in an abortion? He concludes that abortion is not the solution to societal problems.

977.   Heaney, Stephen J., ed. *Abortion: A New Generation of Catholic Responses.* Braintree, Mass.: Pope John Center, 1992.

A collection of articles in which the individual authors present their own views of abortion, but all of them in line with general Catholic teaching on abortion.

978.   Herbenick, Raymond M. "Natural Fetal Dependency States and Fetal Dependency Principles." In *The Ethics of Having Children,* edited by Lawrence P. Schrenk, 173-181. Washington, D.C.: National Office of the American Catholic Philosophical Society, 1990.

The author uses the concept of fetal dependency to argue that elective abortion amounts to the legal and moral abandonment of the fetus.

979.   ———. "Remarks on Abortion, Abandonment, and Adoption Opportunities." *Philosophy and Public Affairs* 5 (1975): 98-104.

The author argues that parents who decide to have an elective abortion can be seen as stating their intent to abandon support of the child, and this fact should be enough for the state to intervene and to eitherprovide for the adoption of the fetus, or to place the child, *in utero,* as a ward of the state.

980.   Hershenov, David B. "The Problem of Potentiality." *Public Affairs Quarterly* 13 (1999): 255-271.

The author claims that granting rights to fetuses because they are potential persons leads to condemning birth control, while devaluing potential persons leads to allowing late term abortions and infanticide. This article tries to navigate between these two. The author claims that there is no cutoff point for permissible abortions which is morally significant, and that therefore we should allow women a grace period of five or six months during which they can ponder whether or not to have an abortion.

981.   Humber, James M. "Abortion: The Avoidable Moral Dilemma." *Journal of Value Inquiry* 9 (1975): 282-302.

The author makes three assertions: (1) that abortion must always be the taking of a human life, (2) that the arguments of those who favor abortion are all so poor that they should not be accepted at face value, but rather should be seen as after the fact rationalizations for beliefs held to be true on other grounds, and (3) the true basis of the moral position of those who favor abortion is such that the view must be rejected out of hand. On the basis of these conclusions, the author then provides some ideas for escaping the dilemma of abortion.

982.   ———. "The Case against Abortion." *The Thomist* 39 (1975): 65-84.

A defense of the thesis that abortion is morally wrong.

983.   Hunt, G. "Abortion: Why Bioethics Can Have No Answer - A Personal Perspective." *Nursing Ethics* 6 (Jan. 1999): 47-57.

Examines whether it is possible, by a strictly rational approach, to solve the abortion debate, by establishing solid grounds for our beliefs once and for all. The author reaches the conclusion that there can be no such philosophically grounded method, and therefore no facts to which everyone must agree. This does not mean that it is impossible for people to reach agreement. It simply means that there is no incontrovertibly rational means by which they must do so.

984.   Hursthouse, Rosalind. *Beginning Lives.* Oxford, Eng.: Basil Blackwell in association with the Open University, 1987

Presents the various arguments made by both those for and those against abortion and examines each.

985.   ———. "Virtue Theory and Abortion." *Philosophy and Public Affairs* 20 (1991): 223-246.

The author outlines, and defends against several criticisms, the virtue theory of ethics, and then discusses the issue of abortion from the point of view of virtue ethics.

986.   Jaggar, Alison. "Abortion and a Woman's Right to Decide." In *Philosophy and Sex,* edited by Robert Baker and Frederick Elliston, 324-337. Buffalo: Prometheus Books, 1975.

The author concerns herself not with the question of whether abortion is morally right or wrong, but rather with the question, given a particular pregnancy, who should decide whether or not it ought to be terminated. She concludes that each woman should have the sole legal right to decide on her own whether or not to have an abortion.

987.   John, Helen J. "Reflections on Autonomy and Abortion." *Journal of Social Philosophy* 17, no. 1 (1986): 3-10.

Using Judith Jarvis Thomson and John T. Noonan as primary examples of the pro-choice and pro-life views respectively, the author surveys the landscape of moral views on abortion, particularly as they relate to autonomy.

988.   Kamm, F. M. *Creation and Abortion: A Study in Moral and Legal Philosophy.* New York: Oxford University Press, 1992.

Begins, for the sake of argument, with the assumption that the fetus is a person, and then examines in what circumstances, and under what conditions, if any, it might be considered morally permissible to have an abortion.

989.   Kenyon, Edwin. "Values, Morals and Religion." Chap. 2 in *The Dilemma of Abortion.* London: Faber and Faber, 1986.

Discusses the different moral concepts employed by those who have evaluated the morality of abortion. Also discusses the views on abortion taken by different religious groups, Christian and non-Christian alike.

990.   Kohl, Marvin. *The Morality of Killing: Sanctity of Life, Abortion and Euthanasia.* London: Peter Owen, 1974.

Examines in what cases it might be moral to kill an innocent human life, and applies that to the issues of abortion and euthanasia.

991.   Kolbenschlag, Madonna. "Abortion and Moral Consensus: Beyond Solomon's Choice." *Christian Century* 102 (1985): 179-183.

Argues that the ethics surrounding both the pro-choice and the pro-life positions are mistaken. She calls for a third ethic which combines the best of both positions.

992.   Koterski, Joseph W., S.J., ed. *Life and Learning: Proceedings of the Third University Faculty for Life Conference.* Washington, D.C.: University Faculty for Life, 1993.

A collection of essays, delivered to an annual conference of pro-life university faculty members, on abortion and related topics.

993.   ———, ed. *Life and Learning IV: Proceedings of the Fourth University Faculty for Life Conference held at Fordham University June 1994.* Washington, D.C.: University Faculty for Life, 1995.

A collection of essays, delivered to an annual conference of pro-life university faculty members, on abortion and related topics.

994.   ———, ed. *Life and Learning V: Proceedings of the Fifth University Faculty for Life Conference, June 1995, at Marquette University.* Washington, D.C.: University Faculty for Life, 1996

A collection of essays, delivered to an annual conference of pro-life university faculty members, on abortion and related topics.

995.   ———, ed. *Life and Learning VI: Proceedings of the Sixth University Faculty for Life Conference, June 1996 at Geortetown University.* Washington, D.C.: University Faculty for Life, 1997.

A collection of essays, delivered to an annual conference of pro-life university faculty members, on abortion and related topics.

996.   ———, ed. *Life and Learning VII: Proceedings of the Seventh University Faculty for Life Conference, June 1997 at Loyola College.* Washington, D.C.: University Faculty for Life, 1998.

A collection of essays, delivered to an annual conference of pro-life university faculty members, on abortion and related topics.

997.   ———, ed. *Life and Learning VIII: Proceedings of the Eighth University Faculty for Life Conference, June 1998, at the University of Toronto.* Washington, D.C.: University Faculty for Life, 1999.

A collection of essays, delivered to an annual conference of pro-life university faculty members, on abortion and related topics.

998.   ———, ed. *Life and Learning IX: Proceedings of the Ninth University Faculty for Life Conference, June 1999 at Trinity International University, Deerfield, Ill.* Washington, D.C.: University Faculty for Life, 2000.

A collection of essays, delivered to an annual conference of pro-life university faculty members, on abortion and related topics.

999.   Kreeft, Peter. *The Unaborted Socrates: A Dramatic Debate on the Issues surrounding Abortion.* Downers Grove, Ill.: InterVarsity Press, 1983.

Using the form of several Platonic style dialogs among Socrates, an abortionist, an ethicist, and a psychologist, the author presents an argument against abortion.

1000. Kuhse, Helga, and Peter Singer. "Abortion and Contraception: The Moral Significance of Fertilization." In *The Beginning of Human Life*, edited by Fritz K. Beller and Robert F. Weir, 145-161. Dordrecht: Kluwer, 1994.

Argues against the traditional dichotomy between contraception and abortion, and concludes that, to be consistent, one cannot treat abortion as morally wrong, and contraception as morally permissible: either both are wrong or both are permissible. Their own conclusion is that the fetus does not have a "right to life," and therefore both contraception and abortion are morally permissible.

1001. Langerak, Edward A. "Abortion: Listening to the Middle." In *What is a Person?*, edited by Michael F. Goodman, 251-263. Clifton, N.J.: Humana Press, 1988.

Presents an argument for a moderate position on abortion that holds, first that there is something about the fetus itself that makes abortions morally problematic, and second that late term abortions are significantly more morally problematic than early abortions.

1002. Lawler, Rev. Ronald D., O.F.M. "Pro-Choice." In *Abortion: A New Generation of Catholic Responses*, edited by Stephen J. Heaney, 313-323. Braintree, Mass.: Pope John Center, 1992.

Presents an argument that (1) those who favor abortion are really arguing that each individual has the right to decide for himself if the fetus is a human being or not, and (2) to be pro-choice is really to be pro-abortion.

1003. Lee, Patrick. *Abortion and Unborn Human Life*. Washington, D.C.: The Catholic University of America Press, 1996.

Presents an argument that abortion, except perhaps to save the life of the mother, is morally wrong. Also presents answers to the arguments of those who favor abortion.

1004. Lockhart, Ted. "A Decision-Theoretic Reconstruction of *Roe v. Wade.*" *Public Affairs Quarterly* 5 (1991): 243-258.

Many times, especially in normative arguments, we are not entirely sure of the premises that are the underpinning of those arguments, as they often include moral values which are very controversial. So if our premises are uncertain, what happens to our conclusions? The author says that we may determine if a conclusion is valid only after we have taken into account the probabilities that the premises are true. He applies this to the Supreme-Court's *Roe v. Wade* decision, and shows that for certain plausible estimates of these probabilities, the exact opposite conclusion should have been reached.

1005.   Lombardi, Louis. "The Legal versus the Moral on Abortion." *Journal of Social Philosophy* 17, no. 1 (1986): 23-29.

Demonstrates the diversity of moral opinion on the abortion issue. He claims that there is no general solution to the abortion problem. In light of that, the author claims that legally, the only choice available is not to make abortion illegal.

1006.   Macklin, Ruth. "Abortion: Contemporary Ethical Perspectives." In *Encyclopedia of Bioethics.* Rev. ed., edited by Warren Thomas Reich. Vol. 1. New York: Macmillan, 1995.

A discussion of the ethical issues involved in the abortion controversy.

1007.   ———. "Ethics and Human Reproduction: International Perspectives." *Social Problems* 37 (1990): 38-50.

The author examines and applies three moral principles that she says form the basis for analyzing ethical issues regarding human reproduction.

1008.   Mahowald, Mary B. "Abortion and Equality." In *Abortion: Understanding Differences,* edited by Sidney Callahan and Daniel Callahan, 177-196. New York: Plenum Press, 1984.

Presents a position on the morality of abortion that falls somewhere between the extreme positions of total condemnation and total permissiveness.

1009.   Marquis, Don. "A Future Like Ours and the Concept of Person: A Reply to McInerney and Paske." In *The Abortion Controversy: 25 Years after Roe v. Wade: A Reader,* 2nd ed., edited by Louis P. Pojman and Francis J. Beckwith, 372-386. Belmont, Calif.: Wadsworth Pub. Co., 1998.

The author replies to two people who have criticized his initial article, "Why Abortion is Immoral." (see citation # 1011).

1010.   ———. "Reiman on Abortion." *Journal of Social Philosophy* 29, no. 1 (1998): 143-145.

A critique of an article by Jeffrey Reiman (see citation # 1050).

1011.   ———. "Why Abortion is Immoral." *Journal of Philosophy* 86 (1989): 183-202.

Argues that abortion, except in rare cases, is seriously immoral, and in the same category as killing an innocent adult human being. He does this on the basis that killing someone is wrong because it deprives him or her of his or her future. Abortion deprives a fetus of its future, and so is immoral.

1012.   Martin, Tracie. *Interests in Abortion: A New Perspective on Foetal Potential and the Abortion Debate.* Averbury Series in Philosophy. Aldershot, Eng.: Ashgate, 2000.

Presents a moderate view of abortion that places the beginning of personhood at 24 weeks gestation. Before that time, abortion is permissible.

1013.   Mathieu, Deborah. "Crime and Punishment: Abortion as Murder?" *Journal of Social Philosophy* 23, no. 2 (1992): 5-22.

Demonstrates that, to be consistent, those who hold to the full personhood of the fetus must also hold that abortion is murder, and so charge all those involved – the woman, people close to her (husband, lover, parents, etc), the abortionist, and nurses – with murder.

1014.   May, William E. "Abortion as Indicative of Personal and Social Identity." *The Jurist* 33 (1973): 199-217.

Commenting that our actions reveal something of who we are, the author portrays abortion as an evil. At the same time, however, he does not condemn women who with reluctance choose abortion, as it is possible that they are choosing it not because it is an act of feticide, but because for them it is something quite different.

1015.   McDonnell, Kathleen. *Not an Easy Choice: A Feminist Re-Examines Abortion.* Boston: South End Press, 1984.

A feminist examines her own views on abortion. Though pro-choice, she admits that the issues are complex, and not easy to answer.

1016.   McInerney, Peter K. Does a Fetus Already Have a Future-Like-Ours?" *Journal of Philosophy* 86 (1990): 264-268.

A critique of the article by Don Marquis "Why Abortion is Immoral." (see citation # 1011). He claims that, whereas Marquis has demonstrated that certain pro-choice arguments fail, he has not shown that a fetus has a future like ours, as the future of the fetus is only potentially so. He claims that the fetus is too weakly connected with its future to be deprived of it.

1017.   McLachlan, Hugh V. "Must We Accept Either the Conservative or the Liberal View on Abortion?" *Analysis* 37 (1977): 197-204.

          Claims that we do not need to adopt either the extreme liberal, or the extreme conservative view on abortion, because we can hold that the fetus is neither a human being nor a person without being committed to the view that abortions are never in need of justification.

1018.   Meehan, Mary. "More Trouble than They're Worth? Children and Abortion." In *Abortion: Understanding Differences,* edited by Sidney Callahan and Daniel Callahan, 145-170. New York: Plenum Press, 1984.

          On the basis of a child's right to life and the parents' obligations to the new child they have brought into existence, the author proposes how the law should deal with abortion. She then outlines the positive values of children, and answers widespread objections.

1019.   Meilaender, Gilbert. "Abortion: The Right to an Argument." *Hastings Center Report* 19, no. 6 (1989): 13-16.

          The author claims that our moral puzzles about abortion will not be resolved by resorting to compromise positions or by seeking some kind of middle ground. He says that the call for a middle ground is really just one substantive moral position among others, and not the voice of reason perched above the battle.

1020.   ———. "The Fetus as Parasite and Mushroom: Judith Jarvis Thomson's Defense of Abortion." *Linacre Quarterly* 46 (1979): 126-135.

          A critique of Judith Jarvis Thomson's article "A Defense of Abortion." (see citation # 1082).

1021.   Meyers, Christopher. "Maintaining The Violinist: A Mother's Obligations to the Fetus She Decides to Keep." *Journal of Social Philosophy* 23, no. 2 (1992): 52-64.

          The author considers this question: If a woman decides to carry her pregnancy to term, is she allowed to do things that would be harmful to the fetus, on the basis that it is "her body?" He answers this in the negative, but stops short of saying that such women should be forced to have an abortion.

1022.   Miller, Hal. *The Abandoned Middle: The Ethics and Politics of Abortion in America.* Salem, Mass.: Penumbra Press, 1988.

Examines the arguments of both pro-choice and pro-life advocates in order to come up with a proposed middle ground which accounts for the virtues of both.

1023. Moore, Harold F. "Abortion and the Logic of Moral Justification." *Journal of Value Inquiry* 9 (1975): 140-151.

The author first examines the conservative position that abortion is morally wrong, and finds the argument weak. He says his position is more in line with that of Daniel Callahan (see citation # 932). He then examines the strengths and weaknesses of the Supreme Court's *Roe v. Wade* decision.

1024. Moreland, J. P., and Norman L. Geisler. "Abortion." Chap. 2 in *The Life and Death Debate: Moral Issues of our Time.* Westport, Conn.: Green-wood Press, 1990.

The authors explain three common views of abortion, and give the most common arguments presented in defense of those views, and the most common objections to them. The three views presented are (1) the fetus is sub-human, and so abortion on demand, for any reason, is acceptable; (2) the fetus is potentially a person, and so abortion is sometimes acceptable; and (3) the fetus is fully human, and so abortion is never acceptable, or only acceptable when the mother's life is in danger.

1025. Muldoon, Maureen. "Philosophical Perspectives on Abortion." Chap. 2 in *The Abortion Debate in the United States and Canada: A Source Book.* New York: Garland Publishing, Inc., 1991.

A survey of the various philosophical and ethical positions usually held on abortion, along with a brief survey of the literature in the field.

1026. Muller, Jerry Z. "The Conservative Case for Abortion." *New Republic,* Aug. 21 & 28, 1995, 27-29.

Presents an argument for saying that abortion can be the right choice to promote healthy family life under certain circumstances. He accuses those who oppose abortion of being "anti-family," in that their policy of not allowing abortions will lead to more dysfunctional families.

1027. Murphy, Julien S. "Abortion Rights and Fetal Termination." *Journal of Social Philosophy* 17, no. 1 (1986): 11-16.

Defining abortion as having two parts – the termination of a pregnancy and the termination of the fetus, the author claims that if advances in reproductive technology make possible the transfer of the fetus from one woman to another, then we will need to re-analyze our arguments for the termination of the fetus.

1028.   Narveson, Jan. "A Contractarian Defense of the Liberal View on Abortion and of the Wrongness of Infanticide." In *Values and Moral Standing,* edited by Wayne Sumner, Donald Callen, and Thomas Attig, 76-89. Bowling Green, Ohio: The Applied Philosophy Program, Bowling Green State University, 1986.

The author points out that those who would support abortion on demand throughout pregnancy, yet also oppose infanticide have a problem, in that there is very little difference between the fetus just prior to birth, and a newborn infant. The author shows, nonetheless, that by using what she calls the contractarian method of philosophy, one can make a legitimate argument for abortion on demand, yet at the same time argue against infanticide.

1029.   ———. "Semantics, Future Generations, and the Abortion Problem: Comments on a Fallacious Case against the Morality of Abortion." *Social Theory and Practice* 3 (1975): 461-485.

A critique of the article by Richard Werner (see citation # 157, 1090). She claims that his conclusions are either pointless, question-begging, or fallacious.

1030.   Noonan, John T. "Abortion is Morally Wrong." In *The Abortion Controversy: 25 Years after Roe v. Wade: A Reader.* 2nd ed., edited by Louis P. Pojman and Francis J. Beckwith, 203-208. Belmont, Calif.: Wadsworth Pub. Co., 1998.

The author takes the conservative view that the fetus is a human being from the point of conception, and that abortion, except to save the life of the mother, is morally wrong.

1031.   ———, ed. *The Morality of Abortion: Legal and Historical Perspectives.* Cambridge, Mass.: Harvard Univ. Press, 1970.

A collection of articles on abortion from the religious, moral, and legal perspectives.

1032.   Norcross, Alistair. "Killing, Abortion, and Contraception: A Reply to Marquis." *Journal of Philosophy* 86 (1990): 268-277

The author presents a critique of the article by Marquis "Why Abortion is Immoral" (see citation # 1011) by demonstrating that if, as Marquis claims, abortion is immoral because it deprives a fetus of its future, then it follows that contraception is also wrong. Marquis had considered this objection in his article, but concluded that contraception did not deprive a fetus of its future.

1033. Overall, Christine. "Abortion." Chap. 4 in *Ethics and Human Reproduction: A Feminist Analysis.* Boston: Allen & Unwin, 1987.

Divides abortion into two distinct events: 1. The premature emptying of the uterus (or the expulsion of the fetus), and 2. the death of the fetus. The author then uses this distinction to present a middle of the road position that she says preserves the rights of the woman without sacrificing a concern for the fetus.

1034. Overduin, Daniel Christian. "The Ethics of Abortion." In *New Perspectives on Human Abortion,* edited by Thomas W. Hilgers, Dennis J. Horan, and David Mall, 357-386. Frederick, Md.: Aletheia Books, University Publications of America, 1981.

The ethics of abortion depends on the individual's point of departure, or presuppositions. The Humanist begins with the view that man is autonomous, and can make decisions for himself without regard to any supposed absolute norms, as there are no absolute norms. The Christian, however, begins with the recognition that man is a creature of God, and in relation to Him; every act is therefore either an expression of faith or of unbelief. The author begins his discussion of abortion from the latter perspective, but also shows that, because there can be no compromise between these two starting points, there will always be an inevitable collision of views.

1035. Paske, Gerald H. "Abortion and the Neo-Natal Right to Life: A Critique of Marquis's Futurist Argument." In *The Abortion Controversy: 25 Years after Roe v. Wade: A Reader.* 2nd ed., edited by Louis P. Pojman and Francis J. Beckwith, 361-371. Belmont, Calif.: Wadsworth Pub. Co., 1998.

A critique of Don Marquis' article, "Why Abortion is Immoral." (see citation # 1011)

1036. Pavlischek, Keith J. "Abortion Logic and Paternal Responsibilities: One More Look at Judith Thomson's 'A Defense of Abortion.'" *Public Affairs Quarterly* 7 (1993): 341-361.

Examines the relationship between abortion and paternal abandonment of children. Using Judith Thomson's article as a basis, the author shows that the call of liberals for paternal responsibility for their children is inconsistent with a policy of allowing abortion on demand.

1037.   ———. "Abortion Logic and Paternal Responsibilities: One More Look
         at Judith Thomson's Argument and a Critique of David Boonin-Vail's
         Defense of it." In *The Abortion Controversy: 25 Years after Roe v. Wade:
         A Reader.* 2nd ed., edited by Louis P. Pojman and Francis J. Beckwith,
         176-199. Belmont, Calif.: Wadsworth Pub. Co., 1998.

         A critique of both Thomson's article (see citation # 1082), and Boonin-
         Vails's defense of it (see citation # 924). This is a revised version of the
         previous citation.

1038.   Perkins, Robert L., ed. *Abortion: Pro and Con.* Issues in Contemporary
         Ethics. Cambridge, Mass.: Schenkman Pub. Co., 1974.

         Essays for and against abortion written from both a religious and a moral
         perspective.

1039.   Perry, Clifton. "Subsidizing Abortions: Additions and Deletions."
         Journal of Social Philosophy 17, no. 1 (1986): 30-38.

         The author presents an argument for saying that while there are some
         abortions for which federal and state funds must be allocated, and some
         for which it is uncertain, there are no good arguments for saying that no
         abortions should be funded.

1040.   Pojman, Louis P. and Francis J. Beckwith, eds. *The Abortion Contro-
         versy: 25 Years after Roe v. Wade: A Reader.* 2nd ed. Belmont, Calif.:
         Wadsworth Pub. Co., 1998.

         A collection of essays on the abortion controversy, presenting both sides
         of the issue.

1041.   Purdy, Laura, and Michael Tooley. "Is Abortion Murder?" In *Abortion:
         Pro and Con,* edited by Robert L. Perkins, 129-149. Cambridge, Mass.:
         Schenkman Pub. Co., 1974.

         The authors argue that abortion is morally unobjectionable, and that
         society benefits if abortion is available on demand.

1042.   Quinn, Warren. "Abortion: Identity and Loss." *Philosophy and Public
         Affairs* 12 (1984): 24-54.

         The author insists that any view on abortion must satisfy two, apparently
         conflicting, ideas. The first is that even a very early abortion demands a
         moral justification that the surgical removal of a mere mass of tissue does
         not. The second is that an early abortion, at least before all the organs of

the fetus are complete, is not morally equivalent to the killing of an adult or the killing of an infant.

1043.   Ramsey, Paul. "Abortion: A Review Article." *The Thomist* 36 (1973): 174-226.

An assessment of the state of the abortion debate. He reviews the writings of several prominent authors on the morality of abortion.

1044.   ———. "Reference Points in Deciding about Abortion." In *The Morality of Abortion: Legal and Historical Perspectives*, edited by John T. Noonan, 60-100. Cambridge, Mass.: Harvard Univ. Press, 1970.

Discusses several points: 1. When does human life begin? 2. Is it possible to make an argument for abortion which is not at the same time an argument for infanticide? 3. The question of viability.

1045.   Rapaport, Elizabeth, and Paul Sagal. "One Step Forward, Two Steps Backward: Abortion and Ethical Theory." In *Feminism and Philosophy*, edited by Mary Vetterling-Braggin, Frederick A. Elliston, and Jane English, 408-416. Totowa, N.J.: Littlefield, Adams, 1977.

Presents the view that no one knows what the moral status of abortion is, as no one has defended an adequate conceptual framework. This being the case, they conclude, no one has the right to coerce others either into having an abortion, or into not having one. Each woman must ultimately make her own decision and take responsibility for it.

1046.   Ray, A. Chadwick. "Humanity, Personhood and Abortion." *International Philosophical Quarterly* 25 (1985): 233-245.

Contends that there is no such thing as a *potential* human being. He presents a defense of the abortion of pre-embryonic human beings.

1047.   Reagan, Ronald, pres., U.S. *Abortion and the Conscience of the Nation.* Nashville: Thomas Nelson, 1984.

A former president of the United States gives his reasons, both legal and moral, for opposing legalized abortion on demand.

1048.   Reeder, John P., Jr. *Killing and Saving: Abortion, Hunger, and War.* University Park, Penn.: Pennsylvania State Univ. Press, 1996.

Presents a general view of killing and saving that is applicable to a variety of cases. He applies this to the issues of abortion, hunger, and war.

1049.   Reiman. Jeffrey. *Abortion and the Ways We Value Human Life.* Lanham,
          Md.: Rowman & Littlefield, 1999.

          The author builds the argument that we value human life *asymmetrically,*
          that is. we believe that the killing of one human being cannot be compen-
          sated for by the procreation of another. He claims that we value human
          beings not because of any good properties they have, nor because of
          intrinsic self-worth, but rather we value that human beings who care about
          their own continuation get what they want. As a result, he claims that
          because fetuses are not conscious that they are alive, abortion is permissi-
          ble. Infants also are not conscious that they are alive, but in this case our
          respect is aimed not at them, but at those who love them.

1050.   ———. "Abortion, Infanticide, and the Asymmetric Value of Human
          Life." *Journal of Social Philosophy* 27, no. 3 (1996): 181-200.

          Asks whether the reasons for which we think it wrong to kill adults and
          children also apply to the killing of fetuses. To answer this, he asks if
          there is anything about the fetus that would make it asymmetrically wrong
          to end its life. He claims that there is something about children and adults
          that provides a plausible basis for the way we value their lives, but that
          there is nothing about fetuses that does the same. As a result, the author
          provides a defense of the pro-choice position on abortion.

1051.   ———. "Abortion, Infanticide, and the Changing Grounds of the
          Wrongness of Killing: A Reply to Don Marquis's 'Reiman on Abortion.'"
          Journal of Social Philosophy 29, no. 2 (1998): 168-174

          A response to Don Marquis' critique (see citation # 1010) of his article
          "Abortion, Infanticide, and the Asymmetric Value of Human Life." (see
          citation # 1050).

1052.   Rodman, Hyman. Betty Sarvis. and Joy Walker Bonar. "The Moral
          Debate." Chap. 3 in *The Abortion Question.* New York: Columbia Univ.
          Press, 1987.

          Without taking sides, the authors explain the moral issues involved in
          abortion, showing how each side of the debate answers these questions:
          When does life begin? Under what circumstances, if any, may life be
          terminated? What is the proper role of women? What role should the law
          play?

1053.   Roleff, Tamara L., ed. *Abortion: Opposing Viewpoints.* Opposing
          Viewpoints Series. San Diego: Greenhaven Press, 1997.

A collection of brief articles on the morality, legality, and safety, of abortion. Articles favoring one viewpoint are followed by an article favoring the opposite viewpoint.

1054. Ross, Steven L. "Abortion and the Death of the Fetus." *Philosophy and Public Affairs* 11 (1982): 232-245.

The author divides abortion into what he claims are two logically, though not factually, separable actions: (1) it terminates a pregnancy, ending a physical dependency relationship the fetus has to the mother, and (2) it terminates the life of the fetus, ending its present functions and its ongoing development. By doing this the author presents a defense of abortion on the basis that the woman has the right to end a dependency relationship she has not willingly entered into, and the death of the fetus is just an unfortunate byproduct.

1055. Roupas, T. G. "The Value of Life." *Philosophy and Public Affairs* 6 (1978): 154-183.

Sets out to answer the question, not whether abortion is right or wrong, but whether abortion is for the best or not. He lays out the principles he will use in assessing that question, and gives the consequences that has for abortion.

1056. Ruddick, William, and William Wilcox. "Operating on the Fetus." *Hastings Center Report* 12, no. 5 (1982): 10-14.

Recounts the success of several medical operations performed on fetuses, *in utero,* and outlines the implications this new technology has for abortion.

1057. Rudy, Kathy. *Beyond Pro-Life and Pro-Choice: Moral Diversity in the Abortion Debate.* Boston: Beacon Press, 1996

The author shows that in our current climate, people are seen as either pro-life or pro-choice. She argues for eliminating that bifurcation, thus opening up new views. She claims that people are not part of only one community, but are a part of multiple, and sometimes, competing communities, making an all or nothing view of abortion impossible.

1058. Schwarz, Stephen D. *The Moral Question of Abortion.* Chicago: Loyola Univ. Press, 1990.

Discusses a number of questions in regard to abortion: Is the fetus a human being? Is it a person? Does the woman have a right over her body? What about the cases of rape, incest, the life or health of the mother?

Should abortion be legal? In all cases the author argues for a pro-life position.

1059.   Schwarz, Stephen D., and R. K Tacelli. "Abortion and Some Philosophers: A Critical Examination." *Public Affairs Quarterly* 3, no. 2 (1989): 81-98.

A critique of the views of several philosophers who have favored abortion rights.

1060.   Scorsone, Suzanne. "Freedom: Choice or Life." In *A Time to Choose Life: Women, Abortion and Human Rights,* edited by Ian Gentles, 19-23. Toronto: Stoddart, 1990.

The author describes the real root of the abortion debate as being in two opposed applications of a single principle – that of freedom. The question is, freedom for which individual, the mother or the child? Given that, the author solves the dilemma in favor of the pro-life side, by showing that the freedom given up by the mother is only temporary, whereas the freedom given up by the child – his life – is permanent.

1061.   Sher, George. "Hare, Abortion, and the Golden Rule." *Philosophy and Public Affairs* 6 (1977): 185-190.

A critique of the article by R. M. Hare (see citation # 975). This critique claims that neither Hare's appeal the Golden Rule, nor any other appeal to an analogous principle is apt to win any ground in the abortion debate.

1062.   Sloan, Don. "Abortion Is not Murder." In *Abortion: Opposing Viewpoints,* edited by Tamara L. Roleff, 40-47. San Diego: Greenhaven Press, 1997. Reprinted from the author's *Abortion: A Doctor's Perspective, a Woman's Dilemma.* New York: Donald I Fine, 1992.

Claims that abortion is not murder because the fetus is not a separate human person, as it is not able to live outside the womb on its own.

1063.   Smith, F. LaGard. *When Choice Becomes God.* Eugene, Ore.: Harvest House, 1990.

Criticizes the Pro-Choice movement by saying that it has made the choice itself as primary. He argues that many choices are not good ones, and that particularly with reference to abortion, the choice involved is to kill.

1064.   Smith, Janet E. "Moral Character and Abortion." In *Abortion: A New Generation of Catholic Responses,* edited by Stephen J. Heaney, 189-208. Braintree, Mass.: Pope John Center, 1992.

Examines the ethical theory that one of the primary considerations taken into account in evaluating whether or not an action is moral is the question of what effect the performance of that act will have on the moral character of the individual. The author then considers abortion and evaluates the likely effects it will have on the moral character of women.

1065.   Spitzer, Robert J., S.J. *Healing the Culture: A Commonsense Philosophy of Happiness, Freedom, and the Life Issues.* With Robin A. Bernhoft and Camille E. De Blasi. San Francisco: Ignatius Press, 2000.

Claiming that the moral assumptions that have given rise to abortion and euthanasia are incomplete and untrue, the author presents new definitions of "personhood" and "happiness," which then lead him to present pro-life views of both abortion and euthanasia.

1066.   Stacy, Tom. "Reconciling Reason and Religion: On Dworkin and Religious Freedom." *George Washington Law Review* 63 (1994): 1-75.

A critique of Ronald Dworkin's book, *Life's Dominion* (see citation # 955), in particular criticizing his notion of intrinsic value.

1067.   Steffen, Lloyd, ed. *Abortion: A Reader.* The Pilgrim Library of Ethics. Cleveland: Pilgrim Press, 1996.

A collection of articles on abortion from the religious, moral, and legal perspectives.

1068.   ———. *Life/Choice: The Theory of Just Abortion.* Cleveland: Pilgrim Press, 1994

The author argues for a moderate position on abortion which views some abortions as morally permissible, and others not. He then proceeds to present the conditions which he believes are necessary for a just abortion.

1069.   Sterba, James P. "Abortion, Distant Peoples, and Future Generations." *Journal of Philosophy* 76 (1980): 424-440.

The author states that those who favor a liberal view on abortion, and thus tend to support abortion on demand, are just as likely to support the rights of distant peoples to basic economic assistance, and the rights of future generations to a fair share of the world's resources. He argues, however, that many of their arguments in support of abortion are inconsistent with a workable defense of these other social goals. Thus, he claims, liberals will have to either moderate their support for abortion, or moderate their commitment to the rights of distant peoples and future generations.

1070.   Stetson, Brad, ed. *The Silent Subject: Reflections on the Unborn in American Culture.* Westport, Conn.: Praeger, 1996.

A collection of articles, which, though all pro-life in orientation, do approach the subject from many points of view and many different angles.

1071.   Stith, Richard. "Nominal Babies." *First Things,* Feb. 1999, 16-20.

Using both legal and ethical reasoning, the author refutes two decisions of the Supreme Court: *Roe v. Wade,* and *Planned Parenthood v. Casey.*

1072.   Strahan, Thomas W. "Induced Abortion as a Violation of Conscience of the Woman." In *Life and Learning VI: Proceedings of the Sixth University Faculty for Life Conference, June 1996 at Georgetown University,* edited by Joseph W. Koterski, S.J., 191-214. Washington, D.C.: University Faculty for Life, 1997.

Demonstrates that in most cases a woman's decision to have an abortion is a violation of, or a denial of, her conscience or ideals, usually for pragmatic reasons, or due to ambivalence, guilt, anger and deep confusion. He argues that those who claim that abortion is a decision based upon conscience are mistaken.

1073.   Strasser, Mark. "Dependence, Reliance, and Abortion." *Philosophical Quarterly* 35 (1985): 73-82.

A critique of the article by Michael Davis (see citation no. 949). In particular, the author argues that Davis' distinction between reliance and dependence does not yield the results which he suggests. Rather, it shows that we need not settle metaphysical claims about the personhood of the fetus before making headway in the abortion controversy.

1074.   Sumner, L. W. "Abortion." In *Health Care Ethics: An Introduction,* edited by Donald VanDeVeer, and Tom Regan, 162-183. Philadelphia: Temple Univ. Press, 1987.

Examines the moral problems posed by abortion, and gives detailed consideration to both the extreme liberal and the extreme conservative approaches to the problem. He then presents his moderate view based on sentience, which would say that abortions are permissible in the first trimester, and impermissible in the third trimester; in the second trimester, however, it is indeterminate.

1075.   ———. *Abortion and Moral Theory.* Princeton: Princeton Univ. Press, 1981.

Criticizes both the extreme liberal and the extreme conservative views on abortion. The author then presents a defense of classical utilitarianism, as providing the necessary foundation for a moderate view of abortion.

1076.   ———. "A Defense of the Moderate Position." In *The Abortion Controversy: 25 Years after Roe v. Wade: A Reader.* 2nd ed., edited by Louis P. Pojman and Francis J. Beckwith, 299-312. Belmont, Calif.: Wadsworth Pub. Co., 1998. First published in *Abortion and Moral Theory.* Princeton, N.J.: Princeton Univ. Press, 1981.

Criticizes both the liberal and the conservative views on abortion, and embraces a moderate position, based on the criterion of sentience.

1077.   ———. "Moderate Views of Abortion." In *New Essays on Abortion and Bioethics,* edited by Rem B. Edwards, 203-226. Greenwich, Conn.: JAI Press, 1997.

Discusses moderate views on abortion in general, and shows that they are morally defensible. He argues for a position which sees abortion as morally permissible before the fetus becomes sentient, which he says occurs at between the twentieth and the twenty-fourth week of pregnancy.

1078.   ———. "A Third Way." In *The Problem of Abortion.* 2nd. ed., edited by Joel Feinberg, 71-93. Belmont, Calif.: Wadsworth Pub. Co., 1984.

Claims that the discussion of abortion has been distorted because of the dominance of two views – the extreme liberal position that abortion is morally innocuous, and the extreme conservative position that abortion is always morally wrong. He then goes on to present and defend a middle ground on the question.

1079.   ———. "Toward a Credible View of Abortion." *Canadian Journal of Philosophy* 4 (1974): 163-181.

The author outlines, and refutes, both the extreme liberal and the extreme conservative views on abortion, and then proceeds to present an argument for a moderate view.

1080.   Tauer, Carol A. "Abortion: Embodiment and Prenatal Development." In *Embodiment, Morality, and Medicine,* edited by Lisa Sowle Cahill and Margaret A. Farley, 75-92. Dordrecht: Kluwer Academic Publishers, 1995.

The author describes two different world-views, by which the moral problems posed by prenatal life are viewed. She reviews the significant positions taken by each world-view, suggesting the most significant areas of debate, as well as presenting her own critical assessment.

1081.   Thomson, Judith Jarvis. "Abortion." *Boston Review* 20, no. 3 (1995): 11-15.

A refutation of the conservative view that the fetus has a right to life from the moment of conception, and that abortion is wrong because of that.

1082.   ———. "A Defense of Abortion." *Philosophy and Public Affairs* 1 (1971): 47-66.

Argues that even if the fetus is a human being from the point of conception, and has a right to life, that fact does not impose an obligation on the mother to carry it to term, unless the mother has voluntarily accepted that obligation. Even then, she is not doing simply what is required of her, but she is going above and beyond the call of duty.

1083.   ———. "Rights and Deaths." *Philosophy and Public Affairs* 2 (1973): 146-159.

A response to John Finnis' critique (see citation # 963) to her article "A Defense of Abortion."

1084.   Tribe, Laurence H. *Abortion: The Clash of Absolutes.* New York: W. W. Norton, 1990.

Describing the abortion controversy as a clash between two absolutes – the life of the fetus versus the liberty of the mother – the author, without taking sides, tries to lay a groundwork for moving beyond this conflict.

1085.   VanDeVeer, Donald. "Justifying 'Wholesale Slaughter.'" *Canadian Journal of Philosophy* 5 (1975): 245-258.

The author shows that, though there are no morally significant differences between successive stages of fetal development, there are such differences between disparate stages of fetal development.

1086.   Vaux, Kenneth L. *Birth Ethics: Religious and Cultural Values in the Genesis of Life.* New York: Crossroad, 1989.

Presents a history and analysis of the ethical principles involved in the issues of sexual activity, pregnancy, abortion, and newborns with life threatening illnesses.

1087.   Von Jess, Wilma G. "Jean-Paul Sartre and the Abortion Debate." In *Life and Learning: Proceedings of the Third University Faculty for Life Conference*, edited by Joseph W. Koterski, S.J., 115-132. Washington, D.C.: University Faculty for Life, 1993.

Shows that some of the philosophical underpinnings of the current abortion on demand movement have their roots in the philosophy of Jean-Paul Sartre.

1088.   Warren, Mary Anne. "The Abortion Issue." In *Health Care Ethics: An Introduction*, edited by Donald VanDeVeer and Tom Regan, 184-214. Philadelphia: Temple Univ. Press, 1987.

Asks two questions: What is the moral status of the fetus, and What are the likely consequences of the legal toleration or prohibition of abortion. As to the first question, she concludes that even late-term fetuses, though they have some moral status, should not be viewed as persons with full moral rights. As to the second question, she concludes that the social effects of maintaining the legality of abortion are much more desirable than the consequences of either restricting it or prohibiting it.

1089.   ———. "Do Potential People have Moral Rights?" *Canadian Journal of Philosophy* 7 (1977): 275-289.

Examines various ways of deciding on whether potential people have any moral rights. She concludes that they do not.

1090.   Werner, Richard. "Abortion: The Moral Status of the Unborn." *Social Theory and Practice* 3 (1974): 201-222.

Presents arguments in favor of three positions: (1) that embryos and fetuses are indeed human beings; (2) that the moral obligation against the taking of human life is strong enough to rule out most abortions; and (3) that being human, rather than being persons is, for abortion, the morally relevant criterion.

1091.   ———. "Hare on Abortion." *Analysis* 36 (1976): 177-181.

A critique of R. M Hare's article "Abortion and the Golden Rule" (see citation # 975).

1092.   Wesley, Patricia. "Re-Visiting Eden: Will We Make the Same Mistake Twice?" In *Life and Learning: Proceedings of the Third University Faculty for Life Conference*, edited by Joseph W. Koterski, S.J., 84-104. Washington, D.C.: University Faculty for Life, 1993.

The author demonstrates that those who favor legalized abortion do so on the basis of a redefinition of life and death. She compares that with the Garden of Eden, where the Serpent redefined good and evil.

1093.   Wilcox, John T. "Nature as Demonic in Thomson's Defense of Abortion." *New Scholasticism* 62 (1989): 463-484.

A critique of the article by Judith Jarvis Thomson, "A Defense of Abortion." (see citation # 1082)

1094.   Wilkins, Burleigh T. "Does the Fetus Have a Right to Life?" *Journal of Social Philosophy* 24, no. 1 (1993): 123-137.

Presents an argument that the fetus has a right to life from the moment of conception because it is a potential person.

THE VALIDITY OF PARTICULAR ARGUMENTS

1095.   Allen, Anita L. "Privacy and Reproductive Liberty." In *Nagging Questions: Feminist Ethics in Everyday Life*, edited by Dana E. Bushnell, 193-239. Lanham, Md.: Rowman & Littlefield, 1995.

Privacy is always pointed to as part of what is at stake in the decision for reproductive rights. The author identifies the most important forms of privacy and explains why respect for these will maximize women's choices.

1096.   Beckwith, Francis J. "Arguments from Bodily Rights: A Critical Analysis." In *The Abortion Controversy: 25 Years after Roe v. Wade: A Reader*. 2nd ed., edited by Louis P. Pojman and Francis J. Beckwith, 132-150. Belmont, Calif: Wadsworth Pub. Co., 1998. Reprinted with revisions from *Politically Correct Death: Answering the Arguments for Abortion Rights*. Chapt. 7. Grand Rapids: Baker Book House, 1993.

Gives a pro-life response to the common argument that a woman has the right to control her own body. The majority of this essay is a critique of the essay by Judith Jarvis Thomson (see citation # 1082). This is a revised version of the paper originally delivered at the Evangelical Theological Society (see citation # 1098).

1097.   ———. "Ignorance of Fetal Status as a Justification for Abortion: A Critical Analysis." In *The Silent Subject: Reflections on the Unborn in American Culture*, edited by Brad Stetson, 33-42. Westport, Conn.: Praeger, 1996.

Some have argued that, since there is disagreement about whether the fetus is a person or not, therefore abortion should be allowed. The author disputes that argument and shows it to be defective.

1098. ———. "Personal Bodily Rights, Abortion, and Unplugging the Violinist." A paper presented at the 42nd National Conference of the Evangelical Theological Society, 15-17 November 1990.

Gives a pro-life response to two pro-choice arguments – that a woman has the right to control her own body, and that abortion is justified because it is statistically less risky than childbirth. Then he presents a critique of the article by Judith Jarvis Thompson (see citation # 1082) who argues that abortion, at least in some cases, is morally justified, even if the fetus is a person.

1099. ———. "Pluralism, Tolerance, and Abortion Rights." In *Life and Learning: Proceedings of the Third University for Life Conference,* edited by Joseph W. Koterski, S.J., 28-44. Washington, D.C.: University Faculty for Life, 1993.

Presents an answer to those who argue for legalized abortion on the basis of pluralism. He claims that tolerance in the abortion controversy is an intellectual impossibility.

1100. ———. "Reply to Keenan: Thomson's Argument and Academic Feminism." *International Philosophical Quarterly* 32 (1992): 369-376.

A reply to Keenan's critique of his paper "Personal Bodily Rights, Abortion, and Unplugging the violinist." (see citation # 1107).

1101. Benn, Stanley I. "Abortion, Infanticide, and Respect for Persons." In *The Problem of Abortion,* edited by Joel Feinberg, 92-104. Belmont, Calif.: Wadsworth Pub. Co., 1973.

Argues that the common presumption that the problem of abortion must be argued in terms of conflict between the mother's rights and fetus' rights, may be a mistake. Rather, he argues that there may be other reasons against infanticide, and perhaps against abortion too, that are not based on the right to life of either the infant or the fetus.

1102. Boss, Judith A. "Pro-Child/Pro-Choice: An Exercise in Doublethink?" *Public Affairs Quarterly* 7 (1993): 85-91.

Claims that the popular pro-choice slogan "pro-child/pro-choice" is an exercise in doublethink, or holding two contradictory beliefs simultaneously.

1103.   Devine, Philip E. "Relativism, Abortion, and Tolerance." *Philosophy and Phenomenological Research* 48 (1987): 131-138.

The author disputes the theory that, if morality is relative, and there is no true morality, that this requires a tolerance of other views. He says that tolerance cannot be a supra-systemic principle, governing relations among diverse moralities. He applies his thesis to the issue of abortion.

1104.   Foh, Susan T. "Abortion and Women's Lib." In *Thou Shalt not Kill: The Christian Case against Abortion*, edited by Richard L. Ganz, 150-193. New Rochelle, N.Y.: Arlington House, 1978.

Presents a critique of the feminist arguments given in favor of abortion; in particular, she criticizes the argument that a woman has the right to control her own body.

1105.   Fox-Genovese, Elizabeth. "Rethinking Abortion in Terms of Human Interconnectedness." *Studies in Prolife Feminism* 1 (1995): 91-104.

The author contends that by grounding the case for abortion in a rhetoric of "rights," feminists have produced a deadlock between competing rights and have ignored a respect for life. The author contends that if we look at abortion from the perspective of life, we will see that it concerns relationships and responsibilities that cannot be captured by a language of individual rights.

1106.   Huffman, Tom L. "Abortion, Moral Responsibility, and Self-Defense." *Public Affairs Quarterly* 7 (1993): 287-302.

An examination of the argument that abortion can be seen as simply a form of self-defense. The author concludes that the principle of self-defense actually argues *against* a woman's right to an abortion, rather than for it, as has been commonly supposed.

1107.   Keenan, James F. "Reply to Beckwith: Abortion – Whose Agenda Is It Anyway?" *International Philosophical Quarterly* 32 (1992): 239-245.

A critique of the paper by Francis Beckwith entitled "Personal Bodily Rights, Abortion and Unplugging the Violinist." (see citation # 1098).

1108.   Kohl, Marvin. "Abortion and the Argument from Innocence." In *The Problem of Abortion*, edited by Joel Feinberg, 28-32. Belmont, Calif.: Wadsworth Pub. Co., 1973. Originally published in *Inquiry* 14 (1971): 147-151.

One popular argument against abortion is the so called argument from innocence, that is, that abortion is immoral because it is the killing of an innocent human being. The author criticizes that argument.

1109. Langer, Richard. "Abortion and the Right to Privacy." *Journal of Social Philosophy* 23, no. 2 (1992): 23-51.

One common critique of Thomson's article "Defense of Abortion" (see citation # 1082) is the "voluntariness objection," that is, that voluntary intercourse constitutes an implied waiver of the woman's right to privacy against the fetus. The article examines that critique for validity, and finds it to be valid in many cases, thus calling into question the moral support for the practice of abortion in general.

1110. Markowitz, Sally. "Abortion and Feminism." *Social Theory and Practice* 16 (1990): 1-17.

The author argues that the autonomy defense of abortion (that the woman has the right to control her own body) , from a feminist point of view, is weak. Rather she presents another defense of abortion, this one derived from an awareness of women's oppression.

1111. McLachlan, Hugh V. "Moral Rights and Abortion." *Contemporary Review* 228 (1976): 323-328.

The author claims that we are mistaken to speak of *rights* in the abortion debate, as when we say that the woman has a right to an abortion, or that the fetus has a right not to be aborted.

1112. Michaels, Meredith W. "Abortion and the Claims of Samaritanism." In *Abortion: Moral and Legal Perspectives,* edited by Jay L. Garfield and Patricia Hennessey, 213-226. Amherst, Mass.: Univ. of Massachusetts Press, 1984.

A critique of the Good Samaritan argument often given in defense of abortion. This argument says that asking a woman to carry a baby to term is to require her to make a sacrifice of the Good Samaritan sort, and that she is under no obligation to do so, and that if she does decide to do so, she is going above and beyond the call of duty. This author claims that this argument in defense of abortion is not valid.

1113. Reiman, Jeffrey. "The Impotency of the Potentiality Argument for Fetal Rights: Reply to Wilkins." *Journal of Social Philosophy* 24, no. 3 (1993): 170-176.

A critique of Wilkins article "Does the Fetus have a Right to Life?" (see citation # ?).

1114.   Rossi, Philip J. "'Rights' are Not Enough: Prospects for a New Approach to the Morality of Abortion." *Linacre Quarterly* 46 (1979): 109-117.

Many view abortion as a question of "rights:" the right of a woman to control her own destiny, or a fetus' right to life. The author says this approach will never solve the problem. He proposes instead an argument based on the question of what is truly good for human persons.

1115.   Roy, Ina. "Defending Abortion: Should We Treat the Body as Property?" *Public Affairs Quarterly* 13 (1999): 309-329.

Some have defended abortion by viewing the body as a piece of property which the woman owns. The author critiques that argument.

1116.   Sherlock, Richard. "The Demographic Argument for Liberal Abortion Policies: Analysis of a Pseudo-Issue." In *New Perspectives on Human Abortion,* edited by Thomas W. Hilgers, Dennis J. Horan, and David Mall, 450-465. Frederick, Md.: Aletheia Books, University Publications of America, 1981.

Some have argued that abortion should be at least allowed, if not actually mandated, as a means of population control. The author claims that this is a very weak argument, because the evidence to support it is weak.

1117.   Smith, Holly M. "Intercourse and Moral Responsibility for the Fetus." In *Abortion and the Status of the Fetus,* edited by William B. Bondeson, H. Tristram Engelhardt, Jr., Stuart F. Spicker, and Daniel H. Winship, 229-245. Dordrecht: D. Reidel Pub. Co., 1983.

Examines the responsibility argument, and finds it wanting. This argument says that if a woman voluntarily engages in intercourse, knowing that pregnancy might result, she has, by that action, waived her right to not have her body used by the fetus.

1118.   Thomas, Laurence. "Abortion, Slavery, and the Law: A Study in Moral Character." In *Abortion: Moral and Legal Perspectives,* edited by Jay L. Garfield and Patricia Hennessey, 227-237. Amherst, Mass.: Univ. of Massachusetts Press, 1984.

The author criticizes those anti-abortion advocates who claim a correlation between the issues of slavery and of abortion. He claims that there are significant differences between the two.

ABORTION IN PARTICULAR CIRCUMSTANCES

1119.   Beabout, Greg. "Abortion in Rape Cases." In *The Ethics of Having Children.* Proceedings of the American Catholic Philosophical Society, 63, edited by Lawrence P. Schrenk, 132-138. Washington, D.C.: National Office of the American Catholic Philosophical Society, 1990.

   The author addresses the moral permissibility of abortion in rape cases. He claims that the woman in such cases is obligated to respect the unborn child, and to abort would be to fail to do so.

1120.   Brody, Baruch A. "Abortion and the Sanctity of Human Life." *American Philosophical Quarterly* 10 (1973): 133-140.

   Centers on the question whether it is morally permissible to perform an abortion in order to save the life of the mother. He concludes that the only situation in which it is permissible to do so is when both the mother and the fetus would die if nothing is done, and the only way to save the mother is to abort the fetus.

1121.   Camenisch, Paul F. "Abortion: For the Fetus's own sake?" *Hastings Center Report* 6, no. 2 (1976): 38-41.

   The author calls into question the argument that in cases where the fetus is severely deformed or handicapped, that we ought to permit abortion, "for the sake of the fetus and the person it will grow up to be."

1122.   Campion, Bridget. "An Argument for Continuing a Pregnancy Where the Fetus is Discovered to be Anencephalic." In *Life and Learning IX: Proceedings of the Ninth University Faculty for Life Conference, June 1999, at Trinity International University, Deerfield, Ill.,* edited by Joseph W. Koterski, S.J., 319-329. Washington, D.C.: University Faculty for Life, 2000.

   By showing that a pregnancy can have value in and of itself, independent of its results, the author presents an argument for continuing a pregnancy where the fetus has no brain.

1123.   Casey, Patricia. "Alternatives to Abortion and Hard Cases." In *Swimming against the Tide: Feminist Dissent on the Issue of Abortion,* edited by Angela Kennedy, 86-95. Dublin, Ireland: Open Air, 1997.

   Argues that having an abortion in the "hard" cases – rape, fetal deformity, and suicide risk – does not really ease the suffering caused by these situations, and may introduce its own set of problems.

1124.   Davis, Nancy. "Abortion and Self-Defense." *Philosophy and Public Affairs* 12 (1984): 175-207.

Can aborting a fetus in order to preserve the life of the mother be seen as a special case of the right of self-defense? The author thinks not. She believes that a fetus may legitimately be aborted in such a case, but not because of the right of the woman to defend herself.

1125.   Gevers, Sjef. "Third Trimester Abortion for Fetal Abnormality." *Bioethics* 13 (1999): 306-313.

Examines the moral and legal issue involved when severe fetal abnormality is discovered in the third trimester, when the fetus is already viable. Should abortion be allowed in such a situation, and if so, what safeguards should be in place?

1126.   Harris, C. E. "Aborting Abnormal Fetuses: The Parental Perspective." *Journal of Applied Philosophy* 8 (1991): 57-68.

The author focuses on the issue of aborting abnormal fetuses from the standpoint of the prerogatives and obligations of parents. He concludes that abortion is justified in cases of severe abnormalities, but not in cases of only slight deformity.

1127.   Holder, Angela R., and Mary Sue Henifin. "Selective Termination of Pregnancy: Commentary." *Hastings Center Report* 18, no. 1 (1988): 21-22.

Using a hypothetical case as a backdrop, two authors present contrasting opinions on the ethics of the selective termination of a multiple pregnancy.

1128.   Schwarz, Stephen D. "Abortion Laws and Exceptions." In *Life and Learning IV: Proceedings of the Fourth University Faculty for Life Conference held at Fordham University June 1994,* edited by Joseph W. Koterski, S.J., 152-167. Washington, D.C.: University Faculty for Life, 1995.

Using both moral and legal arguments, the author presents a case against having an exception for the life of the mother in any law prohibiting abortion.

1129.   Weiss, Gail. "Sex-Selective Abortion: a Relational Approach." In *Feminist Ethics and Social Policy,* edited by Patrice DiQuinzio and Iris Marion Young, 274-290. Bloomington, Ind.: Indiana University Press, 1997.

Examines the ethics of sex-selective abortion (SSA), which is the practice of terminating a pregnancy because the fetus is of the undesired sex. The author pays particular attention to the dilemma faced by feminist ethics: reconciling a pro-choice view of abortion with a negative attitude toward SSA, because most uses of it have been to abort female fetuses.

1130. Wreen, Michael J. "Abortion and Pregnancy Due to Rape." *Philosophia* 21 (1992): 201-220.

Presents moral arguments against the moral permissibility of abortion when the pregnancy is the result of rape.

FEMINIST ETHICS AND ABORTION

1131. "Abortion is not a Selfish Choice." In *Abortion: Opposing Viewpoints*, edited by Tamara L. Roleff, 53-56. San Diego: Greenhaven Press, 1997. Reprint of an editorial in the Jan. 15, 1995 issue of *Revolutionary Worker*.

Presents the view that abortion is not a selfish choice. A woman's physical and mental health, and her right to function in society always take priority over reproduction.

1132. Allen, Anita L. "Privacy and Reproductive Liberty." In *Nagging Questions: Feminist Ethics in Everyday Life*, edited by Dana E. Bushnell, 193-239. Lanham, Md.: Rowman & Littlefield, 1995.

Privacy is always pointed to as part of what is at stake in the decision for reproductive rights. The author identifies the most important forms of privacy and explains why respect for these will maximize women's choices.

1133. Browning, Ali. "The Nature of the Foetus: A Vegetarian Argument against Abortion." In *Swimming against the Tide: Feminist Dissent on the Issue of Abortion*, edited by Angela Kennedy, 57-66. Dublin, Ireland: Open Air, 1997.

The author argues that feminists are being inconsistent when they oppose the killing of animals for food and fur, since it causes pain and suffering to the animals, but at the same time advocate abortion, when it is well known that the fetus also suffers pain in the abortion procedure.

1134. Callahan, Sidney. "Abortion and the Sexual Agenda." *Commonweal* 112 (1986): 232-238

The author. a pro-life feminist. argues that women can never achieve the fulfillment of feminist goals in a society with a permissive attitude toward abortion. She takes four arguments for abortion commonly made by feminists and criticizes them using feminist principles.

1135.   Cohen, Howard. "Abortion and the Quality of Life." In *Feminism and Philosophy*, edited by Mary Vetterling-Braggin, Frederick A. Elliston, and Jane English, 429-440. Totowa, N.J.: Littlefield, Adams, 1977.

Comments that most philosophical arguments about abortion do not address the quality of life concerns of women who are faced with the decision whether or not to bring a fetus to term. The author suggests that quality of life issues should be given equal weight. and he argues that many times they are sufficient by themselves to justify an abortion.

1136.   Darke, Marie-Claire. "Abortion and Disability: Is that Different?" In *Swimming against the Tide: Feminist Dissent on the Issue of Abortion*, edited by Angela Kennedy, 67-74. Dublin. Ireland: Open Air, 1997.

Argues that feminists are being inconsistent when they argue that the abortion of handicapped fetuses is permissible. yet the practice in many Asian countries of aborting female offspring because they are seen as undesirable. is not legitimate. The author maintains that the same reasons Asian countries give for aborting female offspring are the same as the reasons feminists give of allowing the abortion of the handicapped child – cost. stigma. burden, etc.

1137.   De Varent, Marnie. "Feminism and Abortion: A Few Hidden Grounds." In *The Right to Birth: Some Christian Views on Abortion*, edited by Eugene Fairweather and Ian Gentles, 57-68. Toronto: The Anglican Book Centre. 1976.

Demonstrates that. if feminism were true to its feminine principles. it would not support abortion. She claims that if women truly value themselves on their own terms. not on the terms of the patriarchal social order. they will value their unborn children.

1138.   Derr, Mary Krane. "Feminism. Self-Estrangement. and the 'Disease' of Pregnancy." *Studies in Prolife Feminism* 1 (1995): 1-10.

Many in society tend to portray women as deviations from the male norm. and this tends to produce a lack of self-esteem in some women. Feminists have long fought to heal women from this lack of self-esteem. and to see themselves and their bodies in a positive light. The author contends, however. that those feminists who favor legalized abortion have capitulated to the notion that women's distinctive physical powers are the source of their inferior social status, because they portray pregnancy as a "disease" that must be cured by an abortion. She contends that women need to see their pregnancy as something normal and healthy, and in that way appreciate their own distinctive power.

1139.   ————. "A Lost Source of Strength and Power: The Long Feminist Tradition of Non-Violent Response to Crisis Pregnancies." In *Swimming against the Tide: Feminist Dissent on the Issue of Abortion,* edited by Angela Kennedy, 12-27. Dublin, Ireland: Open Air, 1997.

The author points out that, while, since the 1960's, feminism has been linked with abortion advocacy, if one looks at the history of feminism, most feminists up until recent times have actually been anti-abortion.

1140.   Foh, Susan T. "Abortion and Women's Lib." In *Thou Shalt not Kill: The Christian Case against Abortion,* edited by Richard L. Ganz, 150-193. New Rochelle, N.Y.: Arlington House, 1978.

Presents a critique of the feminist arguments given in favor of abortion; in particular, she criticizes the argument that a woman has the right to control her own body.

1141.   Gorman, Michael J. "Abortion and the Biblical Metaphor of God as Mother." In *Life and Learning IV: Proceedings of the Fourth University Faculty for Life Conference held at Fordham University June 1994,* edited by Joseph W. Koterski, S.J., 253-270. Washington, D.C.: University Faculty for Life, 1995.

Examines the Bible's maternal metaphors for God, and shows how these images figure prominently in feminist theology and ethics. The author argues that, contrary to the claim of many feminist theologians, the Bible's metaphor of God as mother implies a comprehensive ethic of protecting all life, including fetal life.

1142.   Harding, Sandra. "Beneath the Surface of the Abortion Dispute: Are Women Fully Human?" In *Abortion: Understanding Differences,* edited by Sidney Callahan and Daniel Callahan, 203-224. New York: Plenum Press, 1984.

An examination of liberalism and Marxism as the philosophical roots of feminism. The author demonstrates that in both liberalism and Marxism, the policies toward abortion have been developed out of a distinctively masculine social experience.

1143.   Harrison, Beverly Wildung. *Our Right to Choose: Toward a New Ethic of Abortion.* Boston: Beacon Press, 1983.

The author argues that women not only have the right to choose whether or not to have an abortion, but they should also have the right to the conditions for procreative choice.

1144.   ———. "Theology of Pro-Choice: A Feminist Perspective." In *Abortion: The Moral Issues,* edited by Edward Batchelor, 210-226. New York: Pilgrim Press, 1982.

A feminist defense of abortion, criticizing the conservative Christian view of abortion as misogynist.

1145.   Harrison, Beverly Wildung, and Shirley Cloyes. "Theology and Morality of Procreative Choice." In *Abortion: A Reader,* edited by Lloyd Steffen, 319-339. Cleveland: The Pilgrim Press, 1996.

A feminist defense of abortion, criticizing the conservative view toward abortion as being misogynist. They say that the typical Christian theology must be converted to one which is more respectful of women.

1146.   Hayden, Mary. "The 'Feminism' of Aquinas' Natural Law: Relationships, Love and New Life." In *Abortion: A New Generation of Catholic Responses,* edited by Stephen J. Heaney, 237-242. Braintree, Mass.: Pope John Center, 1992.

Presents a definition of "feminist" ethics as one based on relationships and of "masculine" ethics as based on justice, impartiality and rights. She points to "feminist" ethics as being relative versus absolute, and of generally favoring abortion. She points to "masculine" ethics as being absolute, rather than relative. She then discusses the natural law approach of Thomas Aquinas. She points out that, contrary to one's expectation, it is just as much based on the "feminist" approach as the "masculine." She shows that the "feminist" ethics of Aquinas actually opposes abortion because it is contrary to "loving thy neighbor."

1147.   Jenni, Kathie. "Dilemmas in Social Philosophy: Abortion and Animal Rights." *Social Theory and Practice* 20 (1994): 59-83.

The author presents a potential conflict between feminists and animal rights activists: the feminist concern for an unrestricted access to abortion appears to be undercut by the animal rights activists who say that we should give legal protection to sentient non-persons. Since fetuses gain a form of sentience in the second trimester, then that claim should mean that fetuses should also be given legal protection. The author of this article presents an approach to abortion that attends to fetal sentience and the insights of animal rights philosophy. She concludes that abortion is nothing more than the sacrifice of one group of beings, the unborn, for the sake of women's liberation.

1148.   Kennedy, Angela, ed. *Swimming against the Tide: Feminist Dissent on the Issue of Abortion.* Dublin, Ireland: Open Air, 1997.

A collection of articles, written from a feminist perspective, which show that to be a feminist does not mean that one has to be pro-choice. Each article, using feminist principles, presents an argument against abortion.

1149.   Kopaczynski, Germain. *No Higher Court: Contemporary Feminism and the Right to Abortion.* Scranton, Penn.: Univ. of Scranton Press, 1995.

The author traces the history of pro-choice feminism, and at the same time presents an argument for a pro-life feminism. He reaches the conclusion that atheism, not feminism, is the real root of the abortion rights mentality.

1150.   Mahowald, Mary B. "As If There Were Fetuses without Women: A Remedial Essay. In *Reproduction, Ethics, and the Law: Feminist Perspectives,* edited by Joan C. Callahan, 199-218. Bloomington, Ind.: Indiana Univ. Press, 1995.

Discusses, from a feminist perspective, the current status of, and the ethics involved in, fetal tissue transplantation from aborted fetuses.

1151.   Maloney, Anne M. "Cassandra's Fate: Why Feminists Ought to Be Pro-Life." In *Abortion: A New Generation of Catholic Responses,* edited by Stephen J. Heaney, 209-217. Braintree, Mass.: Pope John Center, 1992.

Presents the argument that mainline feminists' call for abortion rights will actually destroy the very women who articulate it, and render impossible the very society they are trying to achieve.

1152.   ———. "You Say You Want a Revolution? Pro-Life Philosophy and Feminism." *Studies in Prolife Feminism* 1 (1995): 293-302.

Most feminists take it for granted that, to be a feminist, one must favor abortion rights. The author outlines the major strands in contemporary feminist thought, and shows that a careful reading of the principles underlying it should inevitably lead one to a wholeheartedly anti-abortion position.

1153.   Markowitz, Sally. "Abortion and Feminism." *Social Theory and Practice* 16 (1990): 1-17.

The author argues that the autonomy defense of abortion (that the woman has the right to control her own body) , from a feminist point of view, is weak. Rather she presents another defense of abortion, this one derived from an awareness of women's oppression.

1154.   Matthewes-Green, Frederica. "Compassion and Concentric Circles of Support." *Studies in Prolife Feminism* 1 (1995): 141-154.

The author asks why some women avidly support abortion, whereas other women just as avidly oppose it. She says the answer may well be that women are pro-life or pro-choice for the very same reason. She claims that much of the debate on abortion today has been done on masculine terms of "principle" – the right to life or the right to liberty. Women however, are more often concerned with practical aspects – who will be hurt by this decision? What is the best way to care for all concerned? Starting from this same point, women often reach different conclusions.

1155.   McDonnell, Kathleen. *Not an Easy Choice: A Feminist Re-Examines Abortion.* Boston: South End Press, 1984.

A feminist examines her own views on abortion. Though pro-choice, she admits that the issues are complex, and not easy to answer.

1156.   O'Brien, Brenda. "Empty Rhetoric: A Feminist Enquiry into Abortion Advocacy and the 'Choice' Ethic." In *Swimming against the Tide: Feminist Dissent on the Issue of Abortion,* edited by Angela Kennedy, 28-37. Dublin, Ireland: Open Air, 1997.

The author criticizes the pro-choice position of most feminists on the basis that, while feminism started out seeking freedom from the oppression of patriarchy, it has now, through abortion, adopted the role of oppressor – the oppression of the defenseless unborn child. She also criticizes the ethic of "choice," in that it implies that, whenever a woman makes a choice for abortion because it is "right for her," that choice is automatically the right choice. The logical conclusion, she says, is that a woman can never be held accountable for her freely made decisions, as her decisions, whatever they are, can only be right ones.

1157.   Poppema, Suzanne T. *Why I am an Abortion Doctor.* With Mike Henderson. Amherst, N.Y.: Prometheus Books, 1996.

The author gives her reasons. basically coming from a feminist perspective, why she chose to become, and why she continues to be, an abortion doctor.

1158. Segers, Mary C. "Abortion and the Culture: Toward a Feminist Perspective." In *Abortion: Understanding Differences,* edited by Sidney Callahan and Daniel Callahan, 229-252. New York: Plenum Press, 1984.

Argues that, while abortion should remain legal, we should find ways to reduce the incidence of abortion. She also claims that feminists can and should define the moral standards against which to measure our behavior with respect to abortion.

1159. Smith, Janet E. "Abortion as a Feminist Concern." *Human Life Review* 4, no. 3 (1978): 62-76.

Most feminists view abortion as a basic, fundamental, right of women. The author argues that such a view is a fundamental misunderstanding of women's rights, and that abortion will, in the end prove to be harmful to women.

1160. Soley, Ginny Earnest. "To Preserve and Protect Life: A Christian Feminist Perspective on Abortion." *Sojourners,* Oct. 1986, 34-37.

A feminist Christian presents an argument against abortion.

1161. Strahan, Thomas W. "Studies Suggesting that Induced Abortion May Increase the Feminization of Poverty." *Studies in Prolife Feminism* 1 (1995): 235-246.

Ever since the 1960's, poverty has increasingly become a feminine issue, in that the poverty rate among female-headed households is much higher than it is among male-headed households or husband and wife families. The author notes that it is during this very same period when abortion has been increasingly legalized. This seems to contradict, he says, the argument of pro-choice forces that abortion would lessen this feminization of poverty, because job loss due to childbirth would be avoided, as would the burdens of childcare which clearly contribute to poverty. At the very least, he says, abortion is an inadequate solution to this poverty trend.

1162. Suess, Jennifer Katherine. "The Natural Environment of the Female Body and its Fertility." *Studies in Prolife Feminism* 1 (1995): 45-58.

Many modernists envision a world where people have power over nature and are freed from the natural constrains of their bodies. Many feminists decry this rejection of the natural environment as evidence of a bias towards a male disembodied culture, and a rejection of a female embodied culture. The author contends, however, that on issues having to do with women's fertility, these same feminists have not completely overthrown the modernist notion. Their arguments supporting contraceptives and abortion, she says, adopt the same modernist notion that women need to be freed from the constraints of their bodies.

1163.   Waters, Kristin. "Abortion, Technology and Responsibility." *Journal of Social Philosophy* 17, no. 1 (1986): 17-22.

The author claims that if abortion is a moral wrong, it is a wrong which is not inherent in the act itself, nor is it one which the women who choose it intended. She further argues that current reproductive practices, including abortion, may unnecessarily impede women from pursuing their goals.

1164.   Whitbeck, Caroline. "The Moral Implications of Regarding Women as People: New Perspectives on Pregnancy and Personhood." In *Abortion and the Status of the Fetus,* edited by William B. Bondeson, H. Tristram Engelhardt, Jr., Stuart F. Spicker, and Daniel H. Winship, 247-272. Dordrecht: D. Reidel Pub. Co., 1983.

The author states that as long as women are subservient to men, as long as they are faced with inadequate financial resources, as long as there is rape and fetal defects, then abortion must remain a legal alternative.

1165.   Wolf, Naomi. "Our Bodies, Our Souls." In *The Abortion Controversy: 25 Years after Roe v. Wade: A Reader,* 2nd ed., edited by Louis P. Pojman and Francis J. Beckwith, 400-413. Belmont, Calif: Wadsworth Pub. Co., 1998.

Claims that pro-choice feminists hurt their cause by arguing that the fetus is nothing more than a valueless blob, and thus there is nothing morally problematic with aborting it. Rather, she claims, feminists should admit that abortion is a moral tragedy, though it should be legally permitted in the first trimester.

1166.   Wolf-Devine, Celia. "Abortion and the 'Feminine Voice.'" *Public Affairs Quarterly* 3, no. 3 (1989): 81-97.

First describes the growing movement in feminism to portray women as being nonviolent and nurturing, as opposed to men whom they portray as violent and power-hungry. She then shows the discrepancy between this portrayal of women and the practice of abortion.

FETAL TISSUE TRANSPLANTATION AND RESEARCH

1167.   Benedict, James. "The Use of Fetal Tissue: A Cautious Approval." *Christian Century* 115 (1998): 164-165.

The author presents an argument for the use of fetal tissue for medical research and to save the live of others, provided there are sufficient guidelines to prevent people from aborting their unborn children solely for the purpose of donating the fetal tissue, and provided that the potential recipients can reject it, once informed of its source.

1168. Burtachell, James T. "The Use of Aborted Fetal Tissue in Research and Therapy." Chap. 6 in *The Giving and Taking of Life: Essays Ethical.* Notre Dame, Ind.: Univ. of Notre Dame Press, 1989.

Presents an argument against the use of fetal tissue for research purposes.

1169. Childress, James F. "Ethics, Public Policy, and Human Fetal Tissue Transplantation Research." *Kennedy Institute of Ethics Journal* 1 (1991): 93-121.

Explores various argument for and against the use of fetal tissue for transplantation research, and for and against the use of federal funds for such research.

1170. Fine, Alan. "The Ethics of Fetal Tissue Transplantation." *Hastings Center Report* 18, no. 3 (1988): 5-8.

Presents a moderate view on the ethics of fetal tissue transplantation. He claims that, when circumscribed by appropriate limits, fetal transplantation will not erode ethical values. On the other hand, the pace of scientific progress must not be allowed to preempt societal values.

1171. Human Fetal Tissue Transplantation Research Panel (U.S.) *Report of the Human Fetal Tissue Transplantation Research Panel.* [Bethesda, Md.: National Institutes of Health, 1988].

A report, submitted December 1988, to the director of the National Institutes of Health, advocating the use of fetal tissue for transplantation and research, provided that there be sufficient safeguards to prevent a woman from having an abortion solely for the purpose of fetal research, and that potential recipients be informed of the source of the tissues. The contention of the panel is that the ethics of abortion can, and should be, separated from the ethics involved in using fetal tissue derived from an abortion.

1172. Mahowald, Mary B. "As If There Were Fetuses without Women: A Remedial Essay. In *Reproduction, Ethics, and the Law: Feminist Perspectives,* edited by Joan C. Callahan, 199-218. Bloomington, Ind.: Indiana Univ. Press, 1995.

Discusses, from a feminist perspective, the current status of, and the ethics involved in, fetal tissue transplantation from aborted fetuses.

1173.   Mahowald, Mary B., Jerry Silver, and Robert A. Ratcheson. "The Ethical Options in Transplanting Fetal Tissue." *Hastings Center Report* 17, no. 1 (1987): 9-15.

Presents ethical arguments for saying that, whether or not abortion is morally justified, use of human fetal tissue for research is justified under certain circumstances.

1174.   McCarthy, Donald G., and Albert S. Moraczewski, eds. *An Ethical Evaluation of Fetal Experimentation: An Interdisciplinary Study.* St. Louis: Pope John XXIII Medical-Moral Research and Education Center, 1976.

A report submitted by the Center's Task Force on Fetal Experimentation. It outlines, in light of general Catholic teaching, the moral, ethical and religious aspects of fetal experimentation. It also includes a discussion of the personhood of the fetus.

1175.   Murray, Thomas H. "Human Fetal Tissue Transplantation Research: Conflict in Ethics and Public Policy." In *Abortion, Medicine, and the Law*, 4th ed., completely revised, edited by J. Douglas Butler and David F. Walbert, 704-710. New York: Facts on File, 1992.

Examines the arguments both for and against using fetal tissue in transplantation research.

1176.   Nolan, Kathleen. "*Genug ist Genug:* A Fetus is not a Kidney." *Hastings Center Report* 18, no. 6 (1988): 13-19.

Presents a case against the use of fetal tissue for transplantation.

1177.   Palmer-Fernandez, Gabriel, and James E. Reagan. "Human Fetal Tissue Transplantation Research and Elective Abortion. *Journal of Social Philosophy* 29, no. 1 (1998): 5-19.

Using a specific case from 1990, as well as a report from the National Institutes of Health (see citation # 1171), the authors discuss fetal tissue transplantation research and its relation to elective abortions. They argue that there is a much closer correlation between the two than the National Institutes of Health had reported. They conclude that the participants in, and beneficiaries of, fetal tissue transplantation research are unavoidably complicit in elective abortion. Therefore, those who oppose elective abortion cannot consistently morally participate in, or benefit from, fetal tissue transplantation research.

1178. Rae, Scott B., and Christopher M. De Giorgio. "Ethical Issues in Fetal Tissue Transplants." *Linacre Quarterly* 58, no. 3 (1991): 12-32.

A discussion of the major positions on the use of fetal tissue for transplantation. The authors then present their conclusion that they are opposed to fetal tissue transplants in which the source of the tissue is an induced abortion. They do, however, support the use of tissue from spontaneous abortions or ectopic pregnancies.

1179. Ramsey, Paul. *The Ethics of Fetal Research.* New Haven, Conn.: Yale Univ. Press, 1975.

The author presents an analysis of what fetal research is, and what it entails, along with a discussion of the ethical issues involved. His aim is to aid the reader in thinking through the issue himself, though he does present his own viewpoints along the way.

1180. Robertson, John A. "Fetal Tissue Transplants." *Washington University Law Quarterly* 66 (1988): 443-498.

Examines the key ethical, legal, and policy issues presented by fetal tissue transplants. He concludes that ethical and legal concerns should not preclude research with fetal transplants, especially when the abortion is done for reasons other than for tissue procurement.

1181. ———. "Rights, Symbolism, and Public Policy in Fetal Tissue Transplants." *Hastings Center Report* 18, no. 6 (1988): 5-12.

Outlines the issues involved in fetal tissue transplants, and presents some conclusions.

1182. Sparks, Richard C. "Ethical Issues of Fetal Tissue Transplantation: Research, Procurement, and Complicity with Abortion." *Annual of the Society of Christian Ethics* (1990): 199-221.

Examines the ethical issues surrounding three areas: the legitimacy of fetal tissue research, procurement procedures for research or transplantation, and the question of the complicity of these activities with abortion.

1183. Terry, Nicolas P. "Politics and Privacy: Refining the Ethical and Legal Issues in Fetal Tissue Transplantation." *Washington University Law Quarterly* 66 (1988): 523-551.

The author points out that the debates over abortion and over fetal tissue transplantation are hopelessly intertwined, and that policy makers often become locked into a position on fetal tissue transplantation on the basis of their position on abortion. As long as this continues, he says, the debate on the use of fetal tissue may well be over before it begins.

OTHER RELATED ISSUES

1184.   Belliotti, Raymond A. "Morality and *In Vitro* Fertilization." *Bioethics Quarterly* 2 (1980): 6-19.

An investigation into the morality of *In Vitro* fertilization, particularly with reference to the fact that the process seems inseparable from the destruction of many embryos which are intentionally created.

1185.   Boss, Judith A. "The Moral Justification of Prenatal Diagnosis." In *Life and Learning IV: Proceedings of the Fourth University Faculty for Life Conference held at Fordham University June 1994*, edited by Joseph W. Koterski, S.J., 178-192. Washington, D.C.: University Faculty for Life, 1995.

Presents a moral case against the use of prenatal diagnosis to determine if there are any genetic abnormalities, or possible handicaps in the developing fetus.

1186.   Kallenberg, Kjell, Lars Forslin, and Olle Westerborn. "The Disposal of the Aborted Fetus–New Guidelines: Ethical Considerations in the Debate in Sweden." *Journal of Medical Ethics* 19 (1993): 32-36.

An ethical inquiry into new guidelines passed in Sweden on the disposal of the fetus after an abortion.

1187.   Keyserlingk, Edward W. "Artificial Insemination and *In Vitro* Fertilization." *Bioethics Quarterly* 2 (1981): 35-49.

Examines the ethical and legal implications of artificial insemination and *In Vitro* fertilization. Concludes that in neither case is great optimism or great pessimism warranted.

1188.   Mohler, Albert R., Jr. "Is It Moral to Make 'Test-Tube Babies'? A Response." In *The Befuddled Stork: Helping Persons of Faith Debate Beginning-of-Life Issues,* edited by Sally B. Geis, and Donald E. Messer, 57-66. Nashville: Abingdon Press, 2000.

The author presents a Christian ethical argument against *in vitro* fertilization.

1189.   Paris, Peter J. "Is it Moral to Make 'Test-Tube Babies'? A Response." In *The Befuddled Stork: Helping Persons of Faith Debate Beginning-of-Life Issues,* edited by Sally B. Geis and Donald E. Messer, 50-56. Nashville: Abingdon Press, 2000.

The author gives an endorsement of *in vitro* fertilization, provided that it is conjoined with, and not a substitute for, mutual love. Many of the ethical dilemmas involved in the procedure, he says, can be resolved if this love of a child, whether it be by heterosexual or homosexual couples, is present.

1190.   Sutton, Agneta. *Prenatal Diagnosis: Confronting the Ethical Issues.* London: The Linacre Centre for the Study of the Ethics of Health Care, 1990.

The author examines the current medical and legal aspects of prenatal diagnosis for the purpose of detecting fetal deformity. She notes that most often this is done so as to offer the woman the chance to abort the child. She then discusses the ethical dimensions of prenatal diagnosis.

1191.   Wikler, Daniel I. "Ought We to Try to Save Aborted Fetuses?" *Ethics* 90 (1979): 58-65.

Sometimes, though it is uncommon, abortions performed in the second or third trimesters result in abortuses (aborted fetuses), which might be saved if given vigorous medical care. The author examines the question of whether we should try to save such abortuses, and the relation of that question to the larger question of abortion. He shows that those who oppose abortion do not necessarily have to favor the resuscitation of abortuses. Likewise, those who favor abortion do not necessarily have to oppose such resuscitation.

8   THE ABORTION DEBATE

1192.   Beckwith, Francis J. "Shifting the Focus in the Abortion Debate." In *Life and Learning V: Proceedings of the Fifth University Faculty for Life Conference, June 1995, at Marquette University,* edited by Joseph W. Koterski, S.J., 331-349. Washington, D.C.: University Faculty for Life, 1996.

Shows that there has been a shift in pro-choice argumentation away from saying the fetus is not a person to saying that it is, but, since it is burdensome to the woman, she need not carry it to term. He then provides a critique of the article by Judith Jarvis Thomson, which popularized this view (see citation #).

1193.   Bennett, John, and Robert Hoyt. "Continuing the Discussion: How to Argue about Abortion." *Christianity and Crisis* 36 (1977): 264-266.

Two authors present differing perspectives on the abortion controversy and the rhetoric used in the debate.

1194.   Blackwell, Diana. "Abortion Rhetoric and the Politics of Suffering." *American Atheist* 32 (Jan. 1990): 26-28.

An abortion advocate claims that some of the arguments currently used in favor of legal abortion are weak, and she proposes ways to strengthen them.

1195.   Boss, Judith A. "Pro-Child/Pro-Choice: An Exercise in Doublethink?" *Public Affairs Quarterly* 7 (1993): 85-91.

Claims that the popular pro-choice slogan "pro-child/pro-choice" is an exercise in doublethink, or holding two contradictory beliefs simultaneously.

1196.   Brennan, William. "Confronting the Language of the Culture of Death." In *Life and Learning VI: Proceedings of the Sixth University Faculty for Life Conference, June 1996 at Georgetown University*, edited by Joseph W. Koterski, S.J., 301-322. Washington, D.C.: University Faculty for Life, 1997.

Examines the dehumanizing language used by pro-choice forces to portray the unborn as well as the elderly. He calls for replacing that rhetoric with positive, life affirming, terminology.

1197.   ———. "Female Objects of Semantic Dehumanization and Violence." *Studies in Prolife Feminism* 1 (1995): 203-233.

The author points to many of the atrocities that have been thrust upon women throughout history – the killing of female infants, enforced prostitution, the reduction of women to sex objects, wife beating, etc. He claims that this victimization has been facilitated through the use of dehumanizing language – deficient human, subhuman, etc. He concludes by showing that this same dehumanizing language is being used by pro-choice forces to victimize another class of people – the unborn.

1198.   ———. "Specifying the Abortion-Holocaust Connections." In *When Life and Choice Collide: Essays on Rhetoric and Abortion*, edited by David Mall. Vol. 1. Libertyville, Ill.: Kairos Books, 1994.

Outlines the parallels that can be legitimately drawn between the killing of the unborn today and the killing of Jews in the Nazi era.

1199.   Burt, Donald X. "Facts, Fables, and Moral Rules: An Analysis of the Abortion Debate." *The New Scholasticism* 62 (1988): 400-411.

A suggestion that arguments about the morality of abortion are often subject to errors of facts or principles.

1200.   Callahan, Daniel. "The Abortion Debate: Is Progress Possible?" In *Abortion: Understanding Differences*, edited by Sidney Callahan and Daniel Callahan, 309-324. New York: Plenum Press, 1984.

The author asks the question whether progress is possible in the abortion debate. He defines what he means by progress in this area, and closes with the steps each of the opposing sides must be willing to take if there is to be such progress in the abortion debate.

1201.   ————. "How Technology is Reframing the Abortion Debate." *Hastings Center Report* 16, no. 1 (1986): 33-42

The author claims that, while new technology has not undermined the rationale favoring abortion rights, pro-choice advocates should be willing to continually air the moral question as new technologies may impinge on the moral question.

1202.   Callahan, Joan C. *"The Silent Scream:* A New, Conclusive Argument against Abortion?" *Philosophy Research Archives* 11 (1985): 181-195.

Examines the film. *The Silent Scream,* to see if it does serve, as pro-life forces have contended, as a powerful argument against abortion. The author concludes that it does not.

1203.   Callahan, Sidney, and Daniel Callahan. "Breaking through the Stereotypes." *Commonweal* 111 (1984): 520-523.

Describes the project the authors conducted which resulted in their book, *Abortion: Understanding Differences.* (see citation #) One outcome of the project, they say, is that the participants were able to break through the stereotypes common in the abortion debate.

1204.   Casanova, Judith Boice, Jean Lambert, and Marjorie Suchocki. "What about Abortion?" In *What's a Christian to Do?,* edited by David P. Polk, 113-136. St. Louis: Chalice Press, 1991.

A presentation of both sides of the abortion controversy, concluding that the best theobgical response is that we should have a fundamental trust in God, recognizing that while we make decisions with integrity, likewise others will, with their own integrity, make decisions opposite to ours. The authors also call for an openness and respect for one another in the public debate.

1205.   Cassidy, Keith. "Abortion and the Rhetoric of Legitimacy." In *When Life and Choice Collide: Essays on Rhetoric and Abortion,* edited by David Mall. Vol. 1. Libertyville, Ill.: Kairos Books, 1994.

In the United States, while everyone may participate in public discussion, only those who are perceived to have a form of legitimacy are granted any *effective* participation in public policy debates. This legitimacy may come either from the person having a certain *authority* to speak – social status, education, etc., or from the fact that he is appealing to principles that are widely regarded as legitimate and significant. The author then gives suggestions to pro-life forces on how they may revise their rhetoric so as to best take advantage of theses structures of authority.

1206.   Davis, N. Ann. "Not Drowning but Waving: Reflections on Swimming through the Shark-Infested Waters of the Abortion Debate." In *New Essays on Abortion and Bioethics,* edited by Rem B. Edwards, 227-265. Greenwich, Conn.: JAI Press, 1997.

Many people assume that the abortion debate is deeply polarized because of the intransigence of extremists on both sides of the issue, and that what we need is a moderate view. The author argues against this assumption, claiming, rather, that the debate is polarized because of the inherent complexity of the issue.

1207.   Delgado, Sharon. "Abortion and the Christian Conscience: Twenty-Four Years after *Roe versus Wade* the Debate Continues to Polarize the Country – and the Church." *Christian Social Action* 10, no. 2 (1997): 31-34.

Discusses the Social Principles of the United Methodist Church. She suggests that a discussion of rights is not sufficient to solve the issue, but rather we should talk about what is the loving and compassionate thing to do? Calls on the church to provide grace, forgiveness, affirmation and the love of God, as well as concrete support to women with problem pregnancies.

1208.   DeMarco, Donald. "Grace and the Word." In *When Life and Choice Collide: Essays on Rhetoric and Abortion,* edited by David Mall. Vol. 1. Libertyville, Ill.: Kairos Books, 1994.

Demonstrates that advocates of abortion use words rhetorically, not to shed light on what abortion entails, but to win people over to the pro-choice position. Pro-Life advocates, on the other hand, rely on words to reveal clearly what abortion involves.

1209.   Dillon, Michele. "Cultural Differences in the Abortion Discourse of the Catholic Church: Evidences from Four Countries." *Sociology of Religion* 56 (1996): 25-36.

This essay investigates the cultural themes used by the Catholic Church in arguing against abortion in four different countries: Poland, Ireland, the United States, and England and Wales. The focus is on whether the church differentiates its use of cultural arguments in accordance with its insider/outsider status, or the contested nature of the abortion policy-making environment in that country.

1210.   ———. "Institutional Legitimation and Abortion: Monitoring the Catholic Church's Discourse." *Journal for the Scientific Study of Religion* 34 (1995): 141-151.

Analyzes the abortion policy statements of the National Council of Catholic Bishops in three public fora: the general public, Congress, and the Supreme Court. The statements analyzed were issued between the *Roe v. Wade* and the *Webster v. Reproductive Health Services* decisions. Results show an increasing amount of complexity in the statements issued to the general public and to the court, but a decreasing amount of complexity in statements issued to Congress. Reasons for this discrepancy are offered.

1211. ———. "Religion and Culture in Tension: The Abortion Discourse of the U.S. Catholic Bishops and the Southern Baptist Convention." *Religion and American Culture* 5 (1995): 159-180.

Analyzes the official anti-abortion arguments of the National Council of Catholic Bishops and the Southern Baptist Convention to explore the openness of the two bodies to the American cultural context.

1212. Franz, Wanda. "Abortion through the Eyes of the Beholder: A Cognitive Analysis." In *When Life and Choice Collide: Essays on Rhetoric and Abortion,* edited by David Mall. Vol. 1. Libertyville, Ill.: Kairos Books, 1994.

Discusses the ways in which different people receive and interpret information on abortion. She then makes recommendations on how pro-life arguments may be made so they are most apt to be received and understood by people of differing developmental levels.

1213. Gallagher, Kenneth T. "Abortion and 'Choice.'" *Public Affairs Quarterly* 7 (1993): 13-17.

The author demonstrates that framing the abortion debate in terms of "a woman's right to choose" actually muddies the question, and renders any answer hopelessly confused.

1214. Granberg, Donald. "What Does It Mean to Be 'Pro-Life'?" *Christian Century* 99 (1982): 562-566.

While admitting that he does not know for sure exactly what is meant by the term "Pro-Life," the author claims that it does mean more than simply being "anti-abortion." He claims that the term "Pro-life" should in addition, encompass opposition to militarism, infanticide, euthanasia and capital punishment, as well as supporting gun control and conservation. He then shows that the National Right to Life Committee is, on this scale, only partially "pro-life." Likewise, the National Abortion Rights Action league is also partially pro-life in that it generally opposes capital punishment and favors gun control.

1215.   Harrison, Beverly Wildung, James T. Burtachell, Vivian Lindermayer, and
          Eric Lindermayer. "Continuing the Discussion: How to Argue about
          Abortion II." *Christianity and Crisis* 36 (1977): 311-318.

          Several authors, from varying perspectives, discuss the abortion contro-
          versy and the rhetoric of the debate.

1216.   Hauerwas, Stanley. "Abortion: Why the Arguments Fail." In *Abortion
          Parley,* edited by James T. Burtachell, 323-352. Kansas City: Andrews
          and McMeel, 1980.

          Argues that Christians have failed to convince others that abortion is
          morally wrong because they have assumed that they were required to
          express their opposition to abortion in terms acceptable to a pluralist
          society. They have let those who favor abortion determine the terrain on
          which the battle is to be fought.

1217.   Hodges, Fredrica F. "The Assaults on Choice." In *Abortion Rights and
          Fetal 'Personhood,'* 2nd ed., edited by Edd Doerr and James W. Prescott,
          1-4. Long Beach, Calif.: Centerline Press, in association with Americans
          for Religious Liberty, 1990.

          Examines and criticizes two tactics of the pro-life movement: their
          teaching that the Bible condemns abortion, and their rhetoric.

1218.   Hunt, John. "Abortion and Nazism: Is there really a Connection?" In *Life
          and Learning VI: Proceedings of the Sixth University Faculty for Life
          Conference, June 1996 at Georgetown University,* edited by Joseph W.
          Koterski, S.J., 323-337. Washington, D.C.: University Faculty for Life,
          1997.

          An examination of whether pro-life forces are correct in drawing a
          connection between the current practice of abortion and the Nazi
          Holocaust. The author concludes that the connection is a legitimate one.

1219.   Hunt, William C. "Technological Themes in the Abortion Debate." In
          When Life and Choice Collide: Essays on Rhetoric and Abortion, edited
          by David Mall. Vol. 1. Libertyville, Ill.: Kairos Books, 1994.

          Examines six major themes in our technological society which are often
          merely taken for granted, and which make it difficult for people to think
          ethically about public policy issues. He shows how these themes affect
          the argument in the abortion controversy.

1220.   Joyce, Mary R. "The Dove and the Serpent." In *When Life and Choice Collide: Essays on Rhetoric and Abortion,* edited by David Mall. Vol. 1. Libertyville, Ill.: Kairos Books, 1994.

The author claims that while the pro-life side in the abortion controversy has the truth, it often lacks the rhetorical skill necessary to defend that truth effectively. She calls on pro-life people to sharpen their verbal skills, and to focus on the spot where the opposition is vulnerable.

1221.   Kissling, Frances. "Ending the Abortion War: A Modest Proposal." *Christian Century* 107 (1990): 180-184.

In the wake of the Supreme Court's *Webster v. Reproductive Health Services* decision, the author presents several suggestions to other pro-choice advocates on how they can modify their war to keep abortion legal. In particular, she calls on pro-choice people to begin to examine their own beliefs, and to engage in serious moral discourse on abortion.

1222.   Kulczycki, Andrzej. *The Abortion Debate in the World Arena.* New York: Routledge, 1999.

Examines the status of abortion practice, policy, and debate in three countries: Kenya, Mexico, and Poland. Pays particular attention to the Catholic Church as a transnational player in the abortion debate.

1223.   LaFleur, William R. "The Cult of Jizo: Abortion Practices in Japan and What They Can Teach the West." *Tricycle: The Buddhist Review* 4, no. 4 (1995): 40-45.

Using Japan as a model, the author claims that the abortion debate in the United States does not have to be so intractable, with each side unwilling to give an inch to the other. He suggest that in Japan the issue of abortion has been worked out over the years, without sacrificing its religious dimension.

1224.   "Lies We've Heard Before: The Same Flawed Arguments that Legalized Abortion Are now Being Used to Support Physician-Assisted Suicide." Editorial. *Christianity Today* 13 July 1998, 28-29.

Demonstrates that the same arguments that were used get abortion legalized, are now being used in support of physician assisted suicide.

1225.   MacNair, Rachel Mary. "The Politics of Breast Cancer Research." *Studies in Prolife Feminism* 1 (1995): 29-44.

A number of studies have suggested the possibility that the abortion of a first pregnancy may result in an increased risk of developing breast cancer. Planned Parenthood and other pro-choice forces, fearing that this will dissuade some women from having an abortion, have tried to deny this link by repudiating the studies. The author looks at models that might help predict how these pro-choice forces will react if future studies continue to demonstrate this link between abortion and breast cancer.

1226.   Mall, David. "The Catholic Church and Abortion: Persuading through Public Relations." In *When Life and Choice Collide: Essays on Rhetoric and Abortion,* edited by David Mall. Vol. 1. Libertyville, Ill.: Kairos Books, 1994.

In 1990, the United States Catholic Conference hired a professional public relations firm to help it get across its pro-life message, with the assistance of a group specializing in public opinion research. The author examines the media campaign conducted by this firm, especially in regard to how that campaign was influenced by the research of the firm specializing in public opinion.

1227.   ———. *In Good Conscience: Abortion and Moral Necessity.* Libertyville, Ill.: Kairos Books, 1982.

The author, an anti-abortion advocate, discusses the rhetoric of abortion, and the kind of rhetoric needed to persuade someone of the pro-life position.

1228.   ———., ed. *When Life and Choice Collide: Essays on Rhetoric and Abortion.* With an introduction by Nat Hentoff. Vol. 1. Words in Conflict Series. Libertyville, Ill.: Kairos Books, 1994.

A collection of articles on the rhetoric used in the abortion debate, and on how to improve that debate. Most of the articles are written from the pro-life perspective.

1229.   McCormick, Richard A., S.J. "Rules for Abortion Debate." In *Abortion: The Moral Issues,* edited by Edward Batchelor, 27-37. New York: Pilgrim Press, 1982. Originally published in *America,* 22 July 1978.

The author bemoans the fact that so much of the argumentation over abortion, from both sides of the issue, is at a deplorably low level. He then presents several guidelines for improving the debate, and making it more communicative.

1230.   Muggeridge, Malcolm. "What the Abortion Argument is About." *Human Life Review* 1, no. 3 (1975): 4-6.

Describes the abortion controversy as coming down to this question: Either we go on with the process of shaping our own destiny without reference to any being higher than man, or we drop back and try to both understand and to fall in with our Creator's purpose for us.

1231. National Council of the Churches of Christ in the U.S.A. Commission on Faith and Order. "A Call to Responsible Ecumenical Debate on Controversial Issues: Abortion and Homosexuality." In *Abortion: The Moral Issues,* edited by Edward Batchelor, 48-52. New York: Pilgrim Press, 1982.

A study document which serves as a call to civility on the part of Christians in the debate over the issues of abortion and homosexuality.

1232. Noonan, John T. "Responding to Persons: Methods for Moral Argument in the Debate over Abortion." *Theology Digest* 21 (1973): 291-307.

Contends that abortion arguments that center on principles or theories are wrong headed. Rather we must respond, not to abstract norms, but to persons.

1233. Ooms, Theodora. "A Family Perspective on Abortion." In *Abortion: Understanding Differences,* edited by Sidney Callahan and Daniel Callahan, 81-107. New York: Plenum Press, 1984.

The author points out that though a woman's decision either to abort or to give birth radically affects her family life, these same family considerations are generally not mentioned in public debates. She discusses what these family considerations are, and argues that they should be given greater weight in both legal and ethical discussions of abortion.

1234. Overduin, Daniel Christian. "The Ethics of Abortion." In *New Perspectives on Human Abortion,* edited by Thomas W. Hilgers, Dennis J. Horan, and David Mall, 357-386. Frederick, Md.: Aletheia Books, University Publications of America, 1981.

The ethics of abortion depends on the individual's point of departure, or presuppositions. The Humanist begins with the view that man is autonomous, and can make decisions for himself without regard to any supposed absolute norms, as there are no absolute norms. The Christian, however, begins with the recognition that man is a creature of God, and in relation to Him; every act is therefore either an expression of faith or of unbelief. The author begins his discussion of abortion from the latter perspective, but also shows that, because there can be no compromise between these two starting points, there will always be an inevitable collision of views.

1235.   Rudy, Kathy. *Beyond Pro-Life and Pro-Choice: Moral Diversity in the Abortion Debate.* Boston: Beacon Press, 1996

The author shows that in our current climate, people are seen as either pro-life or pro-choice. She argues for eliminating that bifurcation, thus opening up new views. She claims that people are not part of only one community, but are a part of multiple, and sometimes, competing communities, making an all or nothing view of abortion impossible.

1236.   ———. "Mapping the Moralities of Abortion." Ph.D. diss., Duke University, 1993.

Writing as a Christian feminist, the author contends that abortion has different meanings in different communities. In particular, she contends that abortion means very different things to the feminist community and to the Christian community. She outlines the competing constructions of the term in each of these communities. She then offers suggestions on how feminists can reset the terms of the abortion debate in order to move to what they consider a more desirable future.

1237.   Sernett, Milton C. "Widening the Circle: The Pro-Life Appeal to the Abolitionist Legacy." In *When Life and Choice Collide: Essays on Rhetoric and Abortion,* edited by David Mall. Vol. 1. Libertyville, Ill.: Kairos Books, 1994.

Pro-life forces have drawn an analogy between their efforts to abolish abortion with the 19th century crusade to abolish slavery. The author examines the usefulness of this appeal, and analyzes its strengths and weaknesses.

1238.   Sobran, M. J. "Abortion: Rhetoric and Cultural War." *Human Life Review* 1, no. 1 (1975): 85-98.

A critique of the *ad hominem* argument that characterizes an anti-abortion advocate as a "Roman Catholic," with its implicit assumption that the only reason he is anti-abortion is because he is a Roman Catholic.

1239.   Spitzer, Robert J., S.J. "The Life Principles: A Model for Teaching the Philosophy of the Pro-Life Movement." In *Life and Learning VIII: Proceedings of the Eighth University Faculty for Life Conference, June 1998 at the University of Toronto,* edited by Joseph W. Koterski, S.J., 363-398. Washington, D.C.: University Faculty for Life, 1999.

An outline of the philosophy behind the *Life Principles* Program, a project devoted to explaining the underlying philosophy of the pro-life movement to a secular culture.

1240. Swope, Paul. "Abortion: A Failure to Communicate." *First Things,* April 1998, 31-35.

The author claims that Pro-Lifers have been largely ineffective in getting their message across to people because they have failed to communicate to people where they are. Pro-Life arguments, he claims have largely focused on the baby: trying to prove that the fetus is a human being, and that abortion is the killing of an innocent life. Rather, he says, their arguments should focus on the woman, and demonstrate that abortion is not the answer to the problem she finds herself in.

1241. Wedam, Elfriede. "Splitting Interests or Common Causes: Styles of Moral Reasoning in Opposing Abortion." In *Contemporary American Religion: An Ethnographic Reader,* edited by Penny Edgell Becker and Nancy L. Eiesland, 147-168. Walnut Creek, Calif.: Altamira Press, 1997.

The author examines two very different pro-life groups and shows the different types of moral arguments which these groups use to express their opposition to abortion.

1242. Werpehowski, William. "Persons, Practices, and the Conception Argument." *Journal of Medicine and Philosophy* 22 (1997): 479-494.

Some have argued that human life should be protected from the time of conception. Others have argued that at that point, human life is not fully individuated, as twinning may still occur. The author analyzes this debate and directs the reader's attention to the communal contexts in which the relevant arguments and counter-arguments arise.

1243. Willke, John C. "The Battleground of Semantics." In *When Life and Choice Collide: Essays on Rhetoric and Abortion,* edited by David Mall. Vol. 1. Libertyville, Ill.: Kairos Books, 1994.

Examines in depth the semantics used by both sides of the abortion debate. He also gives pro-life people suggestions on how to counter the semantics of the pro-choice side.

AUTHOR INDEX

References are to the bibliographic citation number, not the page number.

SUBJECT INDEX

References are to the bibliographic citation number, not the page number.

About the Author

GEORGE F. JOHNSTON is Cataloger at the Langsam Library at the University of Cincinnati. He formerly served as Assistant Librarian at Covenant Theological Seminary in St. Louis.